JUL 1 7 2015

Jennifer Kyrnin

D0507395

Sams **Teach Yourself**

Responsive Web Design

in 24 Hours

SAMS 800 East 96th Street, Indianapolis, Indiana, 46240 USA

JUL 1 7 2015

Sams Teach Yourself Responsive Web Design in 24 Hours

Copyright © 2015 by Pearson Education

All rights reserved. No part of this book shall be reproduced, stored in a retrieval system, or transmitted by any means, electronic, mechanical, photocopying, recording, or otherwise, without written permission from the publisher. No patent liability is assumed with respect to the use of the information contained herein. Although every precaution has been taken in the preparation of this book, the publisher and author assume no responsibility for errors or omissions. Nor is any liability assumed for damages resulting from the use of the information contained herein.

ISBN-13: 978-0-672-33838-0
ISBN-10: 0-672-33838-6

Library of Congress Control Number: 2014919261

Printed in the United States of America

First Printing: November 2014

Trademarks

All terms mentioned in this book that are known to be trademarks or service marks have been appropriately capitalized. Sams Publishing cannot attest to the accuracy of this information. Use of a term in this book should not be regarded as affecting the validity of any trademark or service mark.

Warning and Disclaimer

Every effort has been made to make this book as complete and as accurate as possible, but no warranty or fitness is implied. The information provided is on an "as is" basis. The author and the publisher shall have neither liability nor responsibility to any person or entity with respect to any loss or damages arising from the information contained in this book or from the use of the CD or programs accompanying it.

Special Sales

For information about buying this title in bulk quantities, or for special sales opportunities (which may include electronic versions; custom cover designs; and content particular to your business, training goals, marketing focus, or branding interests), please contact our corporate sales department at corpsales@pearsoned.com or (800) 382-3419.

For government sales inquiries, please contact governmentsales@pearsoned.com.

For questions about sales outside the U.S., please contact international@pearsoned.com.

Acquisitions Editor
Mark Taber

Managing Editor
Sandra Schroeder

Project Editor
Seth Kerney

Copy Editor
Kitty Wilson

Indexer
Ken Johnson

Proofreader
Kathy Ruiz

Technical Editor
Jon Morin

Publishing Coordinator
Vanessa Evans

Designer
Gary Adair

Page Layout
Bronkella Publishing, LLC

Contents

About the Author

Jennifer Kyrnin has been teaching HTML, XML, and web design online since 1997. She has built and maintained websites of all sizes, from small, single-page brochure sites to large, million-page database-driven sites for international audiences. She lives with her husband and son and numerous animals on a small farm in Washington state.

Dedication

To Mark and Jaryth. This was much easier because you were around. I love you.

Acknowledgments

I would like to thank all the people at Sams Publishing for the opportunity to write this book and work with you. I would particularly like to thank Mark Taber and Seth Kerney for keeping me moving and the book on track, as well as my fabulous technical editor, Jon Morin, and my amazing and tolerant copy editor Kitty Wilson for all the great suggestions and corrections. Any technical errors you find in the book are mine alone; the editors probably tried to stop me.

I would also like to thank my family for putting up with me while I wrote the book, including my brother Brendan Kirby, who was instrumental in helping me get my thoughts together on one tough section, and the members of the Woodinville Writers Group, who were very kind in letting me interrupt their fiction stories with some cold hard HTML.

We Want to Hear from You!

As the reader of this book, you are our most important critic and commentator. We value your opinion and want to know what we're doing right, what we could do better, what areas you'd like to see us publish in, and any other words of wisdom you're willing to pass our way.

You can email or write to let us know what you did or didn't like about this book—as well as what we can do to make our books stronger.

Please note that we cannot help you with technical problems related to the topic of this book, and that due to the high volume of mail we receive, we might not be able to reply to every message.

When you write, please be sure to include this book's title, edition number, and author, as well as your name and contact information.

Email: feedback@samspublishing.com

Mail: Sams Publishing
800 East 96th Street
Indianapolis, IN 46240 USA

Reader Services

Visit our website and register this book at **informit.com/register** for convenient access to any updates, downloads, or errata that might be available for this book.

Introduction

Responsive web design (RWD) is a way of thinking about web pages that allows designers to work on one website for all visitors but tailor the site to the device each visitor is viewing it on. More and more companies are requiring web designers to build their sites responsively, and knowing how to do it well will help web designers differentiate themselves in the industry.

Making Your Site "Every Device" Friendly

This book covers more than just how and when to build CSS breakpoints to build a responsive site. Once you've finished this book, you will understand all these ideas:

- How the use of RWD got started and why web designers began using it instead of other techniques
- What progressive enhancement is and how important it is to RWD
- Basic HTML5, CSS3, and JavaScript to build a website framework that is easy to make responsive
- How mobile devices affect responsive design and how they aren't the whole story when it comes to creating responsive websites
- The basics of building RWD, including media queries and breakpoints
- How to make your layout, navigation, images, tables, fonts, videos, and forms responsive
- How to test your designs even if you don't have a lot of mobile devices
- The common problems in RWD and how to alleviate them
- How to use RESS and other tools and technologies to improve your designs
- Best practices for using RWD and building a responsive site

How to Use This Book

This book is divided into 24 lessons, called "hours." Each lesson covers a specific topic related to building responsive web pages using responsive web design. Each lesson takes about an hour to complete.

Organization of This Book

The book is divided into three sections:

- Part I, "Introduction to Responsive Design," introduces you to RWD and explains the basic HTML, CSS, and JavaScript you need to know.
- Part II, "Building a Responsive Website," addresses specific aspects of RWD, such as navigation, images, and tables, and shows you how to make them responsive.
- Part III, "Improving on Responsive Web Design," introduces you to some tools and techniques you can use to improve your RWD and describes problems you may have as well as best practices in the field.

Conventions Used in This Book

Code samples are written in `monospaced font` within the text of the book, while blocks of code appear separately, like this:

```
This is a block
Of code
```

Some code samples that are too long to display as one line in the book use the ➥ symbol to indicate that these lines should be all on one line, like this:

```
<link rel="stylesheet" href="styles-320.css"
➥media="only screen and (max-width:320px)">
```

This book has three types of sidebars:

NOTE

Notes provide additional information about the topics that are discussed in the hour.

TIP

Tips share interesting facts or tidbits about the related content.

CAUTION

Cautions alert you to things that can cause problems for your web designs.

You can also use the Try It Yourself sections to practice what you've learned in the hour.

Try It Yourself

Nearly every hour has at least one step-by-step tutorial called "Try It Yourself" to help you use what you've learned.

Q&A, Quiz, and Exercises

Every hour ends with a short question-and-answer section that anticipates follow-up questions you may have after reading the hour. You can also take a short quiz on what you've learned as well as do some suggested exercises to help you get more out of what you learned and apply your new knowledge to your own web designs.

Where to Go to Learn More

This book has a companion website at `http://html5in24hours.com`, where you can go to see the examples, view and download the source code, view and report errata about the book, and continue to learn and ask questions about RWD. You can also find Jennifer Kyrnin online at `http://htmljenn.com`, and she welcomes questions and comments.

HOUR 1
What Is Responsive Web Design?

WHAT YOU'LL LEARN IN THIS HOUR:

- What RWD is
- The history of RWD
- Why RWD is widely used

Responsive web design (RWD) is an approach to web design that attempts to adapt a site's design for optimal viewing on all of a customer's devices. RWD helps web designers and site owners create an "edit once, display anywhere" website. The web designer builds one page that can then be viewed on a wide-screen desktop or a small-screen cell phone without requiring the user to open another site or page. Instead, the content on the page moves around in the design to suit the device being used to view the page.

A website that uses responsive design changes the layout of the website depending on what device is viewing it. But unlike older solutions, RWD does not use scripts or programming to achieve these changes. Instead, RWD uses Cascading Style Sheets (CSS) media queries (more about this in Hour 10, "CSS Media Queries") to define fluid grids, variable font sizes, and flexible images. The media queries define what styles will apply to the design, based on the device being used to view it.

History of Responsive Web Design

When web pages were first being built back in the mid-1990s, most people building them were not designers. Those website builders cared a lot less about how the page looked than if the content was displaying at all.

CAUTION

There Are Better Tools Than the Single-Pixel GIF Trick

The following code listing for the single-pixel GIF trick is provided for interest only. I strongly recommend that you use other techniques, such as CSS, for managing indents. If you don't know CSS, find one of the many great books out there to help you learn, including *Sams Teach Yourself HTML and CSS in 24 Hours* by Julie Meloni.

Web Pages Started with Little Design

The first signs of design starting to have some sway were when someone invented the technique that is now called "the single-pixel GIF trick." This is where you create an image that is 1px by 1px and transparent. Because it is a transparent GIF, it isn't visible on websites and so can be used for spacing content. As you can see in Figure 1.1, when you use a transparent GIF, you can indent paragraphs without using CSS.

This trick was important because CSS wasn't around yet, and web designers didn't have any other way to style or position content on web pages. Web designers used the trick to give paragraphs of text an indent on the first line. But it was also used to move content around on the page. This trick was revolutionary back then as it gave web developers a way to position text and move things around in a way we didn't have before. Listing 1.1 shows the HTML used to create the page in Figure 1.1.

Single Pixel GIF Trick Dem
file:...
Single Pixel GIF Trick Demonstrated
Here is a simple page with two paragraphs (besides this one). The first paragraph uses a single-pixel transparent GIF to indent the first line. The second uses a single-pixel GIF that is not transparent to demostrate the same technique.
Lorem ipsum dolor sit amet, consectetuer adipiscing elit, sed diam nonummy nibh euismod tincidunt ut laoreet dolore magna aliquam erat volutpat. Ut wisi enim ad minim veniam, quis nostrud exerci tation ullamcorper suscipit lobortis nisl ut aliquip ex ea commodo consequat. Duis autem vel eum iriure dolor in hendrerit in vulputate velit esse molestie consequat, vel illum dolore eu feugiat nulla facilisis at vero eros et accumsan et iusto odio dignissim qui blandit praesent luptatum zzril delenit augue duis dolore te feugait nulla facilisi.
Ut wisi enim ad minim veniam, quis nostrud exerci tation ullamcorper suscipit lobortis nisl ut aliquip ex ea commodo consequat. Duis autem vel eum iriure dolor in hendrerit in vulputate velit esse molestie consequat, vel illum dolore eu feugiat nulla facilisis at vero eros et accumsan et iusto odio dignissim qui blandit praesent luptatum zzril delenit augue duis dolore te feugait nulla facilisi. Lorem ipsum dolor sit amet, consectetuer adipiscing elit, sed diam nonummy nibh euismod tincidunt ut laoreet dolore magna aliquam erat volutpat.

FIGURE 1.1
How the single-pixel GIF trick works.

LISTING 1.1 Demonstrating the Single-Pixel GIF Trick

```
<!doctype html>
<html>
    <head>
    <meta charset="UTF-8">
    <title>Single Pixel GIF Trick Demonstrated</title>
    </head>
<body>
    <h1>Single Pixel GIF Trick Demonstrated </h1>
    <p>Here is a simple page with two paragraphs (besides this one).
    The first paragraph uses a single-pixel transparent GIF to indent
    the first line. The second uses a single-pixel GIF that is not
    transparent to demonstrate the same technique. </p>
    <p>
    <img src="images/single-pixel-transparent.gif" width="50"
    height="1" alt=""/>Lorem ipsum dolor sit amet, consectetuer
    adipiscing elit, sed diam nonummy nibh euismod</p>
    <p>
    <img src="images/single-pixel.gif" width="50" height="1"
    alt=""/>Ut wisi enim ad minim veniam, quis nostrud exerci
    tation ullamcorper suscipit lobortis nisl ut aliquip ex ea
    commodo consequat. Duis autem vel eum iriure dolor.</p>
</body>
</html>
```

As you can see, by changing the size with the `width` and `height` attributes on the single-pixel images, you could control the size of the indent.

CSS Gave Designers More Control

Once CSS came on the scene in the mid-1990s, doing design and layout on websites became a little easier. However, CSS level 1 (CSS 1) was fairly limited to just fonts and colors, and it also wasn't widely supported by browsers at first.

CSS 1 was completed as a specification in 1996, but it didn't gain browser traction until 2000, when Internet Explorer 5.0 for Macintosh came out with support for more than 99% of CSS 1. CSS 1 was pretty limited when it came to layout, only supporting aligning text, floating elements, and some box properties (like margins, padding, and borders).

CSS level 2 (CSS 2) came out in the early 2000s, and that's when web designers finally started getting support for layout and positioning of elements on a web page. CSS 2 added properties like `position` and `z-index`. With these properties, web designers could place elements wherever they wanted on the page, including "offscreen" where the elements couldn't be seen at all.

CSS level 3 (CSS3) paved the way for responsive web design. While media queries were first introduced into CSS in level 2, CSS3 media queries came out as a candidate recommendation in 2002, and by 2012 most web browsers and mobile devices supported media queries.

Media queries allow a web designer to create separate CSS documents for devices with different media features. The most commonly used feature is the browser width. For example, a small smartphone might have a width of 640px, while a widescreen monitor might have a width of more than 2000px. With media queries, you can detect that and build designs to suit each size. You will learn more about media queries in Hour 10.

Designers Started Adapting Layouts to the Customers

NOTE

Switchy McLayout Was One of the First Adaptive Designs

Back in 2006, the online magazine *A List Apart* ran the article "Switchy McLayout" (`http://alistapart.com/issue/229`). This article explained how to use CSS media queries to create pages that adapted depending on what browser media was viewing it. This was cutting edge at the time, and only a few desktop browsers recognized media queries, let alone mobile devices. It took a few more years for this type of design to catch on.

While media queries are the basis of responsive web design, it wasn't until 2009 that designers realized that they could use them to develop adaptive websites. Instead, many designers went down a completely different path and created completely separate websites and pages for different browsers and devices.

In the early days of mobile devices and smartphones, it was very common to visit a website on a mobile device and be forced to a "mobile-friendly" version of the site. Often these mobile sites had completely different URLs as well as layouts and even content. Web content owners didn't want to have to maintain two separate sites, so often the mobile site would be left with minimal content, while the primary site business was conducted on the desktop version of the site.

Mobile Browsers Made Things Harder to Design

Mobile-specific websites became very popular a few years later, and almost every website with any mobile customers started using this method to support mobile customers. They often used server-side and local scripts to detect the device being used and redirect the customers there. Some of the sites allowed customers to choose, but most relied on the scripts to direct readers to the "correct" site. But these started losing favor with customers when it became apparent that the mobile versions of the sites were minimal or ignored.

Then in 2010, web designers started discussing the benefits of "graceful degradation" and "progressive enhancement." *Graceful degradation* is a form of fault tolerance web designers use to build sites that continue to operate correctly even in browsers that are not the most modern. In other words, a site looks okay and works correctly, but it might not have all the features. It degrades down to what the browser can support.

TRY IT YOURSELF ▼

Apply Graceful Degradation to a Site

Graceful degradation can be applied to any website. These are the steps you take to determine what needs to degrade and how it should do so:

1. Look at the page to determine what elements are on it. Look for things like navigation, scripts, and modern HTML tags such as in HTML5 and in CSS beyond CSS 1 or CSS 2.
2. Once you have a list of components on the page, evaluate each component to determine how critical it is to the content of the page. For example, an airline site would have a critical need for a flight tracker, but it would not have a critical need for an article about how to pack a suitcase.
3. Using the same list of components, evaluate which elements are most likely to fail. For example, CSS 2 properties are widely supported, even in older browsers, but an Ajax-based flight tracker has a much higher probability of failure in older browsers.
4. Once you have your list of the most critical components and those most likely to fail, this is your list of components that should have some form of degradation. Prioritize this list by criticality and probability of failure.
5. Look at your prioritized list and determine how much time and effort it will take to create a degraded version of the component. This tells you how much it will cost to gracefully degrade the components of your site.
6. Once you know how much time it will take, you should start with your prioritized list and create alternatives to the most important components. Remember that an alternative could be that the component is removed from the page. It is better not to show customers components that could fail, especially if you don't have any better alternative that would work.

The alternatives to your design should be added to your site so that they appear only if they are needed. You can use tools like Internet Explorer conditional comments or JavaScript to display the alternatives only when they are needed.

Steven Champeon introduced the concept of *progressive enhancement* to designers in 2003 at SXSW. This technique turns graceful degradation on its head. Instead of starting with a ton of features and then slowly removing them to let older, less compliant browsers continue to work, designers should start with the absolute minimum required to make the page work and then add features for more feature-rich browsers.

▼ TRY IT YOURSELF

Apply Progressive Enhancement to a Site

Just like with graceful degradation, you can apply progressive enhancement to a website. The steps are similar, but the goals are different:

1. Determine the one component of the web page that is critical for the page. For example, a hotel site would need to have a page to reserve rooms.
2. Build the page using just that component, and do your best to build it for the oldest or least compliant browser your site will be supporting. So, if your site supports Internet Explorer 7 and up, you should focus on getting the feature to work on IE 7. Remember, too, that mobile browsers are often very limited in features.
3. Look at features that are supported by other browsers that would make the component work better and add them to the page. A good place to start is with CSS and scripting.
4. Test your page in as many browsers as possible to make sure the core functionality remains intact.

Progressive enhancement has a goal of supporting as many devices and browsers as possible by focusing on core functionality and using cutting-edge features as improvements on the functionality rather than requirements to get the functionality.

The main difference between progressive enhancement and graceful degradation is how the designers view less functional browsers and devices. Rather than thinking "people should just upgrade to a better browser," designers started recognizing that sometimes the browser people had was the browser they were going to use. And building a web page that supported the browsers that were visiting it was a better strategy.

Responsive Design Finally Entered the Picture

In 2010, Ethan Marcotte coined the term *responsive web design* (*RWD*) in an article on *A List Apart*. He then published a book about RWD in 2011. But RWD didn't start overtaking progressive enhancement as the preferred design technique until late 2012 or early 2013. By the end of 2013, RWD was very popular among web designers and template builders. It is now common to describe a website as being "responsive" or to otherwise imply that it uses RWD.

CAUTION

Newer Doesn't Always Mean Better in Web Browsers

One of the biggest challenges for web designers is the large number of web browsers out there. It's easy to assume that if someone has the most modern browser available, it must have all the most modern features. But the reality is very different. While it's true that desktop browsers have been rapidly incrementing new features, the rise of mobile has been accompanied by a rise in browsers that *don't* support new features. Mobile devices typically have browsers that are one to three revisions back from their desktop counterparts.

Why We Need Responsive Web Design

Responsive web design is a combination of many design techniques, including the following:

- CSS3 and especially media queries. (Cascading Style Sheets are discussed in Hour 6, "Basic CSS," while media queries are discussed in Hour 10, "CSS Media Queries.")
- HTML5 and clean, valid code. (Hour 5, "HTML for Responsive Web Design," discusses HTML5, and all the examples in the book use HTML5.)
- Feature, device, and browser detection using scripts (see Hour 22, "Device and Feature Detection").
- Progressive enhancement (covered in detail in Hour 4, "Progressive Enhancement").
- Server-side components such as RESS to produce faster sites. (RESS is discussed in Hour 23, "Using RESS with RWD.")

These techniques are important because the number of different types of browsers and devices web designs need to support is only growing larger. And instead of the features they support growing more consistent, every day new devices come on the market. But when a customer browses the web on a refrigerator, he wants to be able to do the same things that he can do on his phone or on his laptop.

Responsive web design attempts to respond to the device viewing the page and provide the best experience possible for that device. As you can see in Figure 1.2, a web page might look very different when displayed on a mobile phone than it looks on a desktop computer, but the content remains the same.

FIGURE 1.2
Desktop and mobile phone versions of the same web page.

Summary

In this hour, you've learned about the basic features of responsive web design (RWD). You've gotten an overview of the techniques used in RWD and found out why RWD is so important.

Workshop

The workshop contains quiz questions to help you process what you've learned in this lesson. Try to answer all the questions before you read the answers.

Q&A

Q. Isn't RWD just CSS media queries?

A. In a sense it is, as that is the primary method designers use for creating responsive designs. But there is a lot more to RWD than just media queries, as you'll discover as you read more of this book.

Q. What about fluid or flexible layouts? Aren't they important for RWD?

A. Yes, creating layouts that flow with the width of a web browser is a critical part of RWD. This is covered in detail in Hour 12, "Layout."

Quiz

1. True or False: Graceful degradation is a form of fault tolerance.
2. True or False: Responsive web design is just a form of progressive enhancement.
3. True or False: You can only do responsive web design with CSS3.

Answers

1. True. Graceful degradation in design has been around for a long time as a form of fault tolerance. Designers use it to create sites that continue to operate even under suboptimal conditions.
2. False. Progressive enhancement is often used in responsive design, but websites that use it do not have to be responsive and vice versa.
3. False. Responsive design is done with media queries, which were added to CSS as a part of CSS 2.

Exercises

1. Visit your favorite websites and check to see if they use responsive design. The easiest way to do this is to simply open your computer browser to the page and then resize the browser down as small as it can go. If the page changes layout or design to better support the smaller screens, then the design is responsive.

2. Choose a website you want to make responsive. You should use this website throughout the rest of the book to practice what you're learning. I recommend using a website you both own and feel strongly about. This will help you remain committed to learning RWD so that you can improve your site.

HOUR 2

Alternatives to Responsive Web Design

WHAT YOU'LL LEARN IN THIS HOUR:

- How to build a table-based layout
- How to use CSS positioning for layout
- How to use CSS floats for design
- How CSS3 column properties work
- How to use three types of detection scripts

Using responsive web design is an important way to design web pages, but it is not the only way. In fact, there are many different ways to create web pages that support both mobile and desktop layouts.

In this hour you will learn how to build web pages using several methods that are valid HTML5 and use modern techniques. All these methods can be used in conjunction with RWD, but they are also reasonable solutions on their own.

In this hour you will also learn about detection scripts and how to use them to detect browsers, devices, and objects on your web pages. This hour explains the benefits and drawbacks of these scripts and where to find good resources for using them.

Table-Based Layouts

Using table-based layouts is one of the oldest ways to design a web page layout. Before CSS was widely supported, one of the only ways to get even a mildly complex layout was to use HTML tables.

The basis of a table-based layout was, unsurprisingly, the `table` tag. The benefit of this method of web design is that it is well supported in many HTML editors and web browsers, so it can be very easy to put up. The secret is to turn off the borders, so that the table isn't obvious.

▼ TRY IT YOURSELF

Build a Simple Table-Based Layout

With HTML5, using tables for layout is a valid way of designing web pages. You just need to tell the browser or user agent that the table is not data but rather design. Learn how to use this method in the following steps:

1. Design your web page on paper, in a graphics program, or in your head. In your prototype, be sure to show the borders of each section of your design. Figure 2.1 shows how you might define the tables on a sample web page.

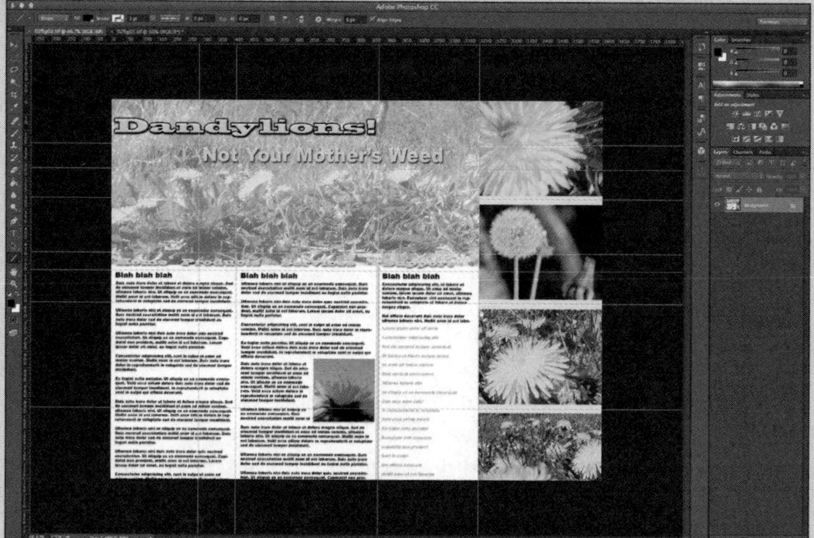

FIGURE 2.1
A preliminary layout with grid lines where the table should be.

2. Once you have your grid lines established, you should determine how the table cells should be displayed. Figure 2.2 shows the table cells in black lines above the guides.
3. Build the table by using the code in Listing 2.1. Note that the table in Figures 2.1 and 2.2 has five columns and eight rows, and Listing 2.1 reflects this.

TRY IT YOURSELF ▼

Build a Simple Table-Based Layout

continued

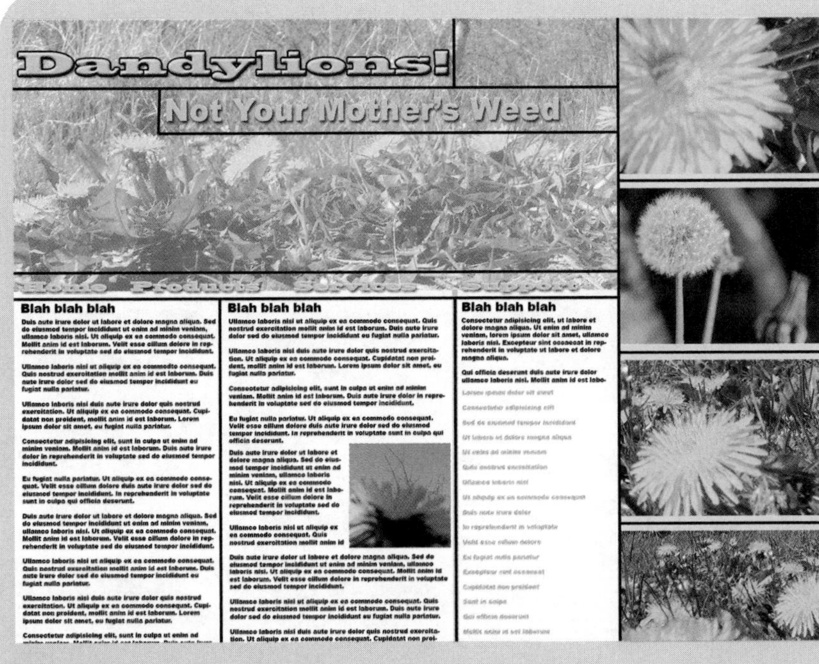

FIGURE 2.2
A layout with the table cells defined.

LISTING 2.1 Basic Table for Layout

```
<!doctype html>
<html>
<head>
<meta charset="UTF-8">
<title>Basic Table for a Layout</title>
</head>
<body>
<table border="1">
    <tr>
        <td> </td>
        <td> </td>
        <td> </td>
        <td> </td>
        <td> </td>
    </tr>
    <tr>
        <td> </td>
        <td> </td>
        <td> </td>
        <td> </td>
        <td> </td>
```

▼ TRY IT YOURSELF

Build a Simple Table-Based Layout
continued

```
    </tr>
    <tr>
        <td> </td>
        <td> </td>
        <td> </td>
        <td> </td>
        <td> </td>
    </tr>
    <tr>
        <td> </td>
        <td> </td>
        <td> </td>
        <td> </td>
        <td> </td>
    </tr>
    <tr>
        <td> </td>
        <td> </td>
        <td> </td>
        <td> </td>
        <td> </td>
    </tr>
    <tr>
        <td> </td>
        <td> </td>
        <td> </td>
        <td> </td>
        <td> </td>
    </tr>
    <tr>
        <td> </td>
        <td> </td>
        <td> </td>
        <td> </td>
        <td> </td>
    </tr>
    <tr>
        <td> </td>
        <td> </td>
        <td> </td>
        <td> </td>
        <td> </td>
    </tr>
</table>
</body>
</html>
```

The ` ` characters are non-breaking spaces used to hold the table cells open. They will be removed from the final table.

4. To tell browsers that this is a layout table and not tabular data, add the `role="presentation"` attribute to the `<table>` tag (for example, `<table role="presentation">`). It's also a good idea to have your table take up the full width of the screen, so add a style to set that (for example, `<table role="presentation" style="width: 100%;">`).
5. Now things get challenging, and you need to start separating the rows and columns by using the `rowspan` and `colspan` attributes. The easiest way is to look at your mockup with the cells blocked out (Figure 2.2) and move from right to left across the columns. In this example, the first cell (with the headline "Dandylions!" in it) spans three columns. Add the attribute `colspan="3"` to the first `<td>` tag and then remove the following two `<td>` tags because they are now spanned by that first tag (for example, `<td colspan="3">`).
6. As you move through the columns, bear in mind that some columns can span rows as well. On the first row, the final cell on the right with the large open dandelion spans three rows. So, to that `<td>` tag add the attribute `rowspan="3"` and then remove one `<td>` tag from the two following rows. Listing 2.2 shows how the HTML looks after all the row and column spanning attributes are added.

LISTING 2.2 Table for Layout Adjusted to the Design

```
<!doctype html>
<html>
<head>
<meta charset="UTF-8">
<title>Basic Table for a Layout</title>
</head>
<body>
<table role="presentation" style="width: 100%" border="1">
    <tr>
        <td colspan="3">Dandylions!</td>
        <td> </td>
        <td rowspan="3">Big Dandelion Pic</td>
    </tr>
    <tr>
        <td> </td>
        <td colspan="3">Not Your Mother's Weed</td>
    </tr>
    <tr>
        <td colspan="4"> </td>
    </tr>
    <tr>
        <td colspan="4"> </td>
        <td rowspan="3">Seeded Dandelion Pic</td>
    </tr>
    <tr>
```

TRY IT YOURSELF ▼

Build a Simple Table-Based Layout

continued

NOTE

Setting the Border Can Indicate a Layout Table

In order to make a layout table valid in HTML5, you need to indicate that it is a layout table rather than a table of data. To do this, you can use the `role="presentation"` attribute. Or, you can instead change the table border to zero, like this: `border="0"`; however, user agents can still misconstrue this, so it is better to use the `role` attribute.

▼ TRY IT YOURSELF

Build a Simple Table-Based Layout
continued

```
        <td colspan="4">Navigation links</td>
    </tr>
    <tr>
        <td colspan="2" rowspan="3">Column 1</td>
        <td rowspan="3">Column 2</td>
        <td rowspan="3">Column 3</td>
    </tr>
    <tr>
        <td>Smaller Dandelion Pic</td>
    </tr>
    <tr>
        <td>Field of Dandelions Pic</td>
    </tr>
</table>
</body>
</html>
```

This listing shows that you can add some text in the cells so that you can remember what goes where in the design. You will replace this text with images and other HTML in the final design.

7. Add the images and HTML to the design. For this design, you need to cut the background image for the headlines into several pieces so that it will fit in the design. Figure 2.3 shows one way to split that image to fit in the design.

FIGURE 2.3
The background image cut up into table segments.

8. Finally, add the rest of the images and other HTML to your web page design. (I leave that for you to do on your own.)

After you've completed this Try It Yourself on your own design, you will have a web page that works in modern browsers. It is not a responsive design, but it is valid HTML5.

The biggest problem with using tables for layout is that they form a very rigid design. Many older cell phones don't display tables, or if they do, they force the designs to scroll horizontally. And many cell phones other than smart phones don't scroll horizontally at all.

CSS Layouts

Using CSS is the modern way of creating a web design layout, but many people find it more difficult to understand than table-based design. There are two main ways to create layouts with CSS: CSS positioning and CSS floats.

CSS Positioning

CSS positioning is often the first place beginning designers start when learning CSS layout because it is easy to understand. With CSS positioning, you treat a web page like it's a paper layout. You decide where you want each individual element and then you position it on the page based on an x,y grid, starting in the upper-left corner. This is called *absolute positioning.*

To use absolute positioning, you use two or three CSS properties. The first property is the `position` style property. This tells the browser that the element is going to be positioned in some way on the page. To specify absolute positioning, you use the value `absolute` (for example, `position: absolute;`).

Then you define where the element will be placed on the screen by using the properties `top` and `left`. For example, if you want an element placed at the upper-left corner of the screen, you add the styles `top: 0px;` and `left: 0px;` to your style sheet.

TRY IT YOURSELF ▼

Create a Layout Using CSS Positioning

CSS positioning allows you to be very explicit about where various elements go on a web page by letting you place them exactly where you want them. In this tutorial you will take the same design you used for the table layout and lay it out by using CSS positioning:

1. Design your web page on paper, in a graphics program, or in your head. In your prototype, make note of the x and y positions for the various elements in your design. Figure 2.4 shows the positions for a few of the elements in this design.

Create a Layout Using CSS Positioning
continued

FIGURE 2.4
The design with the positions of some of the elements indicated.

2. Open your HTML editor and add the `<div>` elements you need to create the web page. Listing 2.3 shows the HTML for this.

LISTING 2.3 HTML Layout with Absolute Positioning

```
<!doctype html>
<html>
  <head>
    <meta charset="UTF-8">
    <title>Using Absolute Positioning</title>
  </head>
  <body>
    <header id="banner">
      <h1>Dandylions!</h1>
      <h2>Not Your Mother's Weed</h2>
    </header>
    <nav>
    Navigation Links
    </nav>
    <article id="column1">
    </article>
    <article id="column2">
    </article>
    <aside id="column3">
```

TRY IT YOURSELF ▼

Create a Layout Using CSS Positioning
continued

```
    </aside>
    <aside id="rightcol">
      <div id="bigflower"></div>
      <div id="seededflower"></div>
      <div id="closeup"></div>
      <div id="field"></div>
    </aside>
  </body>
</html>
```

3. Add your CSS to the HTML, either as an internal style sheet using `<style>` tags or as an external document.
4. For each element to be positioned, include both the width and height as well as the position location. Listing 2.4 shows my CSS styles.

LISTING 2.4 CSS for Absolute Positioning

```
#banner {
  width: 1200px;
  height: 500px;
  position: absolute;
  top: 0px;
  left: 0px;
}
h1 {
  position: relative;
  top: 24px;
  left: 7px;
}
h2 {
  position: relative;
  top: 24px;
  left: 201px;
}
nav {
  width: 1200px;
  height: 45px;
  position: absolute;
  top: 500px;
  left: 0px;
}
#column1 {
  width: 412px;
  min-height: 700px;
  position: absolute;
  top: 545px;
  left: 0px;
}
#column2 {
  width: 466px;
```

▼ TRY IT YOURSELF

Create a Layout Using CSS Positioning
continued

```
  min-height: 700px;
  position: absolute;
  top: 545px;
  left: 412px;
}
#column3 {
  width: 322px;
  min-height: 700px;
  position: absolute;
  top: 545px;
  left: 878px;
}
#rightcol {
  width: 400px;
  min-height: 1312px;
  position: absolute;
  top: 0px;
  left: 1200px;
}
#bigflower, #seededflower, #closeup, #field {
  width: 400px;
  height: 328px;
  position: relative;
  top: 0px;
  left: 0px;
}
```

5. Add your text and other styles to finish the document.

You can cut up the background image similarly to how you cut it up in the Try It Yourself "Build a Simple Table-Based Layout."

NOTE

What Is the Relative Position Style?

You may have noticed in the preceding Try It Yourself that some of the elements have the property `position: relative;` rather than `position: absolute;`. That is because they are elements that are inside other absolute positioned elements.

The `position: relative;` property tells the browser to treat the origin point as the upper-left corner of the current element rather than as the upper-left corner of the browser.

The biggest problem with using CSS positioning for creating web pages is that it creates a very static layout. For example, the site you built in the above two Try It Yourself sections is 1600 pixels wide. This will look fine in a wide-screen device, but it will be hard to read in smaller devices.

CSS Floats

A more flexible CSS layout relies on the CSS `float` property to take elements out of the normal web page flow and let them slide to their position naturally.

When you apply the `float` style property to an HTML element, such as an image, it is removed from the normal flow of the HTML and floated to either the left (`float: left;`) or the right (`float: right;`). The HTML content following it is still in normal flow, so it ends up wrapping around the floated image. Figure 2.5 shows an image with a paragraph of text displayed in normal flow and then with the image floated to the left.

NOTE

What Is Normal Flow?

When you build an HTML web page, *normal flow* is how the browser displays the contents absent any style or positioning directions. Web browsers display the contents of web pages in the order they appear in the HTML document, and they allot them as much space as they need. In other words, a paragraph of text will take up 100% of the browser width and as much vertical space as it requires.

Most web designers use normal flow by placing the content they want at the top of the page first in the HTML and the content they want at the bottom last in the HTML.

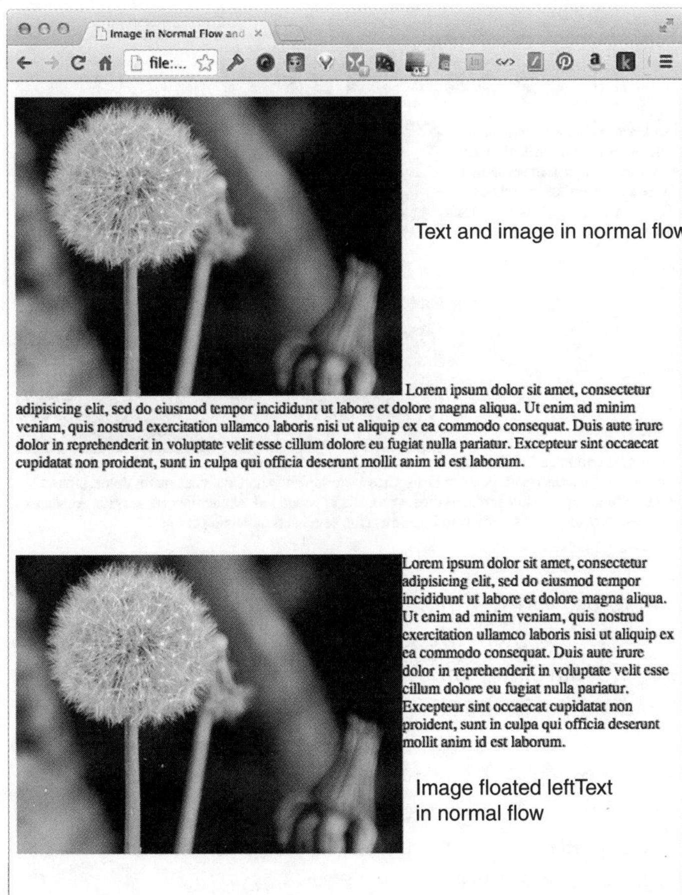

FIGURE 2.5
An image in normal flow and floated left.

In the figure, the same image and text are placed in the HTML. The only difference is that the second image has the `float: left;` style property set on it. As you can see, when an image is in normal flow, any text following it inline is positioned to the right of the image, at the very bottom.

Web designers use the `float` property to position entire blocks of text and images on a page.

To work with CSS floats for design, you also need to know about the `clear` property. This property stops the float and moves all content to below the floated element. For example, Figure 2.6 shows a floated image with two paragraphs following it, but only the first paragraph is alongside the image.

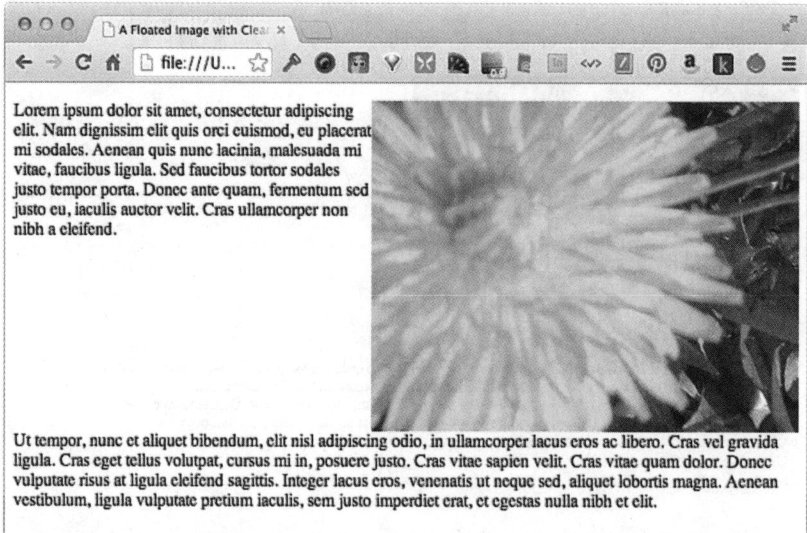

FIGURE 2.6
A floated image with two paragraphs, the second of which is cleared.

The best reason to use CSS float for design is because it is more flexible than other methods. But there are some problems with using just floats for web design. In Figures 2.5 and 2.6, if the browser window is narrower, it can make the text lines very short and hard to read. Floated designs are also very hard to build because they flex and change depending on how much space is available for the non-floated elements. You can alleviate this by setting widths on every element, but if you set explicit widths, you run into the same problems as with CSS positioning and table-based layouts.

Modern CSS Layouts

Modern CSS, and specifically CSS3, gives web designers another very powerful tool for creating interesting web designs: CSS columns or multicolumn layout. CSS multicolumn layout recognizes that most web designs are really just columns of different widths. With CSS3 column properties, web designers can create columns that flow depending on how much content there is but still remain in multiple columns defined by the designer.

You can use 10 CSS3 properties to define columns on web pages:

- `column-count`—Defines the number of columns on an element.
- `column-width`—Defines the width of each column.
- `column-min-width`—Defines the minimum width of each column.
- `column-width-policy`—Defines whether column widths are flexible or strict when there is extra space.
- `column-gap`—Defines the width of the space between columns.
- `column-rule`—Defines the width, style, and color of the line between the columns.
- `column-rule-color`—Defines the color of the line between the columns.
- `column-rule-style`—Defines the style (for example, solid, dashed, dotted) of the line between the columns.
- `column-rule-width`—Defines the width of the line between the columns.
- `column-span`—Defines the number of columns that an element inside the columns should span.

By using the CSS3 column properties, you can create a web page with a lot of content that flows through the columns much as a newspaper layout does. Figure 2.7 shows the four-column layout created in Listing 2.5.

CAUTION

You Must Use Browser Prefixes for the Column Properties

As of this writing, the CSS3 column properties work in all modern browsers. But they work only if you use browser-prefixed versions of the properties. These are the prefixes:

- Firefox: `-moz-`
- Internet Explorer: `-ms-`
- Opera: `-o-`
- Safari and Chrome: `-webkit-`

You should add the browser-prefixed versions first in your CSS and follow them all with the official property. That way the cascade will apply the official property last and keep your web pages up-to-date.

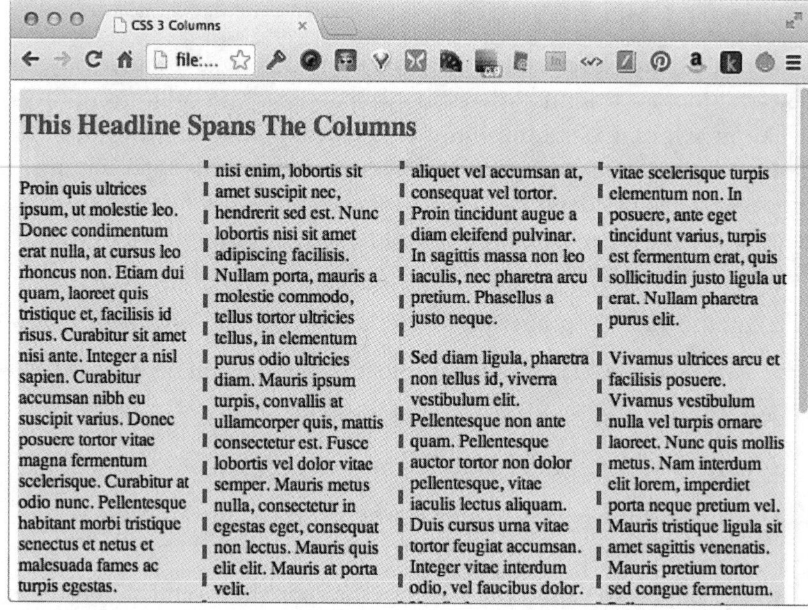

FIGURE 2.7
A four-column layout using CSS3 columns

LISTING 2.5 Four-Column Layout with CSS3

```
<!doctype html>
<html>
<head>
<meta charset="UTF-8">
<title>CSS3 Columns</title>
<style>
#columns {
  width: 100%;
  background-color: #BBF0F9;
  -moz-column-count: 4;
  -webkit-column-count: 4;
  column-count: 4;
  -moz-column-rule: 4px dashed blue;
  -webkit-column-rule: 4px dashed blue;
  column-rule: 4px dashed blue;
}
div h1 {
  color: blue;
  font-size:x-large;
  -moz-column-span: all;
  -webkit-column-span: all;
  column-span: all;
```

```
}
</style>
</head>
<body>
<div id="columns">
  <h1>This Headline Spans The Columns</h1>
  <p>Proin quis ultrices ipsum, ut molestie leo. Donec erat nulla,
  at cursus leo rhoncus non. Etiam dui quam, laoreet et, facilisis
  id risus.</p>
  <p>Quisque ac urna id vehicula iaculis. Nam turpis libero, pulvinar
  faucibus quam suscipit, fringilla semper mi. Quisque cursus tortor,
  non ullamcorper metus accumsan vitae.</p>
  <p>Aliquam sodales volutpat turpis, laoreet ultricies dolor egestas nec.
  Vestibulum vitae tortor massa. Maecenas ultrices consectetur adipiscing.
  felis pretium, pulvinar risus sed, venenatis nunc.</p>
  <p>Sed diam ligula, pharetra non tellus id, viverra vestibulum elit.
  Pellentesque non ante quam. Pellentesque auctor tortor non dolor,
  vitae iaculis lectus aliquam.</p>
  <p>Vivamus ultrices arcu et facilisis posuere. Vivamus nulla vel
  turpis ornare laoreet. Nunc quis mollis metus. Nam interdum lorem,
  imperdiet porta neque pretium vel.</p>
</div>
</body>
</html>
```

The advantage to using CSS3 columns in web page layouts is that they can readily adjust to fit the browser window width. In Listing 2.5, I set the width on the container element (`<div id="columns">`) to 100% so that the layout would flex with the width of the browser. I did not set any column widths so that the browser could make four equally spaced columns.

But this raises a concern with using CSS3 columns for layout. On a narrower browser, such as a smart phone in portrait mode, layouts with more than three or four columns can be very hard to read. The text can get very squished. You can see this in Figure 2.8, with the Chrome browser resized down to its narrowest width.

FIGURE 2.8
A four-column layout in Chrome, with the browser resized to its narrowest width.

Detection Scripts

Detection scripts are scripts usually written in JavaScript or PHP that detect something in the web browser or device viewing the page. They provide fallback programming or even redirect a customer to a completely different page or website.

Browser Detection

One of the most common ways that web designers create web pages that work on mobile as well as desktop devices is through browser detection scripts. The idea behind these scripts is that most web browsers and devices send a signature to the web server that the designer can use to tailor the web page to fit that browser.

On the surface, this sounds like a good idea. If you know that Android phones don't support some feature you want to have on your site, you can detect those phones and give them an alternative.

But browser detection scripts have a huge problem: *There are hundreds if not thousands of different browsers.* And to make matters worse, not all browsers send unique signatures. In fact, some browsers have been known to send false and misleading browser information so that web designers won't block those browsers.

Mobile Detection

One way to deal with the problems caused by browser detection scripts is to use a program for mobile detection. This script looks at the device requesting the page, and if it's a mobile device, like a phone or tablet, does something different than if it's a computer.

One script that is very easy to use is from Detect Mobile Browsers (`http://detectmobilebrowsers.com`). You can download a script and use it to detect many different kinds of mobile phones and tablets. The script lets you do different things for each device, including redirecting users to a new web page.

Another tool that is harder to use is WURFL (Wireless Universal Resource FiLe; `http://wurfl.sourceforge.net`). The WURFL file is a huge repository of devices that is updated regularly to include more mobile devices. It is delivered as an XML file that a web developer can mine to display web pages to very specific devices. This tool is helpful for web designers who need to get very granular in their device detection, but it is harder to use than Detect Mobile Browsers.

Mobile detection suffers from the same problem as browser detection in that there are hundreds or thousands of different mobile devices in use. Detecting for most of them (as WURFL attempts to do) can result in slower pages, while not impacting a large number of customers. However, if you're building a website for the mobile industry, it might make sense to be able to detect exactly what device a customer is using.

Object Detection

Using object detection is the best way to create fallback options for browsers and devices because it doesn't rely on the device or browser to report accurately what it is. Instead, object detection looks at what the device or browser *can do* and builds a web page around those capabilities.

For example, HTML5 offers the ability to create offline web applications using the `applicationCache` object on the `window` or global element. This is useful for creating web applications that don't have to be always online. But you can store information offline only if the browser supports it. Listing 2.6 shows you how you can detect for that object and then provide fallback information when it doesn't exist.

LISTING 2.6 Simple Object Detection Script

```
if (window.applicationCache) {
  document.write("Browser supports offline web apps");
} else {
  document.write("Browser does not support offline web apps");
}
```

As you can see, this JavaScript script uses the `document.write` function to show where you'd place your actual functions using the `applicationCache` and the fallback functions when it isn't available. This script does not need to know what browser or device is viewing the page, just whether the required object is available.

The primary drawback to using object detection is that it assumes that you will know which object is most likely to fail. If you aren't sure which object is most likely to fail, it can be tempting to create scripts that have fallback options for even the most basic objects. While this will make your web pages more compatible with older browsers and devices, the number of people using those browsers is very small, and so the return for the effort required will be small, too.

Summary

In this hour, you've learned about some of the alternatives to RWD that web designers use. You've learned about table-based designs and some of the pitfalls of this technique. You've also learned how to use CSS positioning and floats to create layouts that are laid out with extreme precision or a more flexible format. This hour introduced the CSS3 concepts of columns, and you've learned how to use these new properties to create a newspaper-like layout (see Table 2.1).

In this hour, you've also learned about alternatives to RWD that take the browser or device into consideration, using scripts to detect various features. Browser detection, device detection, and object detection are all good solutions, and while there are certain drawbacks to each, each can serve a purpose.

TABLE 2.1 CSS Properties Covered in Hour 2

Property	Description	Values

`position`	How the element will be positioned.	`absolute`
		`relative`
		`static`
		`fixed`
		`inherit`

`top`	Where to position the element from the top of the browser or container.	`<length>`
		`<percentage>`
		`auto`
		`inherit`

`left`	Where to position the element from the left of the browser or container.	`<length>`
		`<percentage>`
		`auto`
		`inherit`

`float`	Takes elements out of the normal flow to float to the right or left.	`right`
		`left`
		`none`
		`inherit`

`clear`	Stops the floated property and moves all following content below the floated property.	`right`
		`left`
		`none`
		`both`
		`inherit`

`column-count`	Defines the number of columns on the element.	`<number>`

`column-width`	Defines the width of each column.	`<length>`
		`<percentage>`
		`auto`
		`inherit`

`column-min-width`	Defines the minimum width of each column.	`<length>`
		`<percentage>`
		`auto`
		`inherit`

`column-width-policy`	Defines whether column widths are flexible or strict when there is extra space.	`flexible`
		`inherit`
		`strict`

`column-gap`	Defines the width of the space between columns.	`<length>`
		`<percentage>`
		`auto`
		`inherit`

`column-rule`	Defines the width, style, and color of the line between the columns.	`<column-rule-color> <column-rule-style> <column-rule-width>`

Property	Description	Values
`column-rule-color`	Defines the color of the line between the columns.	`<color>`

`column-rule-style`	Defines the style (for example, solid, dashed, dotted) of the line between the columns.	`none`
		`dotted`
		`dashed`
		`solid`
		`double`
		`groove`
		`ridge`
		`inset`
		`window-inset`
		`outset`
		`hidden`

`column-rule-width`	Defines the width of the line between the columns.	`<length>`
		`<percentage>`
		`auto`
		`inherit`

`column-span`	Defines the number of columns an element inside the columns should span.	`<number>`

Workshop

The workshop contains quiz questions to help you process what you've learned in this lesson. Try to answer all the questions before you read the answers.

Q&A

Q. You mention the term *user agent* in this lesson, but what is a user agent?

A. *User agent* is often used interchangeably with the term *web browser*, but it includes any device or program that can view a web page, not just web browsers. For example, some scripts can visit a web page and grab the contents for reading offline. These are not technically web browsers, but they view the page contents and are therefore user agents.

Q. Is it really a good idea to use CSS3 columns if they aren't supported without browser prefixes?

A. If you create your CSS with the CSS3 property last, this will act as a fallback itself. Because the cascade walks through the CSS in order, the last property the browser supports will be the one that is used. When you use browser prefix versions, you are acknowledging that some browsers have not fully implemented the standard (by using the official property), but they do support it. This also allows you to decide what you want to support. For example, if you don't want Internet Explorer to display the columns until it's fully compatible, then you just leave off the `-ms-` prefixed version of the style.

Q. You seem to feel that detection scripts are bad. Why is that?

A. I don't think all detection scripts are bad, but I think they give designers a false sense of security. If you are using a mobile detection script to send all mobile phones to a different site, and a new phone comes out that your script doesn't detect, you may think your site is perfect when some customers aren't getting an ideal solution. In contrast, when you use object detection scripts, you don't have to continually update your scripts for new devices or browsers. You just detect for the objects your site is using and leave it at that.

Quiz

1. What do you need to do to make a table-based layout valid HTML5?
2. What is the difference between CSS positioning and CSS floats?
3. Name the four browser prefixes used on CSS properties.
4. What does an object detection script detect?

Answers

1. The `role="presentation"` attribute defines a table as a layout table, and you can also use the `border="0"` attribute for the same purpose.
2. CSS positioning places elements in a specific location on the page, defined by x and y coordinates. A CSS float removes the element from the normal flow and places it to the far right or far left of the current container and flows all subsequent content around it.
3. The four browser prefixes are `-ms-`, `-o-`, `-moz-`, and `-webkit-`.
4. An object detection script detects elements in a web page that might be problematic for certain browsers and devices. These are typically part of the Document Object Model (DOM).

Exercises

1. Take a look at the web page you decided to work with in Hour 1, "What Is Responsive Web Design?" and decide if it already uses any of the methods described in this lesson: tables for layout, CSS positioning, CSS floats, CSS columns, or detection scripts. Remember that a web page can use any combination of these tools at any time and is not limited to just one.
2. Once you know what the site is using, evaluate how well it's using those tools. For example, if it's using tables for layout, does it have the `role=presentation` attribute set? Does it use the correct browser prefixes? Is it detecting objects or browsers? If you find errors or problems, correct them.
3. Many designers find that CSS float layouts are often the easiest to convert to RWD. If the site you're working with doesn't already use that style of layout, create a new version using CSS float. If you need more help doing this, see my article "Using the CSS Float Property" on my website (`www.html5in24hours.com/2014/09/using-css-float/`).

HOUR 3
The Growth of Mobile

WHAT YOU'LL LEARN IN THIS HOUR:

- How to support several mobile devices
- The size and resolutions of smartphones and tablets
- How Retina screens are changing the way pages are designed
- Why you should consider RWD for supporting mobile devices

Responsive web design (RWD) came about because of mobile devices. Before RWD existed, web designers had few options for creating a website that worked reliably on both small devices like cell phones and large screens like HD monitors. You could use the tools described in Hour 2, "Alternatives to Responsive Web Design," but they were never intended for the vast number of changes that mobile devices added to the landscape.

Designers used to often design pages which assumed that if a browser is "modern," it should support all modern HTML, CSS, and JavaScript (or DOM) features. But mobile browsers often don't support all the features that modern computer browsers do.

In this hour you will learn more about the basic differences between mobile devices. There is more to mobile design than just responsive design. You will also learn more about how to support specific devices.

Basic Cell Phones

Just a few years ago, most people with cell phones had basic cell phones. And while basic phones are not as popular in the West, there are still a lot of countries in the world where simple cell phones are still popular. But many web designers completely discount them.

These phones have the following features:

- They are very small. Some of the older phones have screens 320px wide or even smaller. But they can still browse web pages.
- They don't scroll horizontally. Most basic cell phones that can display web pages only scroll vertically down the page. This

means that wide layouts don't display well on these phones, and customers on these phones will never see any content that is on the right of the main content.

- They don't display tables and other complicated HTML and CSS. While some of the later-model flip phones do support tables and advanced HTML, the majority of these phones either don't support them or do so poorly. Table-based layouts don't display correctly on these phones.
- They have limited scripting capabilities. This is one of the most serious issues with these phones because without scripting, it is very difficult to use fallback options for them.

Basic cell phones often use web browsers that were built for them by the company that sells the phone. This means there isn't a lot of information about what the browser can and cannot support. The Opera Mini browser is the browser most commonly used with these phones. And as of August 2014, Opera Mini still had 3.7% of the worldwide mobile browser market, according to NetMarketShare (`http://www.netmarketshare.com`). That same site said that the market share for other or unrecognized phone browsers was 1.26%.

While the share of Opera Mini and unrecognized browsers has been dropping over the past year or two, 4.96% is still a lot of people on a lot of phones. When you then look at what Opera Mini seems to support on sites like CanIUse.com (`http://caniuse.com`), this number takes on greater significance. And smart web designers consider these users when building their sites.

How to Support Basic Cell Phones

There are many things you can do to support basic cell phones on your website beyond RWD. These are some of the things that I like to do:

- Keep the images as small as possible. Large images take longer to download, and most cell phones have expensive data plans or data limits.
- Use very basic HTML and CSS. As I mentioned above, many of these phones have very basic web browsers that can't support a lot of the newest features of HTML5.
- Avoid frames, tables, Flash, image maps, and JavaScript. Many of these features either won't work well on the phones or won't fit on the screens.

- Build the layout small and narrow. Some cell phones have screens that are no more than 150px wide, and as I mentioned above, many can't scroll horizontally.
- Don't use columns. When a web page is only 150px wide, two columns would each be no more than 75px wide, and text that small is almost impossible to read.
- Test all your pages on a real cell phone. This is a very important step, especially if your website must support basic cell phones. While there are emulators out there you can use, nothing beats trying it out on a real phone to see your site as your customers see it.

The trick to supporting basic cell phones is to keep the sites you build as simple as possible.

Smartphones

Smartphones are growing in popularity every day, and more and more people are using smartphones to access the web. In fact, many people would argue that smartphones are the reason we need RWD.

The best thing about most smartphones is that they use browsers that have good support for modern technology like HTML5 and CSS3. They aren't as large as laptop or desktop computers, but they often have the resolution required to display web pages just as effectively. Table 3.1 shows the resolutions of popular smartphones.

TABLE 3.1 Resolutions of Popular Smartphones (in Early 2014)

Device	Screen Size	Resolution
Apple iPhone 4/4s	3.5-inch Retina	640×960
Apple iPhone 5s/5c	4-inch Retina	640×1136
Blackberry Z30	5 inches	720×1280
Google Nexus 5	5 inches	1080×1920
HTC One X	4.7 inches	720×1280
Motorola Moto X	4.7 inches	720×1280
Nokia Lumia	6 inches	1080×1920
Samsung Galaxy S4	5 inches	1080×1920
Samsung Galaxy S5	5.2 inches	1440×2560
Sony Xperia Z1	4.3 inches	720×1280

When you're planning an RWD site, you should consider both the screen size and the resolution of the devices you're targeting. For example, if a device has a high resolution but a small screen size, even though you can fit a multicolumn layout on the page, it might have text that is completely illegible on the small screen.

How to Support Smartphones

Smartphones are much easier to support than basic cell phones because they have much more sophisticated browsers. But there are still things you need to be aware of when you're designing for smartphones:

- Even a 6-inch diagonal screen doesn't give you a lot of real estate to work with, no matter what the resolution. Keep in mind that the best designs are small and don't require a lot of scrolling.
- Screen size also comes into play when you're dealing with clicking links or filling in forms. The easier you can make these tasks for your customers, the more they will like your website.
- Smartphones are designed to adjust the content display to portrait or landscape mode, depending on the phone's orientation. But if your web design doesn't adjust (or adjusts too much), the page can be difficult to read.
- Font sizes are important, especially on higher-resolution screens. Just because a screen is a Retina display or has a huge resolution doesn't mean that a 12-point font is going to be legible.
- Don't assume that smartphone users are going to be always online. Basic cell phones and smartphones are meant to travel, and while mobile hot spots and cell towers are more widespread today than they used to be, they aren't everywhere. Web pages that must be always online will be frustrating for your customers on the move unless you use technology to handle the offline times.
- Download times and page sizes are often more noticeable on a smartphone than on a laptop or desktop computer. Even the most advanced 4G network isn't as fast as a Wi-Fi cable connection. Pages with huge images or massive text or scripts can take a long time to download, and customers may give up and go elsewhere.
- As with basic cell phones, you should test your designs on a real smartphone rather than just an emulator. This will give you a much better idea of how a design is going to work.

TIP

Some Form Fields Are Ideal for Smartphones

HTML5 brought a lot of new features to HTML, and some of the best new features are related to form input fields. Now web designers can write forms that are easy to fill out even on a small-screen smartphone or tablet. And best of all, these form fields work no matter what browser or device your customers use. I cover this in more detail in Hour 18, "Responsive Web Forms," but here's the basic secret: If you start using the `<input type="email">` for email addresses and `<input type="tel">` for phone numbers in your contact forms today, you will improve them immensely. When you use these two fields on a smartphone or tablet, the input keyboards adjust so that the forms are much easier to fill out. But a customer using even an extremely old browser like Netscape 6 will still see just a text field and will be able to fill it out without issue.

If you're going to support smartphones, then you should remember that they are not just miniature computers.

Tablets

Tablets and tablet computers are where mobile devices have really taken over. Consumers are buying more tablets than they are desktop and laptop computers, and if your website doesn't work on a tablet, you will be in trouble.

Luckily, the tablets on the market now use web browsers that are just as compatible with HTML5, CSS3, and JavaScript as their desktop computer counterparts. But that doesn't mean you should treat these devices just like computers.

Like smartphones, tablets have different screen sizes and resolutions, and these can impact your designs, so you need to take them into consideration. Table 3.2 lists some of the popular tablets and their screen sizes and resolutions.

TABLE 3.2 Resolutions of Popular Tablets (in Early 2014)

Device	Screen Size	Resolution
Amazon Kindle Fire HDX 7	7 inches	1200×1920
Amazon Kindle Fire HDX 8.9	8.9 inches	1600×2560
Apple iPad Air	9.7 inches	1536×2048
Apple iPad Mini 2	7.9 inches	1536×2048
Asus MeMO Pad HD7	7 inches	600×1024
Dell Venue 8	8 inches	1280×800
Google Nexus 7	7 inches	1200×1920
Microsoft Surface	10.6 inches	1080×1920
Samsung Galaxy NotePRO	12.2 inches	1600×2560

How to Support Tablets

As with smartphones, the range of sizes and resolutions varies greatly on tablets. When you're a web designer, it can be tempting to simply assume that if a device has a resolution of more than 1000px wide, it should be able to display web pages without any problem. But there are some aspects of tablets that you need to be aware of:

CAUTION

Scrolling Clickable Banners Can Be Extremely Annoying

A very popular feature on web pages right now is the rotating banner image or carousel. These are clickable images that showcase a featured part of the site. On desktop computers where the pages load very quickly, these work really well. But a common problem on tablets is that pages load more slowly, but the rotation on the banner continues. So when a customer clicks on such a banner, the page continues to load, rotating that banner out and the new banner in. The customer ends up at a page other than the one she wants. If you must use these types of banners, it's best to either give them a very long rotation period (like 60 seconds or more) or to allow customers to rotate them manually.

- Tablets have touch screens and require tap interfaces. This means that if you're building clickable interfaces (such as drag-and-drop), you need to create tap-and-drag interfaces, too.
- Even more importantly, the nature of tapping means that people use their fingers, and not everyone has thin, tiny fingers. You should make sure that your links have sufficient margins and paddings surrounding them so that they are clickable.
- The processors in tablets aren't as powerful as those in desktop and laptop computers, so complex pages may take longer to finish loading on a tablet than on a laptop or desktop.
- Flash is a challenging tool for designers who want to support tablets. Apple has removed all Flash support from iOS, so it won't work at all on Apple devices. And while it will work on Android devices, it's not always very stable.
- Be sure to test your pages on actual tablets. You can do preliminary testing by resizing your desktop web browser down to an approximate tablet size, but this won't give you the feel of using a real tablet.

Many people use tablets as their primary web browsing device, and if your web pages aren't tablet ready, you will lose customers.

Retina Devices

Retina devices are a special subset of Apple iPhone and iPad devices. A Retina display has a much higher pixel density than other computer screens. The density is roughly 300 pixels per inch, which is comparable to the density of a print document.

Apple first introduced Retina displays in the iPhone 4S in 2011. And since then, Apple has come out with Retina iPads and Retina laptops as well as the iPhones. Retina-like screens will probably start coming out for non-Apple devices sometime in 2014.

This means that anyone using a Retina device to view a website that is not optimized for Retina displays will see images that seem fuzzy or blurry. In some cases, the pixels will be visible, such as in a rounded corner or on transparent edges. Pixels are square, and rounded edges where you can see the pixels make those edges look square and blocky, too.

Why Build Retina-Ready Websites?

As I mentioned above, a website that is not Retina-ready can look blurry and pixelated on a Retina screen. Pixelation may not be obvious to a non-designer, but the reality is that even if users don't know they are seeing it, their brains do. When a picture is blurry or pixelated, your customers will need to spend more effort to see the page. And this can be tiring. For example, I am prone to migraines, and I notice that if I spend a lot of time on non-Retina-ready sites, I'm much more likely to get eye strain and then a migraine. Websites should not cause their customers pain.

These are some of the reasons to build Retina-ready pages:

- There are millions of people already using Retina devices. This means that if any of them come to your page and you haven't optimized the page for Retina, they will find the images blurry or pixelated and quite possibly ugly.
- Your fonts will be clearer and easier to read. This means that if you want to work with smaller font sizes, you can because Retina devices will be able to see them more clearly.
- You can get as detailed as you want. I think of this as the fractal method of design. With Retina screens, you can move deeper and deeper into the details of an image or a design element without significant loss of perception.
- And, of course, for the purposes of this book, building Retina-ready sites is a great way to use responsive design. You can detect whether a device is Retina ready and display Retina-ready images to it. You will learn more about this in Hour 15, "Creating and Using Images in RWD."

How to Build Retina-Ready Websites

The majority of work you need to do to get a website Retina-ready involves the images. You want to create images that are at least 220ppi and often twice as large as their non-Retina counterparts.

An easy way to include these images only for your Retina customers is to use the `retina.js` script, which you can find at `http://retinajs.com`. Then you simply create a graphic and give it a name like `image.jpg` and then create a Retina version of that graphic and name it `image@2x.jpg`. When a Retina user visits your page using the `retina.js` script, the images are automatically replaced with the Retina versions. I discuss this in more detail in Hour 15.

Why Responsive Design Is Important

Responsive design is very important to mobile customers because it allows them to see the same website that non-mobile customers see. Before RWD came along, web designers would often create entirely separate sites for mobile customers, which were typically subsets of the full site.

RWD allows designers to create sites that work on many different devices without requiring them to repost the content multiple times.

The thing to remember is that mobile use and the use of different devices to view web pages is growing and, according to some measures, the use of mobile devices will surpass or already has surpassed desktop use. There are already a lot of people who only go on the web using mobile devices.

RWD lets you as a designer build a website that doesn't care what device your customer is using. Rather than having to build a site for mobile, a site for desktop, and a site for smart appliances, you build just one site that is flexible enough to support all those devices and more.

And RWD is more future-proof than standard web design. RWD doesn't look at a device but rather looks at the features. For instance, an RWD site that checks for Retina displays doesn't care if the device is an iPhone 4S or a Google Nexus 11. It just notices that the screen can handle high-resolution Retina images and displays those.

Many people believe that RWD is not a trend but rather the way websites will be built. The expectation is that a site that isn't responsive by 2015 will be considered behind the curve and will lose customers.

Summary

This hour you've learned about the different devices that RWD tries to respond to. You've learned how to support basic cell phones, smartphones, and tablets. And you've learned how Retina screens are impacting the mobile device landscape.

Workshop

The workshop contains quiz questions to help you process what you've learned in this lesson. Try to answer all the questions before you read the answers.

Q&A

Q. I don't know anyone who browses using a basic cell phone. Is it really important to support those devices?

A. The answer really depends on your website and who your customers are. For some websites, basic phones are a nonexistent part of the customer base, but for others they are critical. If you don't know, rather than make a guess, you should watch your stats and see who is visiting your site.

When you're looking at your site stats, bear in mind that if your site focuses on a lot of people from undeveloped countries, you need to support their greater use of basic cell phones.

Also, your site's topic can have an impact in this area. For instance, I work on a site that is visited by a lot of people who don't like modern technology. The site's customers are all from North America, but they tend to use more basic cell phones than do users of my site about HTML5.

Q. Is Retina-ready really as critical as you say? Most of my mobile customers are on Android devices.

A. Again, this is a factor that you'll need to decide based on your site's customers. A good tool to use to find out if you're being visited by a lot of Retina devices is Google Analytics (`www.google.com/analytics/`). After you know how many people are seeing your site as pixelated and blurry, you can make a better decision.

Quiz

1. What is a Retina display?
2. What makes links on tablets and smartphones difficult to click?
3. Can most basic cell phones scroll horizontally?
4. True or False: Testing using an emulator is just as good as testing using a device.

Answers

1. Retina displays have a much higher pixel density than other displays, often more than 300 pixels per inch. This is as dense as print and makes images and text much clearer.
2. Links that are kept close together or that use very small fonts can be hard to tap, especially for customers with larger fingers.
3. Most basic cell phones cannot scroll horizontally, only vertically.
4. False. While an emulator can give you a good initial sense of how your design works, using a device to test is the best way to really understand if your site works or does not work with a basic cell phone, smartphone, or tablet.

Exercise

Using a basic cell phone, smartphone, or tablet—or all three if you have them—visit the website you chose in Hour 1, "What Is Responsive Web Design?" Evaluate how the site looks in the device. Does it work well? Is it easy to use? What can be improved?

HOUR 4
Progressive Enhancement

Progressive enhancement is a buzzword that many web designers bandy about without having a clear understanding of what it is. But with more and more devices and browsers needing to be supported in order to maintain a quality website, understanding progressive enhancement is critical.

Progressive enhancement works with RWD to create a website with a strong foundation that can be used by many devices and browsers. By starting first with progressive enhancement and then converting to RWD, you can create a site that is flexible and works with your customers, not against them.

WHAT YOU'LL LEARN IN THIS HOUR:

- What progressive enhancement is
- How progressive enhancement applies to RWD
- Why you should use progressive enhancement
- How progressive enhancement differs from similar tools
- How to use progressive enhancement on a website

What Is Progressive Enhancement?

Progressive enhancement, as discussed in Hour 1, "What Is Responsive Web Design?" is the process of creating a strong foundation on a website and then adding enhancements to that foundation as browsers and devices can handle them.

Progressive enhancement came as a reaction to graceful degradation. Graceful degradation was a carryover from software engineering, which involves testing for faults and creating a system that is as fault tolerant as possible. In the web design world, graceful degradation became an excuse for web designers to create the most amazing website they could on their browser of choice and then pass on whatever scraps they could scrape together to the browsers that weren't as powerful.

The problem was that this whole idea went against the goals of the web as an accessible medium where everyone has access to information, no

CAUTION

Beware: Graceful Degradation Is Addicting

The challenge with switching from graceful degradation to progressive enhancement is that graceful degradation is often more fun, especially in the initial stages. With graceful degradation, the first thing you work on is creating the most amazing, most advanced website you can. You work in the most advanced or capable browsers, and the design and development phase is heady and fun. But then you get to the testing phase, where you have to shoehorn your designs into the older or less capable browsers, and that part is not fun at all. In fact, it is a common occurrence to dump the testing and fixing phase on lower-level designers, contractors, or even interns, letting them fight with the inferior browsers.

NOTE

Graded Browser Support

Yahoo! decided to implement progressive enhancement as *graded browser support* in its YUI library (`http://yuilibrary.com`). With this technique, a web designer assigns different levels of support to different browsers, depending on their capabilities. A C grade provides the base level of support. C-grade devices get the core content and functionality but nothing more. A-grade devices get the highest level of support. These browsers get additional features and functions beyond just the core content. X-grade browsers have more functionality than C-grade browsers, but they may not get all the features of the A-grade browsers.

matter what their situation. As Sir Tim Berners-Lee said in *Technology Review* in July 1996: "Anyone who slaps a 'this page is best viewed with Browser X' label on a Web page appears to be yearning for the bad old days, before the Web, when you had very little chance of reading a document written on another computer, another word processor, or another network." If you use graceful degradation, that is what you are saying to your customers, even if you don't slap a label on your pages.

When you switch to a progressive enhancement mindset, you switch your focus away from what browsers and devices your customers use. Instead, you focus on *content*. When you're concerned with building a site with progressive enhancement, your first concern is with the content—what the content is, how it will be manipulated on the site, and where the site will get it.

Progressive enhancement lets you create websites that are inclusive and accessible, which is the ultimate goal of the World Wide Web.

How to Use Progressive Enhancement on a Website

As you saw in Hour 1, you can add progressive enhancement to a web page fairly quickly. But to do it well across your whole site, you need to think more strategically.

Separating Content from Presentation and Functionality

The first thing you should think about when adding progressive enhancement to your site is the content. A website has three layers:

- The content stored in the HTML
- The presentation defined by CSS
- The functions written in scripts like JavaScript

While it is possible to add CSS and scripts inline in your HTML, the best sites separate them into three different files and maintain strict distinctions between them.

Starting with the Content Layer

When you build a site, you should start with the content and the HTML that marks it up. Your HTML should be valid, well formed, and semantic.

To create *valid* HTML, you should use the most current version of HTML and write it without deprecated or obsolete elements. The most current version of HTML right now is HTML5.

Well-formed HTML is HTML that is written correctly. Your HTML should have closing tags where required as well as quoted attributes and good nesting. HTML that isn't written correctly can confuse some browsers, and confused browsers don't display web pages correctly.

Semantic HTML provides information about the content via the tags that are used. For example, if the content includes a date or time, you can use the `<time>` element to indicate to the browser that this is a time. The advantage of using semantic HTML is that your content can be used more widely when it's marked up. When you use the `<time>` element, the user agent can then offer to add the event to a calendar because it knows that it's a date or time.

Once the content layer is correct, your web pages will work well even in user agents that don't support CSS or JavaScript, like screen readers and basic cell phones.

You will learn more about how to work with your content and HTML in Hour 5, "HTML for Responsive Web Design."

NOTE

HTML5 Recommended

HTML5 is the current version of HTML, but it is not the only version of HTML out there. HTML5 offers a lot of extra features and tags that make it preferable for RWD websites, but if your site is already built in HTML 4.01 or XHTML, you can continue to use that version and still use progressive enhancement.

Adjusting How the Content Looks

Once you have all your content displayed in correct HTML, you can work with CSS to adjust how the page looks. As with the content, you want your CSS to be as valid and current as possible. This will ensure the widest support.

CSS, because of the way it's written, provides a lot of opportunity for progressive enhancement. There are some things you should be aware of:

- **The cascade**—CSS stands for *Cascading Style Sheets*, and the *Cascading* part indicates that CSS should be evaluated in order, with the last supported feature taking precedence. There's more to cascading than this, but when it comes to progressive enhancement, you should use the cascade by putting the most cutting-edge features last, with fallback options above them in the style sheet.

- **Browser prefixes**—Not all user agents support all the new features of CSS right away, but most provide browser prefixes to give support in the interim. By placing browser-prefixed versions of your style properties first in a rule, you ensure that the final, official version is supported when it can be.
- **Unrecognized properties**—User agents ignore what they don't recognize. This means that if a browser sees a property that is new to it, it will ignore it and not change the style at all.

You can place your CSS in an external style sheet and change it there to change your entire site at once. Hour 6, "Basic CSS," covers CSS in more detail.

Adding Interactivity

Interactivity is often the most fun part of a website to work on because it's what makes the site into an application or an entire experience. By adding in the scripts last, you know that your site already works, whether you have the scripts or not. And to add this interactivity, you want to use unobtrusive JavaScript.

There are four rules of unobtrusive JavaScript:

- The script should be usable without the customer noticing it is there.
- The script should not generate an error message. Even when it fails, it should just disappear and not get in the way of the content.
- The script should never block access to the core content of the page.
- The script should be maintained in a separate document outside the HTML and CSS.

Unobtrusive JavaScript allows you to add interactivity to your web pages without changing the HTML or CSS. And this means that you know the pages already work and look good before you add the interactive elements. You will learn more about this in Hour 7, "Unobtrusive JavaScript."

Benefits of Progressive Enhancement

The most obvious beneficiaries of progressive enhancement are people who use outdated browsers. When designers used primarily graceful degradation to deal with older browsers, they often simply aimed to keep outdated browsers from crashing, and if that meant removing a majority of the content from those browsers, then that's what happened.

In addition to providing more features for those using outdated browsers, there are other benefits to using progressive enhancement:

- Basic cell phones can display HTML content without issue. Since the focus of progressive enhancement is on content, a website using it will display content no matter what is viewing it.
- The same is true for screen readers. These devices handle well-structured HTML more effectively and so are more likely to read these pages without problem.
- Pages built with progressive enhancement are easier to maintain than their counterparts because the content, design, and functionality are kept separate.
- A site built with progressive enhancement is going to get more viewers than one that isn't because the site is not exclusionary in its design.

Earlier in this hour, I warned you that graceful degradation is addictive, but really, progressive enhancement can be just as addictive. The difference is that you give your customers the content they want first, and then you add the fun bells and whistles afterward.

Summary

In this hour you've learned more about what progressive enhancement is and how to use it. With progressive enhancement, you look at the content first, without worrying about the device or browser that is going to view it. Once you've got the content up and working, you can start applying the styles to make it look pretty and then the scripts to add interactivity.

Progressive enhancement makes a website more accessible because it doesn't force your customers to have exactly the right browser or mobile device. Instead, your focus is on the content and then adding features to it to make the content look nicer and be more interactive.

Workshop

The workshop contains quiz questions to help you process what you've learned in this lesson. Try to answer all the questions before you read the answers.

Q&A

Q. If I build a site using progressive enhancement, why do I need responsive web design?

A. Progressive enhancement and RWD work together to create a site that is accessible no matter what device views it. While it's possible to create a site with progressive enhancement that is not responsive, and vice versa, the best sites on the web use both.

Q. Is it possible to tell that a site uses progressive enhancement just by looking at it?

A. It is much easier to tell if a site does not use progressive enhancement (or uses it poorly) by looking at the code. If the site doesn't have valid HTML or has inline styles and JavaScript, you can argue that it is not using progressive enhancement. But even then, the designer may be attempting to keep the content pure and is simply making mistakes. Or the designer may naturally keep content, presentation, and interactivity separate, without knowing this is progressive enhancement.

Quiz

1. Does progressive enhancement require HTML5 to be correct?
2. What is your first concern when doing progressive enhancement?
3. When should you add in CSS when designing with progressive enhancement?

Answers

1. HTML5 is the most current version of HTML, and you are strongly encouraged to use HTML5 in progressive enhancement. But it is not a requirement. As long as your HTML is valid, well formed, and semantic, it will work with progressive enhancement.
2. Your first—and only—concern with progressive enhancement is the content. As long as the content displays correctly, you are doing it right.

3. CSS affects the presentation layer, and so you should add CSS after all the content and HTML are correct. But you add CSS before you write scripts.

Exercises

1. Return to the website you are evaluating and create a new version of one of the pages, using just HTML. Remove all the scripts and styles from the page.
2. Validate your HTML by using an online HTML validator, such as the one at `http://validator.w3.org`. Keep editing the HTML and validating it until it is correct.

HOUR 5
HTML for Responsive Web Design

Responsive web design doesn't add any new HTML tags or attributes: You simply write your HTML so that it is well-formed, valid, and semantic.

The best responsive sites are sites that also use progressive enhancement, as you learned in Hour 4, "Progressive Enhancement." These sites keep the HTML, CSS, and JavaScript separate so that the pages are easier to maintain and load more quickly.

In this hour you will learn the basics of HTML so that you can put together a decent website and make it responsive. However, there is more to HTML than you can learn in just one hour, so if you don't know HTML at all, you should consider a book like *Sams Teach Yourself HTML and CSS in 24 Hours* by Julie C. Meloni.

WHAT YOU'LL LEARN IN THIS HOUR:

- How to write HTML for RWD
- How to build a basic web page with HTML5
- What semantic elements are and how to use them
- Why valid HTML is important

Using HTML5

HTML5 is the most recent version of HTML and provides the most assistance to web designers who want to use progressive enhancement and RWD. While you can build RWD sites using other versions of HTML, it's best to stay as up-to-date as possible. This book uses HTML5 code samples.

Tags Every Page Should Contain

There are several HTML tags that every web page should contain. These tags may not be required for valid HTML, but they provide information about the page to the browser to make them easier to use. Every web page should contain these tags:

- <!doctype>
- <html>
- <head>
- <meta charset>
- <title>
- <body>

If your web page contains these elements, it contains the minimum HTML required to start building a responsive page. Listing 5.1 provides a standard template you can use to start any web page. Note that the tags listed above have both starting and ending tags as well as some attributes.

LISTING 5.1 A Basic HTML Template

```
<!doctype html>
<html>
  <head>
    <meta charset="UTF-8">
    <title>Untitled Document</title>
  </head>
  <body>

  </body>
</html>
```

TIP

HTML Is Not Case-Sensitive

In the past, it was very common to see doctype definitions written in all uppercase, but that is no longer required. In fact, all parts of HTML can be written in upper-, lower-, or even mixed case. The tag `<html>` is the same as `<HTML>` and `<HtMl>`. But the convention is to use all lowercase.

The first line in the code is the doctype. The doctype `<!doctype html>` tells the browser that this is HTML5.

Then you place the opening `<html>` tag. Be sure to surround the entire document with this element by including the `</html>` tag at the very end. This tells the browser that this is an HTML document, and also it tells the browser where it should expect to see HTML tags.

Valid HTML keeps all the content inside the `<html>` and `</html>` tags, but if content slips out, the browser will still parse it. Some content management systems append content to the top or bottom of the HTML, without placing it inside these tags. This content will still be parsed and displayed by browsers, but it could cause problems. Keep your content inside the `<html>` and `</html>` tags, and you'll be safe.

The `<head>` and `</head>` tags contain details about the web page that may not be visible to the browser—things like metadata, the title, and any links to CSS and JavaScript. The basic template in Listing 5.1 includes a `<meta charset>` tag and a `<title>` tag.

The `<meta charset>` tag is an important one for keeping your web pages secure. It should always be the very first tag in the head of your HTML documents. It tells the browser what character set the page uses. If you don't define the character set, or if you define it later in the document, you open up your site to hackers who can manipulate the character set and inject malicious code into the site.

Once you've defined the head information of your document, all you have left is the `<body>` element. This is where all the visible content goes. It contains what most people consider the meat of the web page. Anything that you type inside the `<body>` and `</body>` tags will show in the browser window.

Basic Tags for Web Content

While the tags already listed in this lesson are all you need to create a website, the site would be very plain and hard to read if you used only these tags. While there are dozens of HTML tags you can use (I list the new HTML5 elements at `http://www.html5in24hours.com/2012/04/new-html5-elements/`), there are only a few you need to know about to start creating a decent web page:

- `<h1>`, `<h2>`, and `<h3>`
- `<p>` and `<br>`
- `<a>`
- `<strong>` and `<em>`
- `<img>`, `<audio>`, and `<video>`

Most web pages start with a headline, and in HTML you use the headline tags `<h1>`, `<h2>`, and `<h3>` to define them. They are numbered, and you should use them in order, with `<h1>` first through `<h6>` last. Most sites don't go more than two or three levels deep, so you really only need to know `<h2>` and `<h3>`.

Once you have a headline, you can start adding content in paragraphs by using the `<p>` tag. Browsers typically display a paragraph as a block of text separated by some space. But if you want to drop down just one line of text, you use the `<br>` tag. This is a singleton tag and does not require a closing tag. You will sometimes see it written as `<br/>`, with the additional slash. This is a remnant from XHTML. You don't need the closing slash, and most browsers recognize the tag either way.

CAUTION

Keep Your Tags Closed

Several HTML elements don't require closing tags, like the `<p>` element for paragraphs. While the closing `</p>` is not required, it's a good idea to use it anyway. This helps keep your HTML clean and prevents less compliant browsers from getting confused. It's a small price to pay to ensure that your content is seen by the largest number of people.

You can put these tags together to create a web page. Figure 5.1 shows how a simple web page would look, and Listing 5.2 is the HTML for creating that web page. As you can see, the HTML is still very plain. But because content is the most important part of your website, you need to make sure it is visible and correct first.

The `<a>` tag provides a link to another document. You define a link by using the `href=""` attribute. Then any text or image that is inside the `<a>` element will be clickable in the browser and will take the customer to the new location.

The `<strong>` and `<em>` tags let you provide some emphasis to the text in your paragraphs. In most browsers the `<strong>` tag makes the text bold and `<em>` makes the text italic. But you will be able to define how you want those to display in your style sheets. You'll learn more about that in Hour 6, "Basic CSS."

The last three tags let you add multimedia into your web pages. The `<img>` tag adds an image to the page, using the `src=""` attribute to define the location of the image on your web server. You can add sound files by using the `<audio>` tag and videos by using the `<video>` tag. I cover these in more detail in Hour 16, "Videos and Other Media in RWD."

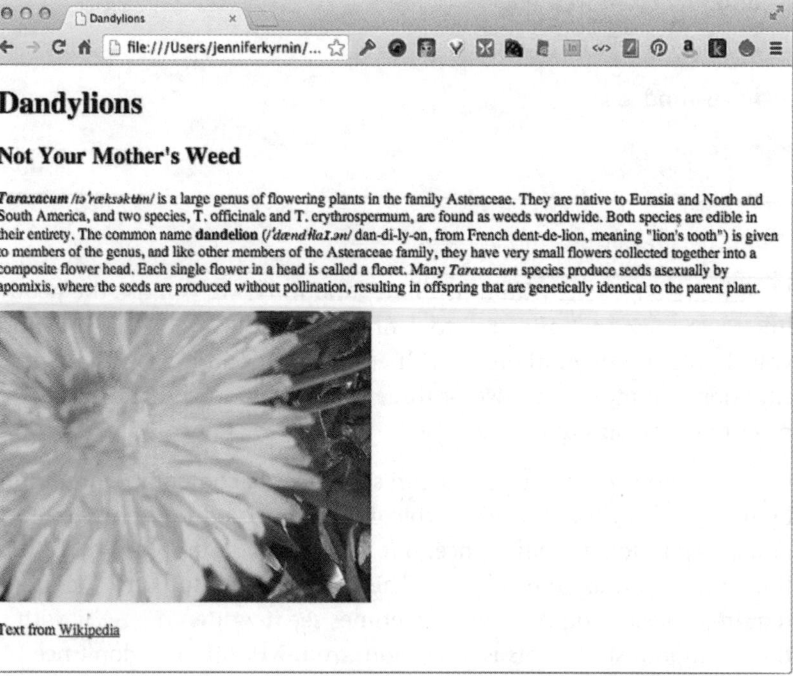
Dandylions
file:///Users/jenniferkyrnin/...
Dandylions
Not Your Mother's Weed
Taraxacum /təˈræksəkʉm/ is a large genus of flowering plants in the family Asteraceae. They are native to Eurasia and North and South America, and two species, T. officinale and T. erythrospermum, are found as weeds worldwide. Both species are edible in their entirety. The common name dandelion (/ˈdændɨlaɪ.ən/ dan-di-ly-on, from French dent-de-lion, meaning "lion's tooth") is given to members of the genus, and like other members of the Asteraceae family, they have very small flowers collected together into a composite flower head. Each single flower in a head is called a floret. Many Taraxacum species produce seeds asexually by apomixis, where the seeds are produced without pollination, resulting in offspring that are genetically identical to the parent plant.
Text from Wikipedia

FIGURE 5.1
A simple web page with content.

LISTING 5.2 Adding Some Content to the Template

```
<!doctype html>
<html>
<head>
<meta charset="UTF-8">
<title>Dandylions</title>
</head>

<body>
<h1>Dandylions</h1>
<h2>Not Your Mother's Weed</h2>
<p><strong><em>Taraxacum</em></strong> <em>/tə'ræksəkʉm/</em> is a large
genus of flowering plants in the family Asteraceae. They are native to
Eurasia and North and South America, and two species, T. officinale and
T. erythrospermum, are found as weeds worldwide. Both species are edible
in their entirety. The common name <strong>dandelion</strong>
(<em>/'dændɨlaɪ.ən/</em> dan-di-ly-ən, from French dent-de-lion, meaning
"lion's tooth") is given to members of the genus, and like other members
of the Asteraceae family, they have very small flowers collected together
into a composite flower head. Each single flower in a head is called a
floret. Many <em>Taraxacum</em> species produce seeds asexually by
apomixis, where the seeds are produced without pollination, resulting in
offspring that are genetically identical to the parent plant.</p>
<img src="images/dandy.jpg" width="400" height="300" alt=""/>
<p>Text from
<a href="http://en.wikipedia.org/wiki/Dandelion">Wikipedia</a></p>
</body>
</html>
```

HTML for Layout

You should also consider learning about some of the tags that are typically used for layout and style. There are two in particular that you should know:

- `<div>`
- `<span>`

These HTML tags provide no semantic meaning to your content and should be used to add hooks for CSS and JavaScript.

The `<div>` element acts like a container element, and you can place large blocks of text in it. It is called a *block* element, and most browsers add a line both before and after, similar to a paragraph.

Most people use `<div>` to create layout sections and then style those sections with CSS. Listing 5.3 shows how you might add some sections to your HTML so that you can style them later.

LISTING 5.3 HTML with Some Divisions

```
<!doctype html>
<html>
  <head>
    <meta charset="UTF-8">
    <title>Dandylions</title>
  </head>
  <body>
    <div id="main">
    <h1>Dandylions</h1>
    <div id="article">
      <h2>Not Your Mother's Weed</h2>
      <p><strong><em>Taraxacum</em></strong> <em>/tə'ræksəkʉm/</em> is a
      large genus of flowering plants in the family Asteraceae. They are
      native to Eurasia and North and South America, and two species, T.
      officinale and T. erythrospermum, are found as weeds worldwide.
      Both species are edible in their entirety. The common name
      <strong>dandelion</strong> (<em>/'dændɨlaɪ.ən/</em> dan-di-ly-ən,
      from French dent-de-lion, meaning "lion's tooth") is given to
      members of the genus, and like other members of the Asteraceae
      family, they have very small flowers collected together into a
      composite flower head. Each single flower in a head is called a
      floret. Many <em>Taraxacum</em> species produce seeds asexually by
      apomixis, where the seeds are produced without pollination,
      resulting in offspring that are genetically identical to the parent
      plant.</p>
    </div>
    <div id="sidebar">
      <img src="images/dandy.jpg" width="400" height="300" alt=""/>
    </div>
    <div id="footer">
      <p>Text from
      <a href="http://en.wikipedia.org/wiki/Dandelion">Wikipedia</a></p>
    </div>
    </div>
  </body>
</html>
```

The <span> element works inside paragraphs to select small blocks of content. It is called an *inline* element. It does not add line breaks, and it allows you to mark up individual words in the content. Listing 5.4 shows a block of text with some words called out with the <span> tag.

LISTING 5.4 A Block of Text with Highlighted Words

```
<!doctype html>
<html>
  <head>
    <meta charset="UTF-8">
    <title>Dandylions</title>
```

```
  </head>
  <body>
    <div id="main">
    <h1>Dandylions</h1>
    <div id="article">
      <h2>Not Your Mother's Weed</h2>
      <p><span class="pronounce"><strong><em>Taraxacum</em></strong>
      <em>/tə'rӕksəkʉm/</em></span> is a large genus of flowering plants
      in the family Asteraceae. They are native to Eurasia and North and
      South America, and two species, T. officinale and T.
      erythrospermum, are found as weeds worldwide. Both species are
      edible in their entirety. The common name
      <span class="pronounce"><strong>dandelion</strong>
      <em>/'dӕndɨlaɪ.ən/</em></span> (dan-di-ly-ən, from French
      dent-de-lion, meaning "lion's tooth") is given to members of the
      genus, and like other members of the Asteraceae family, they have
      very small flowers collected together into a composite flower head.
      Each single flower in a head is called a floret. Many
      <em>Taraxacum</em> species produce seeds asexually by apomixis,
      where the seeds are produced without pollination, resulting in
      offspring that are genetically identical to the parent plant.</p>
    </div>
    <div id="sidebar">
      <img src="images/dandy.jpg" width="400" height="300" alt=""/>
    </div>
    <div id="footer">
      <p>Text from
      <a href="http://en.wikipedia.org/wiki/Dandelion">Wikipedia</a></p>
    </div>
    </div>
  </body>
</html>
```

Some Useful Attributes

Nearly every tag in HTML has attributes. These are keywords that are defined within a tag and give the browser more information about that tag. You have already used attributes with the `<img src="">` tag and the `<a href="">` tag. But there are a couple more attributes that you should know about:

- `id`
- `class`

You can add these attributes to any HTML tag in your document to provide additional information about that element.

You use the id attribute to give an element a unique name. The id must be unique to the page it is on. In other words, there can be only one. But you can give every single tag on your page a unique id.

You use id to identify an element. You can then link to that element by using the pound sign (#) in your URL, followed by the id value you assign. For example, if you had an element `<div id="main">`, you could then write a link to that element by typing `<a href="#main">link to main</a>`.

You can also use the id attribute as a hook for styles and scripts. Because it must be unique on the page, you know that when you attach a style to that id, you will affect only one element. This attribute also makes the style rule more specific, which means it's more likely to be applied. You will learn more about CSS specificity in Hour 6.

Like the id attribute, the class attribute allows you to apply styles and scripts to an element. But it does not have to be unique on the page. This means you can apply a class to multiple elements on the page, and any style rules that are written to that class will be applied to all the elements. For instance, say you want some of your `<h1>` headlines to be red, but others should remain the default color. You could give the red headlines a special class that you would style as red in your CSS: `<h1 class="highlight">`.

One of the nicest things about using classes is that you aren't limited to just one. You can include multiple class names on any element to add styles to the element or hook up with your scripts. To add a second class to an element, simply separate the classes with a space, like this: `<h1 class="highlight fancy">`.

NOTE

Use IDs to Link in Any Page

One thing that many web designers don't realize is that you can use the id attribute to link directly to a specific location in any web page. And because the id attribute can be placed on any element, you can allow direct navigation to almost any portion of a page simply by adding an id attribute to that section. You can also link to external pages by using the id attribute: Simply include the full URL in your href and then include #id at the end.

CAUTION

Get in the Habit of Using Generic Classes and IDs

In the class attribute example I just gave, I suggested that you might want to make some of your headlines the color red. But in the code, I gave it the class name "highlight". It can be tempting to give your elements classes and IDs that describe exactly what they do—for example, `<h1 class="red">`. But doing this can cause problems in the future. What if two years from now, you decide that all the highlighted headlines need to be colored blue rather than red? The fastest thing to do is simply change the class rule in the CSS so that the font color is blue. But anyone coming to the site will look at that rule and think there is an error. The class name is red, but it changes the color to blue? By giving your elements more generic class and id names, you avoid this problem and keep your code more future-proof.

Clean Code

When you're building HTML for RWD sites, you should always strive to keep it as clean and clear as possible. The technical term for this is *well-formed*. Well-formed HTML follows these guidelines:

- There is a doctype at the top of the document.
- Tags should nest correctly, inside to outside; for example, `<b><i>text</i></b>` is correct, and `<b><i>text</b></i>` is incorrect.

- Attributes with spaces in their values should be quoted using single or double quotation marks.
- Comments are not allowed inside tags.
- You should escape special characters used in HTML, such as ampersand (`&`), a less-than sign (`<`), and a greater-than sign (`>`).

Well-formed XHTML involves additional rules, such as always closing every tag and using a closing slash in singleton tags, including an XML declaration, and quoting all attributes. But if you are using HTML5, the rules are not as strict.

The other part of clean code is using only the elements and attributes you need and nothing more. Try to consider what your site needs and limit your HTML to only those elements.

Think about what the content *is* when you are writing HTML. A paragraph should be in the `<p>` element. For a list, you should use one of the list elements. You get the picture. In the next section, you will learn about some of the new HTML5 elements that help define your content right in the HTML, using semantics.

CAUTION

Don't Catch "Divitis"

The most commonly overused HTML element is the `<div>` element. It can be tempting to surround elements with lots of `<div>` tags so that you have lots of things to hook into for your layout and scripts. But most of the time, you can remove these and attach styles directly to the specific elements you want styled. The only exception to this is container elements. Some browsers still have trouble applying container styles to the `<body>` element, and placing a `<div id="container"></div>` around your entire page can help.

I have also seen sites use the `<div>` tag instead of paragraph tags, with a `class="paragraph"` attribute on the `<div>`. This is ridiculous. HTML provides different elements for a reason, and you should use them. And as you'll see in the next section, there are even more elements you can use to mark up your content. You're not limited to using only `<div>`.

Don't Forget Semantic Elements

Semantic elements are elements that describe the content. They provide more information to the browser without requiring any extra attributes.

Standard Semantic HTML Elements

A number of semantic HTML elements have been in use for years—in some cases since HTML level 1. Here are some semantic HTML elements that are valid in HTML5 and earlier versions of HTML:

- `<abbr>` defines abbreviations and acronyms
- `<cite>` defines citations, such as for quotations
- `<code>` defines a code reference
- `<q>` defines a short, inline quotation

There are many more semantic elements in HTML, and you can learn about them in my article "What Semantics Means in HTML and Why You Should Care" (see `http://www.html5in24hours.com/2014/09/what-is-semantic-html/`).

New HTML5 Semantic Elements

HTML5 adds a lot of new elements that you can use to mark up your content semantically. The most useful ones are the sectioning elements:

- `<article>`
- `<aside>`
- `<nav>`
- `<section>`

These elements define areas of the content that are commonly found on web pages. Most web pages have a main article that defines the page (`<article>`); there is usually sidebar information for either the article, the page, or the entire site (`<aside>`); navigation is critical (`<nav>`); and many web pages are divided into separate sections with different semantic meanings that don't fall into the other categories (`<section>`).

There are also two new elements that are not technically sectioning elements. However, they are semantic and help divide a page:

- `<header>`
- `<footer>`

You can add a header or footer to any of the sectioning elements listed above, you can add them to an entire page, or you can add them to both. Listings 5.5 and 5.6 show you how a page written in HTML 4.01 with `<div>` tags as the divisions can be adjusted to use HTML5 and sectioning elements.

LISTING 5.5 An HTML 4.01 Page to Be Converted to HTML5

```
<!DOCTYPE HTML PUBLIC "-//W3C//DTD HTML 4.01 Transitional//EN"
"http://www.w3.org/TR/html4/loose.dtd">
<html>
  <head>
    <meta http-equiv="Content-Type" Content="text/html; charset=utf-8">
```

```
    <title>Dandylions</title>
  </head>
  <body>
    <div id="main">
    <h1>Dandylions</h1>
    <div id="article">
      <h2>Not Your Mother's Weed</h2>
      <p><span class="pronounce"><strong><em>Taraxacum</em></strong>
      <em>/tə'ræksəkʉm/</em></span> is a large genus of flowering plants
      in the family Asteraceae. They are native to Eurasia and North and
      South America, and two species, T. officinale and T.
      erythrospermum, are found as weeds worldwide. Both species are
      edible in their entirety. The common name
      <span class="pronounce"><strong>dandelion</strong>
      <em>/'dændɨlaɪ.ən/</em></span> (dan-di-ly-ən, from French
      dent-de-lion, meaning "lion's tooth") is given to members of the
      genus, and like other members of the Asteraceae family, they have
      very small flowers collected together into a composite flower head.
      Each single flower in a head is called a floret. Many
      <em>Taraxacum</em> species produce seeds asexually by apomixis,
      where the seeds are produced without pollination, resulting in
      offspring that are genetically identical to the parent plant.</p>
    </div>
    <div id="sidebar">
      <img src="images/dandy.jpg" width="400" height="300" alt=""/>
    </div>
    <div id="footer">
      <p>Text from
      <a href="http://en.wikipedia.org/wiki/Dandelion">Wikipedia</a></p>
    </div>
    </div>
  </body>
</html>
```

The HTML in Listing 5.5 has a headline, a main article with a subhead titling it, a sidebar, and a footer. All these are defined in `<div>` elements. Listing 5.6 has these same elements, but it also uses HTML5 sectioning elements to define the sections semantically.

LISTING 5.6 The Converted HTML5 Document

```
<!doctype html>
<html>
  <head>
    <meta charset="UTF-8">
    <title>Dandylions</title>
  </head>
  <body>
    <div id="main">
    <header>
    <h1>Dandylions</h1>
```

```
    </header>
    <article>
      <h2>Not Your Mother's Weed</h2>
      <p><span class="pronounce"><strong><em>Taraxacum</em></strong>
      <em>/tə'rӕksəkʉm/</em></span> is a large genus of flowering plants
      in the family Asteraceae. They are native to Eurasia and North and
      South America, and two species, T. officinale and T.
      erythrospermum, are found as weeds worldwide. Both species are
      edible in their entirety. The common name
      <span class="pronounce"><strong>dandelion</strong>
      <em>/'dӕndɨlaɪ.ən/</em></span> (dan-di-ly-ən, from French
      dent-de-lion, meaning "lion's tooth") is given to members of the
      genus, and like other members of the Asteraceae family, they have
      very small flowers collected together into a composite flower head.
      Each single flower in a head is called a floret. Many
      <em>Taraxacum</em> species produce seeds asexually by apomixis,
      where the seeds are produced without pollination, resulting in
      offspring that are genetically identical to the parent plant.</p>
    </article>
    <aside>
      <img src="images/dandy.jpg" width="400" height="300" alt=""/>
    </aside>
    <footer>
      <p>Text from
      <a href="http://en.wikipedia.org/wiki/Dandelion">Wikipedia</a></p>
    </footer>
    </div>
  </body>
</html>
```

Notice that `<div id="main">` is in both documents. This gives you a hook for styles and scripts on the entire web page.

Considering Microformats

When you're adding semantics into your web pages, you should consider using microformats to add even more meaning, when appropriate. Microformats use human-readable text inside the HTML (usually in the `class` attribute of an element) to define the contents.

These are some commonly used microformats:

- `hCalendar` marks up events for putting in a calendar.
- `hCard` marks up contact information for address books.
- `hRecipe` marks up recipes for making food.
- `hReview` marks up reviews of books, movies, and more.

Microformats add semantic information about the elements, and this information is already being used in certain situations. Figure 5.2 shows a Google search for reviews of the movie *Ender's Game*. The second and third results show "rich snippets," including information like the star rating.

FIGURE 5.2
The second and third results from a Google search for Ender's Game reviews.

Google and Bing are both using these types of rich snippets to enhance their search results, and most of the data they are using to get it is semantically marked-up HTML using microformats. You can learn more about how to use microformats in my book *Sams Teach Yourself HTML5 Mobile Application Development in 24 Hours*.

By writing semantic HTML, you give more information to user agents to use to display the information correctly. For example, if a screen reader sees the `<article>` element, it knows that this is the main point of the page, and it will read it aloud before reading anything in an `<aside>` element. Plus, as web pages get more and more sophisticated, what the user agents do with them gains sophistication. For instance, in the future, your semantically marked-up recipe could tell a web-ready refrigerator what time to alert the robot butler to start the roast.

Validating Your HTML

It is tempting, once you've finished writing the HTML, to start immediately on the CSS. After all, plain HTML is very ugly, and making it pretty with CSS is the fun part! But you should not skip validation. By making sure your pages are valid HTML, you ensure that they are accessible and that your CSS and scripts will work as you intend.

Luckily validating your HTML is easy and takes only a moment. Simply go to `http://validator.w3.org` and fill in the URL of the page. If it's not live yet, you can validate your HTML by uploading a file or pasting it in as direct input. If you've been careful, you should see a green indicator, as in Figure 5.3, that tells you the document was successfully checked as HTML5.

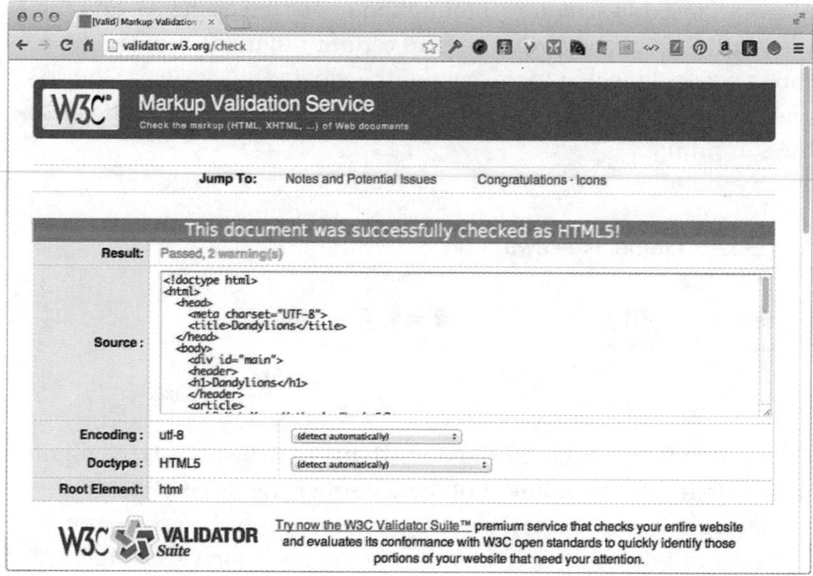

FIGURE 5.3
A successfully validated web page.

Summary

This hour you've learned the basics of HTML and how to create content so that it is ready to be converted to responsive design. You've learned about some HTML5 tags for content, layout, and page setup. Table 5.1 describes these tags and Table 5.2 describes the attributes. You've also learned how to create clean HTML and how to validate it.

This hour you've also learned how semantic HTML can help you create content with meaning. You've learned some HTML5 elements that are semantic as well as how to use microformats to add classes to your HTML to give the content even more semantic meaning. Table 5.3 lists the microformats and what they do.

TABLE 5.1 HTML Elements Covered in Hour 5

Element	Description
`<a>`	A link or an anchor
`<abbr>`	An abbreviation or acronym
`<article>`	An article or a basic block of content that could be syndicated
`<aside>`	A related block of content
`<audio>`	A sound or audio file
`<body>`	The body of an HTML document

Element	Description
 	Line break
<cite>	A citation
<code>	A code reference
<div>	A division of the HTML that doesn't have semantic meaning
<!doctype>	The document type declaration
<em>	Emphasis
<footer>	The footer portion of a page or section
<h1> <h2> <h3>	Headline levels
<head>	The head or metadata of an HTML document
<header>	The header portion of a page or section
<html>	An HTML container element
<img>	An image or a graphic
<meta charset>	A meta character set declaration
<nav>	A navigation section
<p>	A paragraph
<q>	A short inline quotation
<section>	A semantically distinct section of content
<span>	An inline span of content
<strong>	Strong emphasis
<title>	The title of a web page
<video>	A video file

TABLE 5.2 HTML Attributes Covered in Hour 5

Attribute	Description
id	A unique identifier
class	A classification attribute, which need not be unique

TABLE 5.3 Microformats Covered in Hour 5

Microformat	Description
hCalendar	Marks up events and dates for use in calendars
hCard	Marks up contact information
hRecipe	Marks up recipes
hReview	Marks up product and service reviews

Workshop

The workshop contains quiz questions to help you process what you've learned in this lesson. Try to answer all the questions before you read the answers.

Q&A

Q. This hour seems focused on writing HTML from scratch, but I like using a WYSIWYG editor. Will that work?

A. The best editors give you access to the HTML so that you can make sure there aren't extra tags or attributes that you don't want. But as long as you can edit the HTML directly, you shouldn't have a problem using a visual editor rather than a text editor. Hour 21, "Tools for Creating Responsive Web Designs," discusses some other tools, including editors, that you can use to create responsive designs.

Q. My system uses XHTML. Can I create RWD with that?

A. As long as you can add style sheets to your HTML or XHTML, you can use it to build RWD.

Q. You mention microformats, but I already use RDF or Microdata. Is that okay?

A. Using RDF and using Microdata are both acceptable ways to add semantics to your HTML. Microdata is a standard proposed by the W3C, and RDF is a more complicated system for defining metadata of all kinds.

Quiz

1. Is this well-formed HTML: `<strong><em>My dog is</strong> big</em>`?
2. Is it better to use a `<p>` or a `<div>` tag when marking up a paragraph?
3. Is the `<header>` element semantic?

Answers

1. No, this is not well-formed HTML because the `<strong>` and `<em>` tags do not nest correctly. Designers commonly make the error of closing the outermost tag first. Here's the correct version of this HTML: `<em><strong>My dog is</strong> big</em>`.

2. When you're marking up a paragraph, you should use the `<p>` tag because it defines paragraphs.
3. The `<header>` element is semantic because it describes the content as being the header section of a web page, section, or element.

Exercise

Go through the HTML for the site you are evaluating. Convert it as much as possible to semantic HTML5. Remove unnecessary tags and then validate it with an HTML5 validator. If the validator finds errors, fix them until the page is valid.

HOUR 6
Basic CSS

WHAT YOU'LL LEARN IN THIS HOUR:

- How to add CSS style rules
- The basics of CSS syntax
- How to style text and images
- How to use CSS for layout
- What cascading is and how specificity works

You use Cascading Style Sheets (CSS) to adjust how web pages look. This is often called the *presentation layer* of web design. Once you have the content developed in HTML, you can use CSS to affect how it looks.

Some people find CSS difficult because they expect it to work the same as HTML, but as you'll learn in this hour, while CSS can get extremely complicated, there are only a few rules for how to do it, and you can quickly learn the ins and outs.

How to Write CSS Rules

The first thing you need to learn when writing CSS is how to write a CSS style rule. A CSS style is made up of two parts: the selector and the style properties. The properties are the styles themselves, and they tell the user agent how to style the text, such as to change the text color to red or the font to Arial. The selector tells the user agent where to apply those rules.

A simple style rule for changing all paragraph text to red would look like this:

```
p {
  color: red;
}
```

On the first line is the selector, in this case `p`. This means that every `<p>` element on the page will be styled this way. The curly braces (`{ }`) surround the style properties. There is only one property here, `color: red;`, but you can include as many as you need to make your paragraphs look as you want them to.

CAUTION

Get in the Habit of Using the Semicolon

The semicolon is only required to separate multiple properties in one rule. So you will often see designers remove the last semicolon. But when you're writing CSS, it's a good idea to leave them in. That way, if you come back later and add more properties to the rule, it will still work. If you leave off the semicolon between two properties, your CSS will break.

CSS Syntax

The syntax of a property is `style : value;`. You separate the style and the value with a colon (`:`), and you end the line with a semicolon (`;`). You can write style rules all on one line, or "minified," with all the spaces and newlines removed, or you can write them over multiple lines and indent as I did above to make them more readable.

The selector syntax involves a lot of complex rules that define different situations in HTML. These are some of the common selectors:

- An element selector selects the element listed. You can define a style rule on any HTML element by simply writing that element name in your selector. For example, `blockquote` would select all `<blockquote>` elements, `h1` would select all `<h1>` elements, and `span` would select all `<span>` elements.
- An ID selector selects an element with a specific ID. To define an ID selector in CSS, you precede the `id` name with a pound sign (`#`). To select the `<div id="main">` element, for example, you would use `#main`.
- A class selector works in much the same way as an ID selector, but it selects elements with the named class. To define a class selector, you include a period (`.`) before the class name. To select the `<p class=plain">` element, for example, you would use `.plain`.

You can also create combination selectors to select very specific parts of your HTML. These are some of the most common combination selectors:

- A child selector selects the elements that are children of the other element. An element is considered a child when it appears directly within a container element. For example, an unordered list (`<ul>`) has several child list items (`<li>`). You could select all links (`<a>`) inside a list item (`<li>`) by using `li > a`. The two selectors are separated by a greater-than sign (>).
- Descendant selectors are similar to child selectors, but they select all the elements below the other element. These are most useful when you want to select all of an element inside a section of the page. For instance, if you wanted to style all elements with the class `important` that were in the element identified as `sidebar`, you would use `#sidebar .important`. The two selectors are separated by a space.

- An attribute selector lets you select elements with a specific attribute. For example, to select all links with a `title` attribute, you use `a[title]`. The attribute is enclosed in square brackets ([]).
- The universal selector is denoted by an asterisk (*). It selects all the elements in the document.

There are many other style selectors, and to make things even more complicated, you can combine selectors to define exactly the rule you need. Listing 6.1 shows a style sheet that uses all the above selectors in some way, and it includes comments to detail which one is which.

LISTING 6.1 A Style Sheet with Many Different Selectors

```
/* universal selector */
* {
  font-size: 86%;
}
/* element selector */
p {
  font-family: Baskerville, "Palatino Linotype", Palatino,
    "Century Schoolbook L", "Times New Roman", serif;
}
/* id selector */
#main {
  width: 80%;
  margin: 0 auto;
}
/* class selector */
.alignright {
  float: right;
  margin-left: 1em;
}
/* child selector */
div > h1 {
  font-family: "Lucida Grande", "Lucida Sans Unicode", "Lucida Sans",
    "DejaVu Sans", Verdana, sans-serif;
}
/* descendant selector */
p > .bold {
  font-weight: bold;
}
/* pseudo-class selectors */
a:link { color: blue; }
a:visited { color: gray; }
a:hover { color: red; }
a:active { color: pink; }
/* attribute selector */
a[title] {
  background-color: #dfdfdf;
}
```

As you can see in Listing 6.1, CSS allows comments. You add a comment by placing the text you want commented in between `/*` and `*/`.

Embedded and External Style Sheets

After you've written your styles, you need to include them in a style sheet. You can include individual styles on an element to style only one tag; this is called using *inline* styles. To add an inline style, you simply add the style property to the opening tag in the `style` attribute. For example, here's an inline style for changing a paragraph color to red:

```
<p style="color: red;">
```

Inline styles are best used only for testing. As you learned in Hour 4, "Progressive Enhancement," using inline styles goes against the rules of progressive enhancement. For live websites, it's better to use an embedded style sheet. And the best choice is to use an external style sheet.

Embedded Style Sheets

You include embedded style sheets in the `<head>` of an HTML document. As you can see in Listing 6.2, they are surrounded by the `<style>` and `</style>` tags.

LISTING 6.2 An Embedded Style Sheet

```
<style>
  /* universal selector */
  * {
    font-size: 86%;
  }
  /* element selector */
  p {
    font-family: Baskerville, "Palatino Linotype", Palatino,
      Century Schoolbook L", "Times New Roman", serif;
  }
  /* id selector */
  #main {
    width: 80%;
    margin: 0 auto;
  }
  /* class selector */
  .alignright {
    float: right;
```

```
    margin-left: 1em;
  }
  /* child selector */
  div > h1 {
    font-family: "Lucida Grande", "Lucida Sans Unicode", "Lucida Sans",
      DejaVu Sans", Verdana, sans-serif;
  }
  /* descendant selector */
  p > .bold {
    font-weight: bold;
  }
  /* pseudo-class selectors */
  a:link { color: blue; }
  a:visited { color: gray; }
  a:hover { color: red; }
  a:active { color: pink; }
  /* attribute selector */
  a[title] {
    background-color: #dfdfdf;
  }
</style>
```

Embedded style sheets have an advantage over inline styles in that they affect more than just one element on a page. When you use an embedded style sheet, if you change the style on your paragraphs, for instance, the style will change on all the paragraphs on that page, not just the one with the inline style.

External Style Sheets

If you want to make sure every paragraph on an entire website looks the same, you should use external style sheets. External style sheets are stored in a separate file from the HTML document. They don't take any additional tags inside them, just the style rules shown in Listing 6.1.

There are two ways to apply external style sheets to HTML: by using the `<link>` element or by using `@import`. To link a style sheet in the `<head>` of your HTML, you use this:

```
<link rel="stylesheet" href="styles.css">
```

Then you change `styles.css` to the location of your style sheet. To import a style sheet, you add the following to the `<head>` of your HTML:

```
<style>
@import url("styles.css");
</style>
```

CAUTION

`@import` Can Slow Your Pages

Many designers store their CSS in separate files and then use the `@import` rule to load them into the page. But if your page uses both a `<link>` tag and the `@import` rule, the style sheets will not load simultaneously. Instead, the linked file will load, and then the imported file will load. If you have multiple imported files, the browser will have to wait until each file has downloaded before the page is finished rendering. With a lot of files, this can slow your page considerably.

NOTE

The Fastest Pages Use Just One Style Sheet

Many web designers like to manage style sheets by keeping them in separate files, depending on what they do, such as all fonts in one file and all layouts in another. But speed optimization experts recommend linking to as few CSS files as possible. Every time you link to a file, you are making an HTTP request to the server, and this adds download time to the whole page. It might not seem like much, but all those requests add up, and fast pages are better than slow ones.

You can also add `@import` lines to the top of external style sheet files if you want to use multiple style sheets or import styles from other locations, such as web font files.

Styling Fonts and Colors

Fonts and colors are easy to work with, and styling them can make a big difference in how your web pages look.

There are lots of style properties you can use to adjust the fonts and typography on your web pages. But there are six properties that every web designer should know:

- `font-family`
- `font-size`
- `font-weight`
- `font-style`
- `background-color`
- `color`

The `font-family` property defines what most people think of as "the font" of the text. What's interesting about CSS is that you can define a list of fonts for the user agent to choose from. That way, if the browser doesn't have access to your first-choice font, it will use the second choice and so on down the list. This is called a *font stack*.

Here is a typical font stack for a list of sans serif fonts:

```
font-family: Arial, Geneva, Helvetica, sans-serif;
```

In this stack, the browser would look first for the Arial font, and if that wasn't available, the browser would look for Geneva and then Helvetica. The last value, `sans-serif`, is a generic font face value that tells the browser "use whatever font face you have that is sans serif."

These are the generic font faces:

- Cursive
- Fantasy
- Monospace
- Sans-serif
- Serif

Each web browser has a default size it uses to display fonts that aren't styled with the `font-size` property. This property takes relative values like ems or percentages as well as explicit values like pixels or inches. You can also use points, but I don't recommend that because points are a print size and don't have much meaning on websites.

For RWD, your best bet is to use relative font sizes like percentages or ems. An em is equivalent to the current default font size. So 1 em will display at whatever size the browser is using. This is usually around 16px, but sometimes customers adjust their fonts.

Most web designers find the default size of 16px to be fairly large, and you may want to make it smaller. You can use ems to do that directly, by saying `0.8em` (or 80% of the default font size), but that can be hard to manage. I don't know about you, but I can't do the math to determine 80% of 16 in my head (it's 12.8px, by the way). You can use a simple trick to reset the default font size to 10px. Just add the following style rule to your CSS at the top:

```
body {
  font-size: 62.5%;
}
```

This sets the default font size for the body element (and all elements within it) to 10px, which is 62.5% of 16px. Yes, 10px is small, but it's easy to multiply. So if you set a font size to 1.2em, you know that that will be 12px in most browsers. Then you can set your paragraphs and headlines using ems and be confident about the size they'll end up being. As an example, here's how you make a headline 18px:

```
h1 { font-size: 1.8em; }
```

The `font-weight` property defines the boldness of the font. Most typefaces include only two boldness levels—bold and not bold—but CSS allows for relative weights. To make a selection bold, here's what you use:

```
font-weight: bold;
```

And then to make it normal again, you use this:

```
font-weight: normal;
```

You can also specify that the weight be `lighter` or `bolder` to tell the browser to look at how the font would display without any direction and make it either lighter or darker.

The `font-style` property tells the browser to make the font italic or normal. You can also specify that the font be switched to oblique, but most typefaces don't support that. To mark text as italic, you use this:

```
font-style: italic;
```

The last two font properties you should know are the `background-color` and `color` properties. The `background-color` property tells the browser what color to make the element's background. The `color` property tells the browser what color the foreground should be. The foreground is almost always the text, so I consider this a font property, even though it doesn't have the `font-` prefix.

You can change the colors on web pages in several ways. You can use color keywords like `red` or `blue`, you can use hexadecimal codes like `#ff0000` or `#0000ff`, and you can use RGB codes like `rgb(255,0,0)` or `rgb(0,0,255)`. Using hexadecimal and RGB codes are more flexible than using named colors because there are millions of colors but only a couple dozen color names. You can see all the color names listed on my website (`http://www.html5in24hours.com/reference/color-codes/`), and a good place to find RGB and hexadecimal codes is ColorPicker.com.

▼ TRY IT YOURSELF

Adjust the Fonts on a Web Page

It's one thing to read about how to change fonts, and it's a different thing to actually do it online. In these steps, you will add some styles to some plain HTML to make it look much nicer:

1. Copy the following HTML into your web editor and save it to your hard drive as `dandelions.html`:

```
<!doctype html>
<html>
  <head>
    <meta charset="UTF-8">
    <title>Dandylions</title>
  </head>
  <body>
    <div id="main">
    <header>
    <h1>Dandylions</h1>
    </header>
    <article>
      <h2>Not Your Mother's Weed</h2>
      <p><span
        class="pronounce"><strong><em>Taraxacum</em></strong>
      <em>/tə'ræksəkʉm/</em></span> is a large genus of flowering
```

```
      plants in the family Asteraceae. They are native to Eurasia
      and North and South America, and two species, T. officinale
      and T. erythrospermum, are found as weeds worldwide. Both
      species are edible in their entirety. The common name
      <span class="pronounce"><strong>dandelion</strong>
      <em>/'dændɨlaɪ.ən/</em></span> (dan-di-ly-ən, from French
      dent-de-lion, meaning "lion's tooth") is given to members of
      the genus, and like other members of the Asteraceae family,
      they have very small flowers collected together into a
      composite flower head. Each single flower in a head is called
      a floret. Many <em>Taraxacum</em> species produce seeds
      asexually by apomixis, where the seeds are produced without
      pollination, resulting in offspring that are genetically
      identical to the parent plant.</p>
    </article>
    <aside>
      <img src="images/dandy.jpg" width="400" height="300"
        alt=""/>
    </aside>
    <footer>
      <p>Text from
      <a href="http://en.wikipedia.org/wiki/Dandelion">
        Wikipedia</a></p>
    </footer>
    </div>
  </body>
</html>
```

As you can see, there are a lot of HTML tags and attributes you can use to style the page.

2. Add a link to the style sheet in the `<head>` of the document:

```
<link rel="stylesheet" href="styles.css">
```

You can put the link anywhere in the `<head>` element, but I recommend placing it just above the closing `</head>` tag. Do not put it above the `<meta charset>` tag.

3. Open a new CSS file in your web editor and name it `styles.css`. Save the file in the same directory as your HTML file.

4. In your CSS file, change the default font size:

```
body { font-size: 62.5%; }
```

5. Give your paragraphs a font size and family:

```
p {
  font-size: 1.4em;
  font-family: "Lucida Grande", "Lucida Sans Unicode",
    "Lucida Sans", "DejaVu Sans", Verdana, sans-serif;
}
```

TRY IT YOURSELF ▼

Adjust the Fonts on a Web Page

continued

▼ TRY IT YOURSELF

Adjust the Fonts on a Web Page
continued

6. Style your headlines with a size and family as well:

```
h1, h2, h3 {
  font-family: Impact, Haettenschweiler,
    "Franklin Gothic Bold", "Arial Black", sans-serif;
}
h1 { font-size: 2.4em; }
h2 { font-size: 2.0em; }
h3 { font-size: 1.8em; }
```

I prefer to give my headlines the same font but different sizes. As you can see above, I styled the `<h1>`, `<h2>`, and `<h3>` elements by separating the selectors with commas: `h1, h2, h3`.

7. Make sure that any `<strong>` or `<em>` emphasis elements are bold and italic, respectively:

```
em { font-style: italic; }
strong { font-weight: bold; }
```

8. Add a yellow color to anything with a class of `pronounce` on it:

```
.pronounce { color: #767703; }
```

Figure 6.1 shows the page before and after I added the styles, and Listing 6.3 shows the full `styles.css` file.

FIGURE 6.1
Before and after adding the styles.

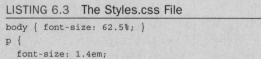

LISTING 6.3 The Styles.css File

```
body { font-size: 62.5%; }
p {
  font-size: 1.4em;
  font-family: "Lucida Grande", "Lucida Sans Unicode",
```

```
    "Lucida Sans", DejaVu Sans", Verdana, sans-serif;
}
h1, h2, h3 {
  font-family: Impact, Haettenschweiler,
    "Franklin Gothic Bold", "Arial Black", sans-serif;
}
h1 { font-size: 2.4em; }
h2 { font-size: 2.0em; }
h3 { font-size: 1.8em; }
em { font-style: italic; }
strong { font-weight: bold; }
.pronounce { color: #767703; }
```

TRY IT YOURSELF ▼

Adjust the Fonts on a Web Page
continued

Creating a Layout with CSS

Layout is a big part of RWD. Pages that look great on a wide-screen desktop monitor can be torture to read on a narrow smartphone. So it's a good idea to understand some basics of layout using CSS. In Hour 2, "Alternatives to Responsive Web Design," you learned a little about how to use CSS floats and positioning. Most RWD sites use some aspect of CSS floats for layout. In Hour 12, "Layout," you will learn more advanced techniques, including grid layouts, fixed and liquid layouts, and more, as well as which types are best used with RWD.

But beyond the CSS `float` property, there are a few other properties that are useful for laying out web pages:

- `margin`
- `padding`
- `border`
- `width`
- `height`
- `clear`

The `margin` property is a short-hand property that defines the top, right, bottom, and left margin around an element. The margin is the space between the element and other elements on the page. As you see in Figure 6.2, it is outside the border.

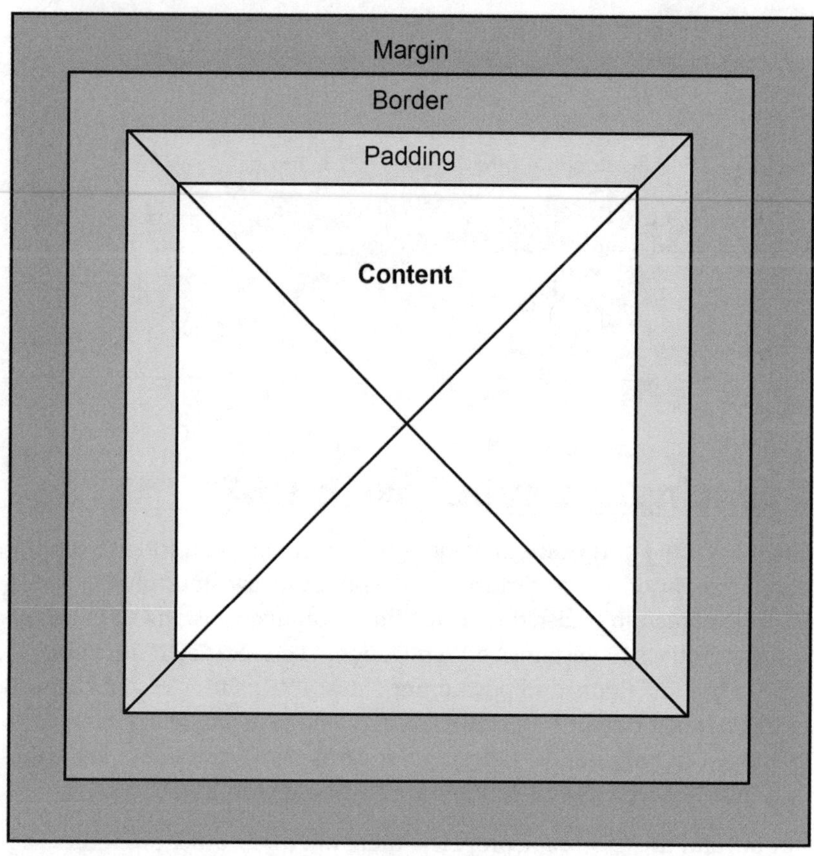

FIGURE 6.2
The CSS box model, showing the margin, border, padding, and content of an element.

You can define the margin with one value, like `margin: 1em;` or you can use up to four values to define the different sides, like this: `margin: top right bottom left;`. To give an element a top and bottom margin of 1em and a left and right margin of 0.5em, you use this:

```
margin: 1em 0.5em;
```

NOTE

Use the Margin Property to Center Elements

You can use the `margin` CSS property to center any element that has a defined width. You set the margins on the right and left to `auto` to tell the browser to center that element. This example sets a margin of 1em at the top and bottom, and it centers the margin on the right and left:

```
margin: 1em auto 1em auto;
```

The `padding` element is part of the content box and is inside the border, as you can see in Figure 6.2. It gives space around the content. It is defined in the same way as the `margin` element: `padding: top right bottom left;`. If you use three values, the padding will be set on the top, right and left, and bottom—in other words, `padding: top right/left bottom;`. You can use two values to set first the top and bottom and then the right and left. And you can use one value to set all four sides. To set the padding to 0.75em on all four sides, you use this:

```
padding: 0.75em;
```

The `border` property is a bit trickier. It is also a shorthand property, and it defines the border width, style, and color. You can set your border widths in ems as I've been doing up until now, but most designers like to keep the borders consistent in size, no matter how small or large the screen is, so this is one place where it's appropriate to use pixels.

You can set the style of the `border` property to one of several values. Here are the five most commonly used:

- `none`
- `dotted`
- `dashed`
- `double`
- `solid`

You set the color of the `border` property the same way you set foreground colors, with hexadecimal, RGB, or named color codes. For example, here is how you set a 2px-wide solid dark green border:

```
border: 2px solid rgb (11,85,1);
```

The last two styles you should know are the `width` and `height` styles. You use these styles to define the dimensions of layout blocks, and `width` is more important because web pages can be almost any height. If you specify both a width and a height and your content overflows the space provided, most browsers will default to making the content block taller and leave the width alone.

These two properties take standard sizes like percentages, ems, pixels, and inches. I recommend using a relative value like percentages so that your pages flex with the browser width. However, as you will see in Hour 12, fixed-width layouts can work in RWD as well.

To define an element as 30% of the width of its parent element, you can use this:

```
width: 30%;
```

The last property you need to know about for creating layouts with the CSS `float` property is `clear`. This is a very important property to know because it stops the floating, so you can move parts of your design down below the floated elements.

▼ TRY IT YOURSELF

Create a Two-Column Layout

Two-column layouts are fairly easy to create using CSS floats. You simply float one element to the side, and the other page elements stay in a column. Here's how you do it:

1. Open the HTML and CSS you edited in the last Try It Yourself.
2. Adjust the margins on the paragraphs by adding `margin: 0px auto 0.25em auto;` to the paragraph style.
3. Add `margin: 0px auto 1em 0px;` to the `<h1>` style rule.
4. Add `margin: 0px auto 0.4em 2em;` to the `<h2>` style rule.
5. Add new style rules to create the columns. To have the header cover the whole page, set the width of that to 100%:

```
header { width: 100%; }
```

6. The `<article>` element serves as the main column in this design, so set its width and float it to the left:

```
article {
  width: 65%;
  float: left;
}
```

7. Use the `<aside>` tag as a sidebar and float it to the right:

```
aside {
  width: 25%;
  float: right;
}
```

   In this case, you don't set the `<article>` and `<aside>` widths to add up to 100%. This ensures that there is a gutter in the middle between the two columns.

8. Set a width and height on any images inside the `<aside>` element, so that they take up 100% of the `<aside>`:

```
aside img {
  width: 100%;
  height: auto;
}
```

   The `<img>` inside the `<aside>` is defined in the HTML with a large width and height, but to keep the design flexible, you can use a flexible width and have the height set automatically based on that width.

TRY IT YOURSELF ▼

Create a Two-Column Layout

continued

9. Clear the footer so that it winds up below both floated elements and give it a width of 100%, just like the header:

```
footer { width: 100%; clear: both; }
```

Listing 6.4 shows what the CSS looks like all put together, and Figure 6.3 shows what the page looks like with these new styles.

LISTING 6.4 The Updated Styles.css File

```
body { font-size: 62.5%; }
p {
  font-size: 1.4em;
  font-family: "Lucida Grande", "Lucida Sans Unicode",
    "Lucida Sans", "DejaVu Sans", Verdana, sans-serif;
  margin: 0px auto 0.25em auto;
}
h1, h2, h3 {
  font-family: Impact, Haettenschweiler,
    "Franklin Gothic Bold", "Arial Black", sans-serif;
}
h1 { font-size: 2.4em; margin: 0px auto 1em 0px; }
h2 { font-size: 2.0em; margin: 0px auto 0.4em 2em; }
h3 { font-size: 1.8em; }
em { font-style: italic; }
strong { font-weight: bold; }
.pronounce { color: #767703; }
header { width: 100%; }
article {
  width: 65%;
  float: left;
}
aside {
  width: 25%;
  float: right;
}
aside img {
  width: 100%;
  height: auto;
}
footer {
  width: 100%;
  clear: both;
}
```

▼ TRY IT YOURSELF

Create a Two-Column Layout

continued

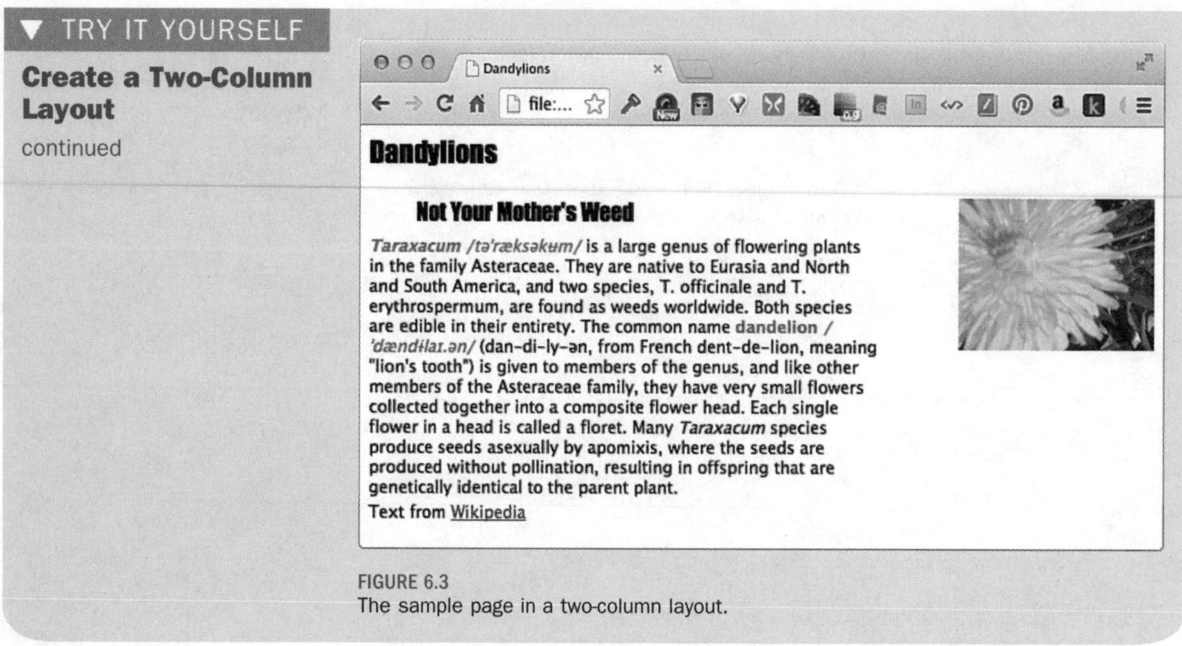
Dandylions
file:...
Dandylions
Not Your Mother's Weed
Taraxacum /tə'ræksəkʉm/ is a large genus of flowering plants in the family Asteraceae. They are native to Eurasia and North and South America, and two species, T. officinale and T. erythrospermum, are found as weeds worldwide. Both species are edible in their entirety. The common name dandelion /'dændɨlaɪ.ən/ (dan-di-ly-ən, from French dent-de-lion, meaning "lion's tooth") is given to members of the genus, and like other members of the Asteraceae family, they have very small flowers collected together into a composite flower head. Each single flower in a head is called a floret. Many Taraxacum species produce seeds asexually by apomixis, where the seeds are produced without pollination, resulting in offspring that are genetically identical to the parent plant.
Text from Wikipedia

FIGURE 6.3
The sample page in a two-column layout.

Understanding Cascading and Specificity

The number-one reason that many people find CSS difficult is because it doesn't always act as you might expect. A lot of the confusion comes from not understanding cascading (also called *the cascade*) and how specificity affects your style rules. When designing RWD pages, you will be working in the CSS a lot, so it's important to understand these aspects of CSS.

What Is the Cascade?

A user agent uses the cascade to read CSS and apply it to a web page. If you understand the rules whereby a style can be applied and when, you will start to understand why some styles don't take effect when you think they should.

User agents use the following steps to determine precedence of a style rule. These steps are the cascade:

1. Find all style rules that apply to the element in question for the current media type. (You'll learn more about media types in Hour 10, "CSS Media Queries.")

2. Determine what type of style sheet the rule is in. Author style sheets (style sheets web designers write) come first, followed by user style sheets (style sheets created by the customer and applied to the pages they view), and finally user agent style sheets (default styles the browser uses if no other rule applies).
3. Look at how specific the style rule is. The more specific a rule, the more precedence it gets.
4. Sort the rules in the order in which they were written in the style sheet. Rules closer to the top of the style sheet have higher precedence than rules that come later.

The only exception to this cascade order is if the style rule has the `!important` keyword attached to it. This indicates that that style rule should have precedence over another rule in the cascade. You can learn more about the cascade on the W3C (see: `http://www.w3.org/TR/css3-cascade/#cascading`).

As a web designer, you can affect the order in which the styles show up in the style sheets and how specific they are.

CAUTION

Avoid Using `!important`

When many new web designers first learn about the `!important` keyword, they use it on every style rule in their CSS as a way to force the browser to show the styles they want. But this is lazy coding and can make things more difficult to manage later. Plus, if everything is important, then nothing really is important, and the browser goes right back to the standard cascade.

I recommend using the `!important` keyword only for testing. Then once you know what styles you need in order to get the look you want, you should remove it and increase the specificity of your selectors or move your styles farther up the document until they display without needing that keyword.

What Is Specificity?

Specificity is where CSS can seem really complicated. But when you understand the rules, it becomes clear and makes sense. Specificity is the idea that the more specific your CSS selector is, the higher precedence it should get.

For example, if you have three paragraphs in a document and one has the `highlight` class (that is, `class="highlight"`), any styles that point at the `highlight` class point to a more specific paragraph than styles that just point at any old `<p>` element. So in that case, if there is a conflict, the more specific rule displays.

Several things make a rule more specific:

- Multiple elements in the rule
- Classes, pseudo-classes, and attribute selectors in the rule
- `id` attributes because there can be only one element with a particular ID

But say that you have two style selectors, like this:

```
div > p.class1 span a[name]:hover
p span a[name].class2:hover
```

How do you know which one has a higher precedence? Here are the steps for determining the precedence:

1. Count the number of element names (like `p` or `span`) in the selector. Give each of them 1 point.
2. Count the number of classes, pseudo-classes, pseudo-elements, attributes, and other non-ID selectors. Multiply this by 10.
3. Count the number of ID selectors and multiply by 100.
4. Add all three numbers together.
5. Do the above steps for the second rule you are checking. The number that is higher has the higher specificity and will have precedence.

When you apply these rules, the first selector (`div > p.class1 span a[name]:hover`) has a score of 34 (4 + 30 + 0), and the second selector (`p span a[name].class2:hover`) has a score of 33, so the first selector is more specific.

Summary

In this hour you've learned how to write CSS rules and how to apply them to your web pages by using embedded and external style sheets.

You've learned some basic CSS for styling fonts and changing colors. You've also learned how to create simple layouts using CSS and the `float` property.

And you now understand the basics of cascading and specificity and how they affect your style sheets.

Table 6.1 describes all the CSS properties discussed in this hour.

TABLE 6.1 CSS Properties Covered in Hour 6

Property	Value(s)	Description
`background-color`	Color name, hexadecimal code, or RGB code	Defines the background color of the selected element.
`border`	A length, color, and style	Defines the border color, border width, and border style around the element.

`clear`	`both`
	`right`
	`left`
		Clears floated elements.

`color`	Color name, hexadecimal code, or RGB code	Defines the foreground color (text) of the element.
`font-family`	A comma-separated list of font faces	Defines a list of fonts in preferential order for styling the text.
`font-size`	A length	Defines the size of the font.
`font-style`	`italic` `normal`	Defines whether the font should be displayed in italic or normal.
`font-weight`	`bold` `normal`	Defines whether the font should be displayed bold or normal.
`height`	A length	Defines the height of an element.
`margin`	A length	Defines the margin around an element.
`padding`	A length	Defines the paddings around an element.
`width`	A length	Defines the width of an element.

Workshop

The workshop contains quiz questions to help you process what you've learned in this lesson. Try to answer all the questions before you read the answers.

Q&A

Q. I want to learn more about CSS. Where do you recommend I start?

A. A great book for learning CSS is *Sams Teach Yourself HTML and CSS in 24 Hours* by Julie C. Meloni.

Q. My two-column layout looks really awful on wide-screen monitors because the page is so wide that it's hard to read. Is there anything I can do about that?

A. A good solution is to use the CSS property `max-width` on the `<body>` element or the container `<div>`. This sets the maximum width to which the whole page should open. You'll learn more about it in Hour 12.

Q. Are any of the properties you mentioned too advanced for some browsers?

A. All the properties you've learned this hour have been around for a long time—some since CSS level 1 and some since CSS level 2. They are all well supported by all modern browsers.

Q. What about CSS3? I heard that I can use it to do cool things like shadows and rounded corners and so on. Should I learn CSS3 and where can I do that?

A. CSS3 does add a lot of great new features for styling and designing your web pages. You can do things like rounded corners without images, gradient colors, and multi-column layouts. The book I mentioned above will also help you with CSS3.

Quiz

1. What is the syntax of a style property?
2. What is the difference between a child selector and a descendent selector?
3. Is `handwriting` a generic font family?
4. If you use `margin: 1em 5em 2em;`, what is styled?

5. Which rule would be applied if you saw a style sheet written in this order:

```
p.important { color: red; }
p#unimportant { color: blue; }
```

Answers

1. The syntax of a style property is `style : value;`.
2. A child selector selects elements that are immediately under the parent element in the document tree. A descendent selector selects any elements that are under that parent branch on the document tree.
3. No, `handwriting` is not a generic font. The closest generic font is `script`.
4. The `margin: 1em 5em 2em;` property says to make the top margin 1em, the bottom margin 2em, and the right and left margins both 5em.
5. This style sheet has a selector that selects paragraph with a class and a paragraph with an ID. Since an ID refers to only one element on a page, this is the most specific rule. If you use the steps outlined in this hour, you see that the first line is 11 points, while the second is 101 points. That also tells you that the second is more specific.

Exercises

1. In the Try It Yourself exercises in this lesson, I had you change the color of the text. Using the same format (`color: color name;`) go into the CSS file and change the background of the `<header>` element to yellow. You can use the color keyword or choose an RGB or hexadecimal color.
2. You are now ready to add some styles to the HTML you worked with in Hour 5, "HTML for Responsive Web Design." Adjust the headlines and the fonts to create a more interesting design. Add some color, either background or text color, and see if you can adjust the layout to make the page more pleasing.

HOUR 7
Unobtrusive JavaScript

WHAT YOU'LL LEARN IN THIS HOUR:

- What unobtrusive JavaScript is
- How unobtrusive JavaScript relates to progressive enhancement
- How to use unobtrusive JavaScript on your web pages

JavaScript is the third pillar of a web page, along with HTML (for content) and CSS (for the look and feel). JavaScript is what you use to make your site do things. It adds interactivity to your pages and often makes the pages more fun.

But until recently, JavaScript was so difficult to use without generating at least a few bugs that most designers would either forgo it completely or simply ignore the bugs as long as the scripts worked in most situations. Then Ajax emerged, creating a style of web interactivity that we had never seen before.

But with that interactivity came problems. Ajax wasn't, by default, accessible to everyone. And while more and more clients were demanding rich internet applications (RIAs) for their websites, the scripting to create them was becoming more and more difficult to manage. Then the idea of unobtrusive JavaScript came along.

What Is Unobtrusive JavaScript?

Unobtrusive JavaScript is a general approach to how you add JavaScript to your web pages. It involves several components:

- Separating the structure (and design) from the behavior
- Adding a layer to support usability
- Writing clean, semantic HTML

Separating Structure from Behavior

As you learned in Hour 4, "Progressive Enhancement," you should always separate your content from your presentation and behavior.

Unobtrusive JavaScript helps you do this by having you remove all your JavaScript from your HTML. This includes

- Scripts embedded in the `<body>`
- Scripts embedded in the `<head>`
- Scripts included in the HTML elements (except the one file that contains the scripts)

A good rule of thumb is to only use the `<script>` element at the very bottom of the `<body>` element of your document to point to *one file* that contains all your scripts. If you must include a script in the `<head>` element, you should place it right before the `</head>` tag. You should never have any `<script>` elements amid the body elements of your web pages, as doing so means mixing up content and behavior.

The trickier part for many designers is removing scripts from the elements themselves. After all, HTML includes a bunch of event attributes like `onclick` and `onmouseover`, and it can be challenging to understand how to make scripts activate on the events without using those attributes. But by using the DOM, you can identify elements in your scripts and then assign events to them there.

For example, say that you have a block of code that you want to hide when someone clicks a link. Without unobtrusive JavaScript, you would write this:

```
<a href="#" onclick="hide();" id="hidden1">
```

Then when that link is clicked, the `hide()` function runs, hiding the content. With unobtrusive JavaScript, your HTML looks like this:

```
<a href="#" id="hidden1">
```

Then, in your script file, you write this:

```
var hidden1 = document.getElementById('hidden1');
if (hidden1) {
  hidden1.onclick = hide;
}
```

Yes, this is slightly longer than the other version, but it's much easier to manage. If you decide tomorrow to add this to another link, you just add a few more lines to your JavaScript. If you decide to switch it so that it happens when the user hovers over the link, you just edit the event in your JavaScript. You never have to edit your HTML.

NOTE

You Aren't Limited to Identified Elements

You can select any DOM element in your script and add behavior to it. For instance, if you want every element that has the `hide` class assigned to it to run the `hide()` function, then you change `document.getElementById('hidden')` to `document.getElementsbyClassName('hide')`. You'll have to modify the rest of the script to accept an array, but the principle is the same.

Supporting Usability

Usability is the backbone of both progressive enhancement and unobtrusive JavaScript. This is because JavaScript is not supported on 100% of the browsers and operating systems out there. And JavaScript can be turned off by the user, so even if your customers all use the most modern browsers, if they've turned off JavaScript, they won't see your behaviors.

You should never think that using JavaScript is the only way to make something work on your website. You should use it to add features. In other words, you use JavaScript to progressively enhance your website for customers and browsers that can use it.

When you're thinking about adding JavaScript, you should consider the following basic principles:

- Your website should work correctly without JavaScript. It's okay if it's not as smooth or easy to use without JavaScript. But you should never rely on using JavaScript as the only way to do a task.
- When your customers have JavaScript enabled, you should use it to add another layer of usability to the site. JavaScript might speed things up (like an in-browser form validator) or make the page easier to use.
- You shouldn't use JavaScript as the only way to do something on your site. This is because JavaScript is unsafe. For example, if you set up form validation using only JavaScript, a malicious user could simply turn off JavaScript and bypass your defenses.

What you should take away from this section is that it's not critical that a user without JavaScript see the identical site or have exactly the same functionality as a user with JavaScript. Instead, you should ensure that both customers get the experience they need to use the site.

Usability also refers to browser compatibility. When you're writing unobtrusive JavaScript, it should work in as many browsers as possible. When it doesn't work, it should simply go away without any error messages, leaving the customer with a site that still works but without the script bells and whistles.

Writing Clean and Semantic HTML

This was covered in Hour 5, "HTML for Responsive Web Design," but it bears repeating: If you create clean HTML that has lots of identifying markers including `class` and `id` attributes and other semantic identifiers, you will have much more to connect to with your JavaScript.

Some things to look for:

- Use headline tags like `<h1>`, `<h2>`, and `<h3>`.
- Create lists using list elements (`<ul>`, `<ol>`, `<li>`, and so on).
- Use the HTML5 sectioning elements (`<article>`, `<section>`, `<figure>`, and so on) where appropriate.
- Add `id` and `class` attributes to elements.
- Validate your HTML to make sure it's correct.

If you think that clean HTML isn't really critical for writing JavaScript, you're correct. It's not that you can't write a script to accommodate poorly written HTML, it's that it's easier in the long run if you don't have to.

How to Implement Unobtrusive JavaScript

If you're building a website from scratch, implementing unobtrusive JavaScript is reasonably easy. Just keep your JavaScript out of the HTML and think of your scripts as an enhancement to your website rather than as a critical part of the infrastructure. If you're following this book in order, you already have a good base structure for your content in the HTML.

NOTE

You Don't Need the Type Attribute

Many websites include the attribute `type="text/javascript"` in the `<script>` tag, but with HTML5, that is no longer required. It is required only if your script is not JavaScript (or ECMAScript) because web browsers assume JavaScript unless told otherwise.

The challenge comes when you're converting an existing site to unobtrusive JavaScript. Here are the steps I take to convert a site:

1. Open a new external JavaScript file and save it to your website as `scripts.js`.
2. Move all the scripts stored inside `<script>` tags into the `scripts.js` file.
3. At the very bottom of your web page, add a single `<script>` tag that will load all your scripts:

```
<script src="scripts.js"></script>
```

4. Run an initial test of your web page by loading it in a browser. You may have to upload it and the script file to your web server. You should test your page now to identify any possible problems and fix them in your script. For instance, some scripts don't work if they aren't called in exactly the location on the page where they are to display.
5. Fix any obvious problems using the DOM to identify where your scripts should display or activate.
6. Go through the HTML, looking for event attributes like `onmouseover` and `onclick` and remove them.
7. In your script file, add the events you removed using the DOM to define what elements are affected.
8. Test your page again and fix any additional problems you find. Remember to test in as many web browsers as you can, including browsers on mobile devices.

NOTE

Putting Scripts at the Bottom Speeds Up Your Pages

When web browsers load JavaScript, they do it without performing any other requests. This means that if you put your script at the top of a page (or in the `<head>` of your document), the browser will download the script before downloading any of the following HTML or CSS. This can cause your page to appear to load more slowly. If you're using unobtrusive JavaScript, it shouldn't affect the content of the page and so isn't as vital if it loads last.

Those steps are a high-level overview of how to implement unobtrusive JavaScript, but there are some specific rules of thumb you should be familiar with as well:

- Make sure that objects exist before you use them.
- Don't write browser-specific JavaScript.
- Use local variables.
- Use JavaScript as an enhancement only.
- Don't assume that everyone is using a mouse.

If an object doesn't exist and you perform an action on it with JavaScript, you will get an error message, which is the opposite of unobtrusive. But luckily it's easy to fix. All you do is add an `if` statement to checking that an object exists before you do anything to it. In my earlier example, I used this line to ensure that the `hidden1` object had a value:

```
if (hidden1) {
```

If it had a value, then the `if` statement functions (inside the curly braces) would run otherwise they wouldn't run.

Before unobtrusive JavaScript, it was very common to see browser-specific JavaScript. And often it was coupled with long browser-detection scripts to determine whether the browser viewing the page could even use the script feature. Instead of checking for features like `document.layers` or `document.all`, you should check to make sure the DOM is supported and simply test for that. The easiest way to test this is with the following line:

```
if (document.getElementById) {
```

Then place all your DOM operations inside that `if` statement.

CAUTION

Older Versions of Opera Need a Bit More

Some early versions of Opera (pre-version 5 or earlier) reported that they supported the `document.getElementById` method, but they didn't do it correctly. If you're concerned about this or have a lot of Opera customers, you should change the DOM check line to this:

```
if (document.getElementById &&
document.createTextNode) {
```

Using local variables is good coding practice as it keeps your scripts maintainable. But sometimes it can be tempting to treat a variable as a global variable and use it everywhere.

When you do this, you run the risk of some other function on the page changing the variable without your realizing it. This can break your functions or generate unexpected results.

I've mentioned several times that you should treat JavaScript as an enhancement rather than as a critical part of your web pages, but it bears repeating: JavaScript is not a trustworthy source and can be bypassed.

Beginning web designers are often tempted to use JavaScript for passwords. It can be hard to add passwords to a web page if you don't have access to the server, but JavaScript is a poor solution. Beyond the fact that it can be turned off, as mentioned earlier, it is also written in clear text on the website. This means that if you password protect a page, that password is written right in the JavaScript code for anyone to see.

If you must use JavaScript, for security purposes, you should have a backup like a web server script or `.htaccess` file as well.

Finally, a lot of JavaScript functions rely on the mouse. You see lots of `onmouseover` events for rollover effects and `onclick` events for click effects. And these are great. But remember that not everyone uses a mouse. This is especially true as more and more people use touch-screen tablets and smartphones to access the web. For example, if some of your web page content is visible only when a mouse hovers over a link, someone on an iPad is going to be hard-pressed to see that. When you hover your finger over the iPad, you aren't touching it, so the iPad does nothing.

Summary

In this hour you've learned the basics of unobtrusive JavaScript. Unobtrusive JavaScript is important both for your customers and for yourself as it makes it easier for your pages to be used and maintained. You've learned why unobtrusive JavaScript is important as well as some tips for implementing it on both new and existing websites.

Workshop

The workshop contains quiz questions to help you process what you've learned in this lesson. Try to answer all the questions before you read the answers.

Q&A

Q. Unobtrusive JavaScript is hard to do, and many scripts don't seem to use it. Is it really that important?

A. Of course, how you build your website is your choice. But it's important that you understand the choices you are making. I only started using unobtrusive JavaScript a few years ago. Before that I found it easier to use just JavaScript in my pages. But as I worked on larger and more complicated sites, unobtrusive JavaScript made more sense.

Q. It sounds like what you're saying is that JavaScript shouldn't be used for anything important on a website. Is that true?

A. JavaScript is risky. While it has much better support in 2014 than it did in 2004, there are still browsers out there that handle JavaScript calls in unexpected ways. Plus, because the user can turn off JavaScript, you can't be sure that a customer will have JavaScript, even with the most recent version of Chrome. So if your site requires JavaScript, there are going to be some customers who won't get the full experience. And that goes against the philosophy of progressive enhancement.

Quiz

1. What are two aspects of unobtrusive JavaScript?
2. Is this bit of HTML unobtrusive JavaScript?

```
<p>My dog is <script src="dogsage.js"></script> years old</p>
```

3. Why is the above HTML unobtrusive or why is it not?
4. How do you select an element with an `id` attribute with JavaScript?

Answers

1. The three things that define unobtrusive JavaScript are that it is separate from the content and presentation, it supports usability, and it is built on clean, semantic HTML.
2. No, it is not.
3. It is not unobtrusive because the script is being called from directly within the HTML.
4. You use the `getElementbyId()` function to select an element by a specific `id` attribute.

Exercise

For the site you've been working with, move all the scripts to an external JavaScript file. Then apply the rules of unobtrusive JavaScript to add the interactivity back into the site.

HOUR 8
Planning a Responsive Website

Every web designer I've ever worked with has been way more interested in diving into the code of a website than in planning how to build that site. Planning, for most of us, is boring and gets in the way of the meat of the project. But even doing a little bit of planning before you dive in can prevent a lot of problems.

Here are some examples, from real sites that I've worked on. In most of these situations, we did a little bit of planning, but often the planning was along the lines of asking the content writers "How many articles do you have ready to go on the site?"

- On one site I worked on, we spent two weeks designing an amazing navigation menu. It was responsive, flexing with the width of the browser window, and it contained sections for all the areas of the website. However, when we made the site live, we learned that one of the site sections was rolling out a new section name that was more than 30 characters long. The content team had tested this name, gotten it approved by upper management, and had already spent a lot of money on it; they were waiting for the redesign to make it live. But 30 characters didn't fit in our design. If we had gone to the content teams at the beginning of the process, we would have known about this name, but because we didn't, we had to spend another two weeks reworking the menu to make it fit.
- On another site, my team worked hard to create a mobile version of the site. The company had done research and felt that having a separate mobile site was more cost-effective than doing RWD. It wasn't until we made the new mobile site live that anyone thought to look at current mobile usage. It turns out that only 3% to 5% of the traffic was from mobile. When the mobile site

WHAT YOU'LL LEARN IN THIS HOUR:

- How to determine if RWD is right for your site
- How to create a site plan
- How to use analytics to evaluate your current site
- How to look at your content critically with regard to responsive design

went live, it ended up getting only a fraction of the page views that the desktop site got, and when I left after six months, that number had not increased significantly.

- I once worked on an ecommerce site where the site owner was convinced that he was losing customers by not offering his products for sale in a mobile-friendly manner. From my discussions with him, it seems he had visited his site on a smartphone and didn't like how it looked. So we spent five months creating a more mobile-friendly storefront. When we were done, we took a look at the usage by customers, and nearly all of the mobile customers were coming to the site, clicking the "show desktop version" link, and then going to a completely different section than the storefront.

All these scenarios could have been prevented if we had done more planning and analysis before we started working on the designs. This hour you'll learn how to evaluate your site and then come up with a plan for creating a responsive web design for it.

Should You Make Your Website Responsive?

Chances are, if you've bought this book, you already plan to make your website responsive. But before you leap ahead, you should make absolutely sure that this is the best solution for your website. As I will discuss in Hour 20, "Problems with Responsive Web Design," RWD is not a panacea for all web problems. And RWD can cause problems of its own.

There are some things you should evaluate before deciding to build a responsive website, including these:

- Who's viewing your site
- What you want your site's audience to look like (more mobile? less mobile?)
- How much time you have to build the site
- What kind of content you already have on the site
- What changes you will need to make

I recommend that websites with a large mobile audience (for example, where more than 20% of current visitors use a mobile device to view the site) and sites that want to attract a large mobile audience use RWD. Sites with a smaller mobile audience can still benefit from responsive design, but they need to recognize that the time it takes to build a responsive site and modify or add content to support it might be expensive.

How to Plan for a Responsive Website

Once you've decided to go ahead with a responsive web design, you should make a plan for how you're going to implement it. If you're like most other web designers, you think planning is boring, and you want to get straight to the implementation. But if you plan things first, you'll spend less time later fixing problems.

Check Site Analytics

You need to check your website analytics to see if your site is a good candidate for RWD. As mentioned above, sites with more than 20% of their current visitors on mobile (both phone and tablet devices) make good candidates for responsive web design because a lot of people already want to read the site, and making the site more mobile friendly will encourage them to visit and stay longer.

There are many analytics packages that will tell you what percentage of viewers are viewing your site on mobile devices. Figure 8.1 shows analytics on two different sites: one that doesn't and one that does get a lot of mobile traffic. On one site I manage, the traffic is primarily desktop customers, while on another site, 25% are coming from mobile devices. Neither of these sites are optimized for mobile customers right now.

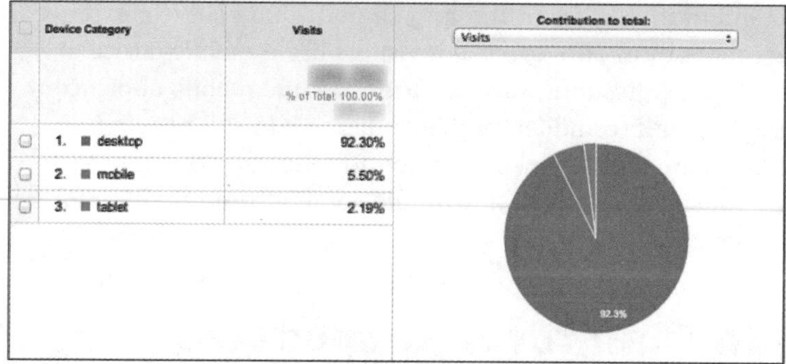

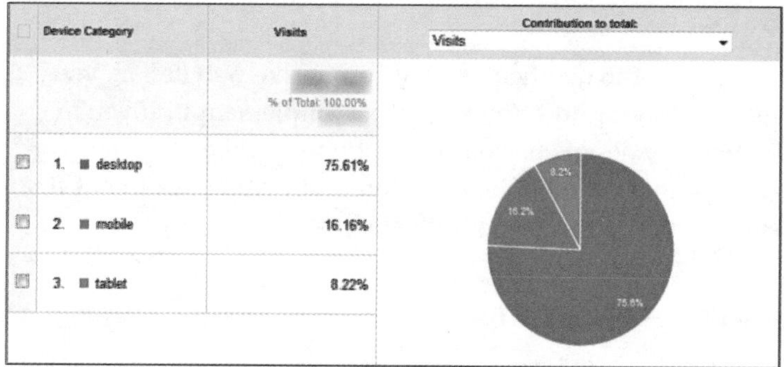

FIGURE 8.1
The top image shows a site in Google Analytics with only around 7% mobile traffic, while the bottom shows another site with almost 25% mobile traffic.

▼ TRY IT YOURSELF

How to Find Mobile Traffic in Google Analytics

Google Analytics is a popular analytics tool. You can set it up by going to `http://www.google.com/analytics` and following the instructions there. Once you have collected data on a month's worth of traffic, you are ready to evaluate your site's mobile trends. Follow these steps:

1. Open your Google Analytics account to your site's reports.
2. In the left column, select Audience.
3. Choose the Mobile area and open the Overview report.
4. Click the pie chart icon above the table to see how many mobile users your site has.

The results will give you an idea of how your current customers are viewing the site. If you want to know exactly what devices are viewing it, you can switch to the Devices report. And if your site gets a lot of visitors, it can be fun to watch the real-time overview report as well. Figure 8.2 shows how that might look.

TRY IT YOURSELF ▼

How to Find Mobile Traffic in Google Analytics

continued

FIGURE 8.2
For this site, Google Analytics shows only 6% non-desktop users in real-time analytics.

Evaluating Existing Content

The next thing you want to do is evaluate what content you currently have. You need to decide whether you have content that works well for mobile devices and whether it's content that your customers (or the customers you hope to attract) will want to view on their mobile devices.

Remember that content isn't just the words on your pages. For your plan, you should create a list or spreadsheet that includes the following:

- All the pages on your site that contain text
- The navigation elements (a list of what's in them and where they point)
- All the images that are content related—in other words, not including design elements like icons
- Multimedia elements like sound files and video, including their formats
- Special text content pages like tables and forms
- Other content items like PDFs or Word documents
- The font families and styles preferred or required by the company
- Advertising blocks—not necessarily what ads you serve, as that changes, but rather what ads you generally serve and where they are in the design

NOTE

Don't Forget Retina Devices

Retina display is a brand of screens from Apple that has a high pixel density. While Retina is an Apple brand, there are other companies that have high resolution displays that have the same issues as Retina. I will cover high resolution displays and how they affect images in more detail in Hour 15, "Creating and Using Images in RWD," but for now you should be aware that you are probably going to need a second set of images to make your site Retina-ready. It's a good idea to include in your plan a list of what images you absolutely want crisp on retina devices so that you can have them created.

If you have a large site, you might want to do this in aggregate rather than list the exact files. But you want to have a general overview of what your content consists of. For example, you might find that you have a site with 80% text and only two form pages, 90% of your pages include at least one image that can't be removed from context, and you have more than 100 videos and PDFs. Or you may find that your site is 95% videos, with only a few text pages.

Don't forget to catalog your advertising. Advertising can be a problem on responsive websites because ad blocks are usually sold in very specific sizes that can't be changed. I discuss more about what to do with advertising on responsive sites in Hour 20.

Making Decisions About Content

Once you know what you have on your site, you need to decide whether the site needs to be available to a mobile user. Remember that sites that use progressive enhancement make the site accessible to everyone, regardless of what browser or device they are using. So it's easy to think that all your content should be available to all your customers.

But some content works better for mobile customers than others, and your design should respond to that, too. Figure 8.3 shows you how eBay adjusts content for mobile users and desktop users. The screen shots were taken at the same time, but as you can see, the design is significantly simplified for mobile customers.

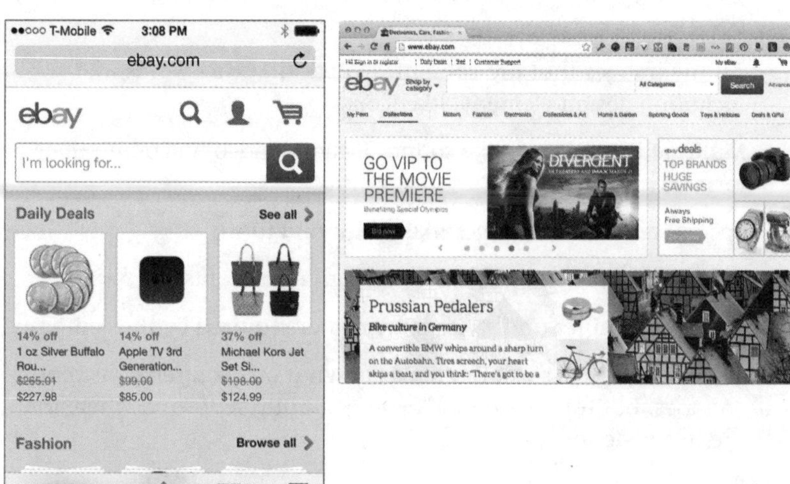

FIGURE 8.3
The eBay website viewed on an iPhone and on a desktop computer.

While there may be some mobile customers who want to access an entire site, the majority of them are only going to do one or two things. If your site is already live, and you're getting traffic from mobile customers, you can use your analytics software to determine what pages mobile users like best so you know what to showcase in your smaller-screen designs.

TRY IT YOURSELF ▼

Find the Popular Pages on Mobile in Google Analytics

Google Analytics can help you see what pages are most popular to your mobile customers. Follow these steps:

1. Log in to your Google Analytics account.
2. Go to Behavior and then Site Content and open the All Pages report.
3. At the top of the table, choose Device Category under Secondary Dimension. This will give you an additional column indicating what type of device is used to view the page.
4. Then click Advanced on the right side of the top of the table.
5. Set the filter to say Exclude Device Category Containing Desktop, as shown in Figure 8.4.

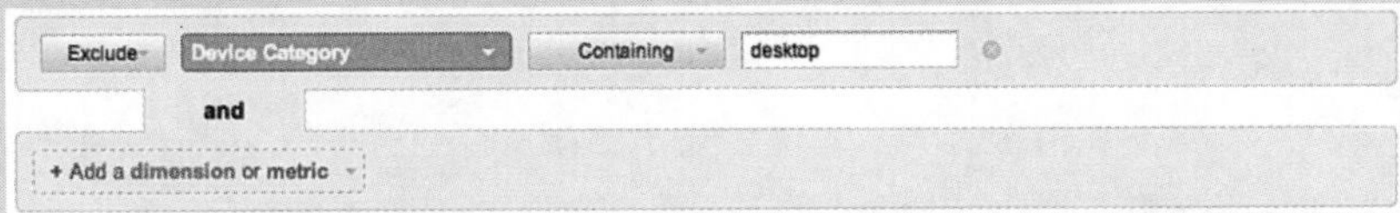

FIGURE 8.4
Google Analytics advanced filter.

6. Click Apply.

Google Analytics then shows you the 10 most popular pages for any device that isn't a desktop computer. Google separates the views out by both tablet and mobile. If you want to see just one or the other, you can change the filter to include or exclude only the devices you want to see.

Try to evaluate every piece of content or at least every type of content you have on your site. You want to decide whether it needs to be on mobile or tablet devices, whether it can be resized (many videos and most advertising cannot be resized), and how critical the content is for mobile, tablet, and desktop users.

Writing a Site Plan

Once you have your content listed and evaluated, the plan is nearly written. You will realize as you're evaluating the content that some of it doesn't need to be highly visible on smaller-screen devices, and some of it can't be displayed there because it won't fit and can't be resized.

Your site plan should include what you will do to make the critical parts of your pages accessible no matter what. Remember that this isn't a design plan. You don't have to worry about how the pages will look or where elements will be placed. You just need to know that you have images that will need to be adjusted, you have advertising alternatives, and the forms need to be accessible and look good.

Summary

In this hour you've learned about some tools to help decide whether responsive web design is right for your site as well as how to plan for building a responsive website. You've learned that planning is a critical, if boring, part of the web design process, but by planning before you start doing the design, you can avoid problems after the site is live.

Workshop

The workshop contains quiz questions to help you process what you've learned in this lesson. Try to answer all the questions before you read the answers.

Q&A

Q. In this hour you focus on Google Analytics for evaluating the site, but are there other options?

A. Google Analytics is one of the most popular website analytics tools available, but it's not the only tool. If you host your site on WordPress, you can get a lot of information from the analytics available in the JetPack plugin (`http://wordpress.org/plugins/jetpack/`). Another good analytics tool you can install on your own server is Piwik (`http://piwik.org`).

Q. If my site doesn't get any mobile viewers, do I still need to make it responsive?

A. Ultimately, it's your website, and you can do what you like with it. But I recommend that you consider making your site responsive even if you don't get a lot of mobile users. A responsive site doesn't have to be extremely complicated to be useful to mobile customers. In fact, if all you do is convert a multiple-column site into a single column for mobile customers, you'll have made it much easier for your mobile customers to use. And mobile is growing more and more popular as more people get smartphones.

Quiz

1. What five things should you evaluate to decide whether RWD is right for your site?
2. Why is planning important?
3. What kind of site is a good candidate for RWD?
4. How much data should you have before you start using analytics for customer analysis?
5. Name three types of content that you should list in your content plan.
6. Why should you list advertising blocks in your content plan?

Answers

1. You need to know what your site's customers are using to view the site right now, who you want to cater to, how much time you have to build and maintain the site, what kind of content you currently have, and what content you need to make your site better for mobile customers.
2. Planning is important because it helps you identify trouble spots and fix problems before they cause a lot of trouble.
3. Any site that gets more than 20% of its visitors from mobile devices is a good candidate for RWD.
4. While you can start using site analytics immediately, it's good to wait at least a month to make sure you're seeing a good overview of your customer base.
5. You should list your web pages with text content, navigation elements, content images, multimedia elements, PDFs and Word documents, tables and forms, and advertising blocks.
6. You should list advertising blocks in your content plan because they cannot be resized and can cause problems in responsive designs.

Exercise

Return to the site you're working on and create a site plan for it. Include all the content types along with how important they are for mobile customers and any other information you think is important. I use a spreadsheet to evaluate my site content; check it out at `http://www.html5in24hours.com/siteplan.xlsx` and see if it helps you.

HOUR 9
Mobile First

WHAT YOU'LL LEARN IN THIS HOUR:

- Why mobile first is important for RWD
- What to consider when deciding to design for mobile first
- What makes a website mobile friendly

Traditionally, web designers first build a website for desktop users and then modify that site for mobile users. Mobile-first web design turns that formula on its head: It says to build a site for mobile users first and then adjust it to work for desktop users.

In this hour you will learn more about mobile first responsive web design and how you can begin to think in a way that is counterintuitive for many designers. You will also learn why mobile first is so important and how mobile design needs to be different from desktop design. Finally, you'll take a look at a design method that is even more cutting edge: mobile-only design.

Why Design for Mobile First?

One of the things many designers forget when building a website is that they are not the site's customers. Most designers build web pages on desktop or laptop computers. They test their pages in the most up-to-date browsers and operating systems and expect their customers to use the site the same way.

But the reality is that more and more people are moving to mobile and tablet devices. As you can see in Figure 9.1, the mobile and desktop stats as compiled by StatCounter (`http://gs.statcounter.com`) are converging on one another, and they appear to be converging more rapidly as time moves on. More and more people worldwide are buying mobile devices with web browsers and using them to browse the web.

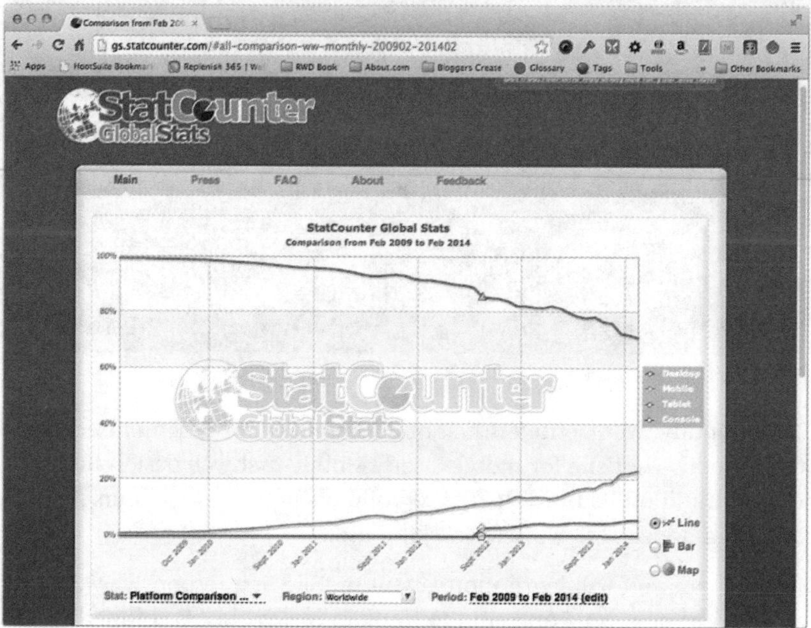

FIGURE 9.1
Platform comparison of mobile, desktop, and tablet browsers from August 2013 to August 2014 from StatCounter.

But while more and more people are browsing the web using mobile devices, it is still difficult to design web pages on mobile devices. So it's not surprising that most web designers start by building their pages for the machine they are using.

But if you start your design by focusing on mobile, you are immediately changing your focus to a much larger market, worldwide. According to SmartPlanet (`http://smartplanet.com`), which gets its data from the United Nations, there are almost as many cell phone subscriptions today as there are people on the planet. And nearly every phone sold has a web browser. In developing countries, using smartphones is often the only way people get online.

The global penetration of cell phones is between 89% and 97%. So if you want your website to be accessible to people all around the world, a mobile-first design strategy is a smart way to go.

Changing the Focus to Content

When you design first for mobile devices, you have to focus on the content first. You have to determine what content is the core content for a page because the screen size on a mobile device is much smaller than most desktop computers. If you don't know what the core content or functionality is for every page on your site, then your mobile customers won't know either.

In Hour 8, "Planning a Responsive Website," you created a site plan that lists all the content on your site. But chances are, not all of it is critical to your mobile customers. By using your website statistics, you can promote articles that mobile customers prefer to mobile customers, and promote other articles to non-mobile customers.

But while it's good to highlight different content to different users, you should provide a way to get to all the content for all your users. As discussed in Hour 4, "Progressive Enhancement," that is the key to progressive enhancement. So if you're going to reduce the main navigation or remove links or other elements for mobile users, you need to decide where you're going to put them so that they can be found if they are needed.

Experimenting with New Technologies

A lot of new technologies have appeared on mobile devices first or are more widely used on mobile. Here are some examples:

- Geolocation
- Touch screen interfaces
- Web storage
- Offline applications
- Mobile web applications

While more of these technologies are appearing on desktop computers, there are still a lot more uses for them on mobile devices. For example, geolocation isn't terribly useful on a machine that never leaves its current position.

Why Mobile First Works

Mobile first is primarily an implementation of progressive enhancement (explained in Hour 4), which means that you focus on getting the required content and functionality to as many customers as possible. A lot of different devices out there can display web pages, including these:

- Mobile devices, including smartphones, basic cell phones, and tablets

> NOTE
>
> **What Is "The Internet of Things"?**
>
> The Internet of things (IoT) involves objects, animals, or humans that are given unique identifiers and the capability to transmit data over a network without requiring a human to initiate anything. Examples are heart monitors, farm animals with embedded microchips, and refrigerators that transmit their contents so you know when you're almost out of milk.
>
> The first "thing" in the IoT was a Coke machine at Carnegie Mellon University in the 1980s. It was connected to the Internet, and programmers could access the data to determine whether there would be a cold drink available. No more getting to the machine only to find that all the root beer was gone!

- Specialized devices, such as gaming consoles, ebook readers, televisions, and refrigerators and other things in the "Internet of things"
- Traditional computing devices, such as netbooks and laptop and desktop computers

But just because we have a list of common devices in use today doesn't mean that there won't be something new invented tomorrow. By having a mobile-first mindset and using progressive enhancement, you can ensure that any web-enabled device will have at least basic access to the content and functionality of your website, *no matter what that device is.*

What Makes a Site Mobile Friendly?

Mobile-friendly designs always start by looking at the content. Once you know what content is the most important for any page on your site, you know what you need to make front-and-center in a mobile-friendly design. But there are other things you should bear in mind as well, to avoid driving away your mobile customers. These are some of the basic things you should remember when designing for mobile:

- Keep your layout simple. One column is all most basic phones can handle. And while smartphones can often display more columns, the smaller the screen, the harder those columns will be to work with.
- Limit the navigation choices. The best mobile sites provide access to everything on the site, but the main navigation is slimmed down to just the three or four most popular (to mobile customers) elements, with other links relegated to lower positions on the page.
- Keep the total file size as small as possible. While it's true that download speeds keep getting faster, viewing web pages, even on the most advanced 4G networks, can be painfully slow. And most cell phone connections charge for data download. Your huge images will take forever to download and cost your customers money, which will not win you any friends.
- Shorten URLs and lengthen link text. If your customers need to type in a URL, you should make it as short as possible. But if they need to tap a link, then the longer that text is, the easier it is to

tap. Remember too that multiple links stacked one above the other can be very hard to tap for anyone with fingers larger than a five-year-old's.

- Avoid Flash, frames, and nested tables. Many mobile devices won't display Flash or frames, so you shouldn't use them. And nested tables can be very hard for basic cell phones to display.
- Test your design on as many devices as possible. Don't assume that because your design works fine on your iPhone 6+, it'll look equally great on a Samsung Galaxy S5. It probably will, but if you can test on both, you can find problems before your customers do.

Giving Your Users Options

One major mistake that many designers make when designing for mobile is to make all the decisions for their users. It can be tempting to want to limit what pages they can see, what applications they can use, and so on. But doing that upsets people. It is very frustrating to *know* that a site has a certain feature because you've used it on your laptop and be completely unable to find it when browsing on your smartphone.

It's okay to create a minimal site for mobile viewers, but you should provide a way for users to find the hidden content if they want it.

Accounting for Zooming

The other thing to remember is that your customers can affect how your pages are displayed. The easiest way is through zooming. You might spend days getting a design exactly the way you want it, with everything positioned precisely, and then your customers can't read the text, so they zoom in on just what they want to see. Figure 9.2 shows the same web page viewed on an iPad at normal size and zoomed in so that only a small portion of the content is visible.

People viewing on computers can do even more to affect how your pages look because they can use user style sheets to style every page they visit. Most customers don't use this feature, but you should be aware that it's possible. On a computer, zooming is still the most common adjustment to web pages because it's so easy.

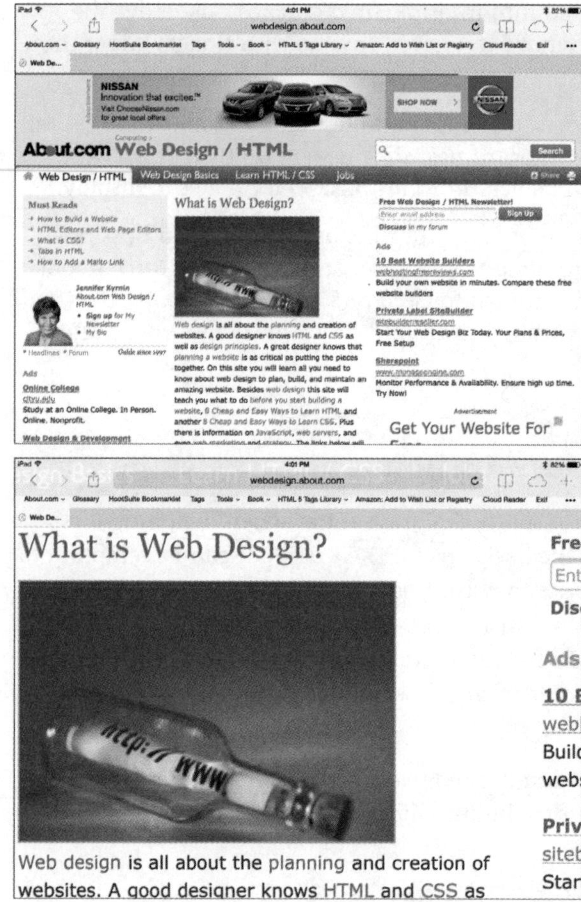

FIGURE 9.2
The same web page viewed on an iPad at the default size and zoomed in.

It is possible to block mobile devices from zooming on your web pages. You add a meta tag to the <head> of your documents, like this:

```
<meta name="viewport"
content="width=device-width, initial-scale=1, maximum-scale=1, user-
scalable=no">
```

This meta tag says a number of different things:

- `viewport` is the meta name, and it defines the different values you want applied to the viewport.
- `width=device-width` tells the browser to set the width the same as the device width. Otherwise, some mobile devices will set it to a default size, much as on a desktop, which can make the text very hard to read.

- `initial-scale=1` says that you want the page set to 100% scaling when it first loads. If you set it larger, the page will appear zoomed in, and if you set it smaller, the page will appear zoomed out.
- `maximum-scale=1` tells the browser to leave the zooming at 1. When you've set `initial-scale` to `1`, this acts the same as not allowing zooming. There is also a `minimum-scale` attribute you can use to define how zoomed in the screen can get.
- `user-scalable=no` also explicitly says that the user is not allowed to zoom in or out.

CAUTION

Blocking Zooming Annoys Readers

When you block zooming for your users, you can make your site very difficult to read. Even if the font size is perfectly legible to you, that doesn't mean it's legible to everyone. I have a friend who has vision in the 20/100 range, but she can still read an iPad when it's zoomed in enough. To allow people to scale their devices, you can change your `viewport` meta tag to this:

```
<meta name="viewport"
content="width=device-width,
initial-scale=1>
```

This sets the `viewport` width to the same as the device width and the initial scaling to 100%, but it doesn't block users from changing it to something else, if necessary.

What About Mobile Only?

Another method of doing web design that is gaining popularity is mobile-only design. With mobile only, rather than build a site that will work for both desktop and mobile customers, you focus only on mobile and let the desktop customers fend for themselves.

One benefit of this method is that it takes a bit less work to create a mobile-only design that will work effectively than it does to create a multi-breakpoint responsive web design. In addition, you can customize the content to be 100% mobile friendly.

But most web design clients are not going to be interested in running just one site optimized for mobile. Chances are they will eventually visit the site from a wide-screen desktop monitor and then be very upset with the minimalist style.

However, if 75% or more of your users are using mobile devices to visit your site, then a mobile-only design makes a lot of sense. In this scenario, it makes sense to worry about desktop last or not at all. After all, most desktop browsers will handle any of the designs and scripts that work on mobile browsers.

Summary

In this hour, you've learned why mobile-first design is so important. You've learned that you'll probably need to change your way of thinking about web design to start thinking about the mobile site before you worry about the desktop site. You've learned some of the key features of a mobile-friendly site, and you've learned about the strategy of mobile-only design and when you might decide to build a site that way. You also learned a number of elements and attributes you can use to adjust your site for mobile-first design. These are listed in Table 9.1.

TABLE 9.1 HTML Tags and Attributes Introduced in Hour 9

Element Name	Attributes	Description
`<meta name=viewport>`		Defines how the viewport should be customized for mobile browsers.
	`initial-scale`	Specifies how the browser should first scale the page when it loads. The default is 1, or 100%, but it can be set to any multiplier of 0.0 to 10.0.
	`maximum-scale`	Specifies the maximum amount the user can zoom in. It can be set between 0.0 and 10.0, and the default is 1.6 on iOS Safari.
	`minimum-scale`	Specifies the minimum amount the user can zoom out. It can be set between 0.0 and 10.0, and the default is 0.25 on iOS Safari.
	`user-scalable`	Specifies a Boolean (yes/no) value that indicates whether the user is allowed to scale. The default is yes.
	`width`	Specifies the width of the `viewport` in pixels (or using the keyword `device-width`). The default is similar to a desktop width on mobile devices.

Workshop

The workshop contains quiz questions to help you process what you've learned in this lesson. Try to answer all the questions before you read the answers.

Q&A

Q. Why should I care about mobile users more than desktop users?

A. In reality, you don't need to care more about them, but by focusing on mobile first, you are acknowledging that mobile users have issues that are often completely ignored by desktop designers. Chances are you've been doing website design for several years and are already familiar with how pages should and will look on a desktop browser. By thinking about mobile browsers first, you can make sure that mobile customers are not an afterthought.

Q. What's the first thing I should do to implement mobile-first design?

A. The first, and possibly most important, thing you should do is change how you think about web design. In fact, if you do nothing other than consider mobile devices first in your design plan, you'll be taking a huge leap forward. By thinking about mobile, you are forced to think of the content, and that will help you design a site that showcases that content in the best way.

Quiz

1. How is mobile-first design a change from traditional web design?
2. Why should you design for mobile first?
3. Name three technologies that were first introduced on mobile devices or that work better on mobile than on desktop devices.
4. Name a type of specialized device that can display web pages.
5. What are two elements of a good mobile design?

Answers

1. Traditional design involves building a desktop design first and then turning to mobile. Mobile-first design turns that on its head and does the work for the smallest, least capable screens first.

2. Mobile devices are becoming more and more popular. There is nearly one cell phone subscription for every person on Earth. And all modern phones support web browsing in some way. Plus, in developing countries, using cell phones is the most common way people access the web.

3. Geolocation, touch screen applications, offline applications, web storage, and mobile web applications are all examples of technology that are more popular on mobile devices.

4. Many specialized devices can view or use web pages, including gaming consoles, ebook readers, televisions, and even refrigerators and other things in the Internet of Things.

5. Good mobile designs bear in mind the total download size of a page and its elements; they keep the layout and navigation as simple as possible; they keep the URLs short and the link text long; they avoid Flash, frames, and nested tables; and they are tested on as many devices as possible.

Exercises

1. For this hour, you should use several mobile devices—at least a cell phone or smartphone and a tablet—to evaluate the site you're looking at. What mobile-friendly design elements are present, and what elements are missing? How can you improve the design and layout so that a person visiting on a basic cell phone can use the site?

2. Look at the content plan you created in Hour 8. With your list of the most important content on the site, evaluate how you will showcase that content to your mobile users.

3. Use your site analytics to determine what pages are most popular with your mobile users. Compare those pages to what pages the design displays to mobile and desktop customers. How will you change the design for mobile customers?

HOUR 10

CSS Media Queries

WHAT YOU'LL LEARN IN THIS HOUR:

- How to write a CSS media query
- Using the different media types
- How to create expressions
- Understanding logical keywords in your queries

This may be the hour you've been waiting for. In this hour, you will learn how to get started applying the rules and theories discussed in the earlier lessons.

For many people the term *responsive web design* is synonymous with *CSS media queries*. And while it's possible to have a responsive site without using media queries, using them is the most common way of doing RWD. This hour will take you through how to write a media query, as well as the different types of queries, keywords, and expressions.

What Is a Media Query?

According to the W3C, a *media query* is a "logical expression that is either true or false. A media query is true if the media type of the media query matches the media type of the device." There's more, but what the W3C is saying is that a web designer can use a media query to define if/then statements based on the characteristics of the device viewing a page.

CSS media types were introduced into the CSS specification in CSS level 2. Media queries were added in CSS3, and they became a full-fledged recommendation in June 2012; however, they have been supported by many browsers since 2010 and earlier. CSS media queries are a stable tool, and web designers should feel confident that most if not all the user agents that view web pages today support them.

When you are building a media query, you use the `@media` rule. You then define the media types this rule applies to and then the features of that type you want to focus on. You place these rules right in your CSS style sheet, using this syntax:

```
@media mediaType and (mediaFeature) {  }
```

CAUTION

Most Small-Screen Devices Do Not Use the `handheld` Media Type

The `handheld` media type was originally used to apply to cell phones and PDAs and other handheld devices, but most cell phone manufacturers wrote their devices to report a `screen` media type because they didn't want their customers to be penalized by web designers not wanting to give handheld customers the full experience. So you cannot rely on this media type to detect mobile devices.

Media Types

There are 10 media types you can test for with CSS media queries:

- **`all`**—All media
- **`braille`**—Braille and tactile feedback devices
- **`embossed`**—Paged braille printers
- **`handheld`**—Small-screen, low-bandwidth handheld devices
- **`print`**—Paged media and documents in print preview mode
- **`projection`**—Projected presentations
- **`screen`**—Color computer screens
- **`speech`**—Speech synthesizers
- **`tty`**—Teletypes and media with a fixed-pitch character grid
- **`tv`**—Television

The most common media type web designers use is `screen` because most modern cell phones, tablets, and all computer monitors use this designation.

▼ TRY IT YOURSELF

Use the `print` Media Type to Create a Print Style Sheet

The `print` media type allows web designers to control how a web page looks when it's printed out. The following steps show how easy it is to create a basic print style sheet:

1. Create a style sheet for your print styles. Best practices recommend that you do things like remove advertising, change the color of links to the text color, add underlines to links if they are removed, and remove the background colors so they don't print.
2. Save your print style sheet as `print.css`. This isn't ideal, and later this hour you'll learn how to include this style sheet in your master style sheet so that only one document is requested and loaded.
3. In the `<head>` of your document, add this line:

```
<link href="print.css" rel="stylesheet" media="print">
```

TRY IT YOURSELF ▼

Use the `print` Media Type to Create a Print Style Sheet

Continued

The media type is listed right in the `<link>` tag with the attribute `media="print"`.

4. To test that your styles are applied, open the page in a browser and choose Print Preview.

You write the style sheet exactly as you write any other style sheet. However, because it is a style sheet for print, you can use a few styles you otherwise might ignore, like `page-break-before`, `page-break-after`, and `page-break-inside`. Since web pages don't have page breaks, these styles aren't used in screen style sheets.

You can set the media type in any style sheet link by using the `media` attribute. But most designers leave it off because the default is `all`.

Setting the media type in the `<link>` tag is not the best way to define styles for media types because this forces the browser to request and load multiple style sheets. The same is true if you use the `@import` rule. Table 10.1 shows how to use the three different methods to include media queries.

TABLE 10.1 Three Ways to Add Media Queries

Method	Description
`<link media="type" href="url" rel="stylesheet">`	Use the `media` attribute on a link tag to define media queries as the style sheet is loaded.
`@import url("url") type;`	Include the type in the `@import` command to define media queries when a style sheet is imported.
`@media type { ... }`	Include media-specific styles directly in another style sheet to limit the scope of those styles.

Best practices indicate that you should define styles for different media types all in the same style sheet document by using the @media rule. Here's how:

1. Open your style sheet file in a web page editor or text editor.
2. Add the styles you want to apply to all media types.

3. To include a print style sheet, enter this:

```
@media print {
  // put print styles here
  a:link { color: black; text-decoration: underline; }
}
```

4. Include as many different media types as you need. Just remember to include all their styles in a separate curly braces block ({ }).

NOTE

Speed Is Important

Requesting multiple CSS documents slows down a website. By keeping your media queries all in one CSS document, you reduce the number of requests to the server, and this improves the speed at which your documents load. For example, if you need to load three 1KB CSS files, if you use `@import` or `<link>` tags to include them all, the browser sends three separate requests for each file and has to wait for three responses from the server. If each request and response takes 0.5 second, you've added an extra 2 seconds to the download time for all three files.

Here's how it would look:

```
request file 1 (.5s)
response file 1 (.5s)
download file 1 (1KB)
request file 2 (.5s)
response file 2 (.5s)
download file 2 (1KB)
request file 3 (.5s)
response file 3 (.5s)
download file 3 (1KB)
```

This gives you a total of the time it takes to download 3KB plus 3 seconds of request and response time. If you combine all three files into one 3KB file, you'll have the same download time (for 3KB), but only one request and response (1s). While most request and response times are much faster than 0.5s, all those requests add up. If you have 10 CSS files, plus another 10 JavaScript files, plus other server requests (for example, images, media), your site can be slowed way down.

Media Features

Media features are where CSS media queries get really interesting. Rather than limit your designs just to specific media types (screen versus print, for example), media features let you look at the specific features of the media and style your pages accordingly.

You can test for 13 media features:

- **`aspect-ratio`**—A ratio of the width of the device to the height
- **`color`**—The number of bits per color component
- **`color-index`**—The number of colors in the device's color lookup table
- **`device-aspect-ratio`**—The ratio of the `device-width` to the `device-height`
- **`device-height`**—The height of the rendering surface
- **`device-width`**—The width of the rendering surface
- **`grid`**—Whether the device is grid (such as TTY devices or phones with only one font) or bitmap
- **`height`**—The height of the display area
- **`monochrome`**—The number of bits per pixel in monochrome devices; if the device isn't monochrome, the value is `0`
- **`orientation`**—Whether the device is in portrait or landscape mode
- **`resolution`**—The pixel density of the device; in print, this would be the dots per inch (dpi) of the printer
- **`scan`**—The scanning process of TV output devices, such as progressive scanning
- **`width`**—The width of the display area

Nearly all the media features also have two prefixes you can use to evaluate: `min-` and `max-`. These prefixes evaluate a feature based on whether it is a minimum amount (`min-`) or a maximum amount (`max-`). For example, to set a style sheet to apply to all browsers with at least a width of 320px, you use this:

```
@media (min-width: 320px) { ... }
```

And if you want to target devices with browsers no wider than 1024px, you use this:

```
@media (max-width: 1024px) { ... }
```

As you can see, you add on the media features to your `@media` rule with the word `and`, and you enclose your features in parentheses. If you want to get more specific, you add more features. For example, to target browsers between 640px and 980px wide, you use this:

```
@media (min-width: 640px) and (max-width: 980px) { ... }
```

Notice that none of the expressions above use a media type. This is the case because if the media type is left off, it applies to all devices, regardless of type.

CAUTION

There Is a Difference Between `width` and `device-width`

The `device-*` features are confusing to most web designers at first, as it doesn't seem like there is any difference between them, especially on mobile devices. But there are differences, and they're important. `width` is the width of the browser window, while `device-width` is the width of the device itself. You can see this most effectively on a computer. When you set a media query with `max-device-width` and then resize the browser, the page will not change, no matter how much you resize. This is because the device width is the computer monitor, and that doesn't change.

This may not seem to matter on mobile devices, but on iOS devices, `device-width` is always the width in portrait mode, *even if the device is in landscape*. On Android devices, `device-width` changes when the device is rotated; the same goes for `device-height` and `device-aspect-ratio`.

Media Query Expressions

In order to use media queries effectively, you need to know how to write expressions. Earlier this hour, you learned three basic expressions to target browsers above a certain minimum width, browsers below a maximum width, and browsers that fall between minimum and maximum widths. But you can create much more complicated expressions.

Media query expressions use logical operators to define complex scenarios. These are the operators you can use:

- **`and`**—Combines features and types together. The query matches if all elements are present. For example, this would match a device in landscape mode with a 768px browser window:

  ```
  @media (min-width: 760px) and (orientation: landscape) { ... }
  ```

- **Comma-separated list**—Using a comma-separated list is equivalent to using the OR logical operator. In a comma-separated list of features or types, if any of them are true, the query matches. For example, this would match both a 480px browser in landscape mode and a 800px wide browser in portrait mode:

  ```
  @media (min-width: 760px), (orientation: landscape) { ... }
  ```

NOTE

The `not` Operator Only Applies to the Entire Expression

The `not` operator can be confusing to use, but one thing to remember is that it applies only to the entire expression, not to individual features. In other words, if you use `@media not screen and (max-width:400px)`, your query matches everything that is both not a screen-based device and has a width larger than 400px. It helps if you remember to evaluate the `not` last. So you write the expression the opposite of what you want and then apply the `not` operator at the front.

- **`not`**—Negates the entire query. The query matches if the query would normally return `false`. For example, this would match a 480px-wide browser that is in portrait mode:

```
@media not (min-width: 760px) and (orientation: landscape) { ... }
```

- **`only`**—Prevents browsers that don't support media queries from applying the styles. For example, this will block extremely old browsers from using the style sheet:

```
@media only screen { ... }
```

Media query expressions are the basis of responsive web design. With them you can define very complex formulas for your style sheets and make sure that the designs look exactly the way you want them to.

Summary

This hour introduced you to the meat of responsive web design. With CSS media queries, you create style sheets that are written explicitly for the devices that you want to define. You learned several media features that are explained in Table 10.2.

TABLE 10.2 Media Features in CSS

Feature	Uses `min-` and `max-` Prefixes	Usage and Example
`aspect-ratio` `device-aspect-ratio`	Yes	Two positive integers separated by a slash. They represent the width and height. This example finds devices with at least a 4:3 aspect: `@media all and (min-aspect-ratio: 4/3)`
`color`	Yes	Either a number indicating how many colors or an indication to select all color devices. This example selects all color devices: `@media all and (color)`
`color-index`	Yes	An integer indicating the number of indexed colors. This example selects all devices that have at least 256 colors: `@media all and (min-color-index: 256)`

Feature	Uses `min-` and `max-` Prefixes	Usage and Example
`device-height` `height`	Yes	A length indicating the height of the browser or device. This example selects all devices that are 6in. or smaller in height: `@media all and (max-device-height: 6in)`
`device-width` `width`	Yes	A length indicating the width of the browser or device. This example selects all browsers that are 320px or smaller in width: `@media all and (max-width: 320px)`
`grid`	No	Either `1` if the device is a grid device or `0` if the device is a bitmap device. This example selects all devices that are TTY or grid devices: `@media handheld and (grid)`
`monochrome`	Yes	An integer indicating the number of bits per pixel on a monochrome display. This example selects all devices that have monochrome displays with 16 bits per pixel or more: `@media all and (min-monochrome: 16)`
`orientation`	No	Either the value `landscape` or `portrait`. This example selects all devices in portrait mode: `@media all and (orientation: portrait)`
`resolution`	Yes	Resolution value of the device. This example selects all devices with a 96dpi or higher resolution: `@media all and (min-resolution: 96dpi)`
`scan`	No	Either the value `progressive` or `interlace`. This example selects all television devices with interlaced scanning: `@media tv and (scan: interlace)`

Workshop

The workshop contains quiz questions to help you process what you've learned in this lesson. Try to answer all the questions before you read the answers.

Q&A

Q. Is there a media feature to detect Retina displays?

A. Yes, there is a feature to detect Retina displays, but it's not standardized on all browsers, nor is it a part of the specification. This feature is `-webkit-device-pixel-ratio`. To select only Retina displays, you use this:

```
@media screen and (-webkit-min-device-pixel-ratio: 2)
```

As you can see, this is a browser-prefixed feature selector (`-webkit`), and you can add the `min-` and `max-` prefixes as well. I cover how to handle Retina displays in more detail in Hour 11, "Breakpoints," and in Hour 15, "Creating and Using Images in RWD."

Q. What's the difference between CSS level 2 media queries and CSS3 media queries?

A. CSS level 2 doesn't really have media *queries*. CSS level 2 allows you to define a style sheet as being for a specific media type, but it wasn't until CSS3 that media *queries* were developed. Media queries let you define test structures surrounding media types and features that allow only the user agents that fit the query criteria to use the styles.

Quiz

1. What is the W3C definition of *media query*?
2. When did CSS media queries become an official recommendation?
3. What is the syntax of a media query?
4. What are five of the media types?
5. What are five of the media features?
6. What are two of the logical operators?

Answers

1. According to the W3C, a media query is a "logical expression that is either true or false. A media query is true if the media type of the media query matches the media type of the device."
2. CSS media queries got to Recommendation status at the W3C in June 2012.
3. The syntax of a media query looks like this:

   ```
   @media mediaType and (mediaFeature)
   ```

4. The 10 media types are `all`, `braille`, `embossed`, `handheld`, `print`, `projection`, `screen`, `speech`, `tty`, and `tv`.
5. The 13 media features are `aspect-ratio`, `color`, `color-index`, `device-aspect-ratio`, `device-height`, `device-width`, `grid`, `height`, `monochrome`, `orientation`, `resolution`, `scan`, and `width`.
6. The four operators are `and`, comma-separated lists, `not`, and `only`.

Exercise

Start practicing writing CSS media queries. Look at the site you've been evaluating through the book and decide what types of media features you want to focus on for your styles. For example, decide whether you need designs for different widths, different orientations, or different aspect ratios. Your analytics program can help by giving you information about what your current customers are using.

HOUR 11
Breakpoints

WHAT YOU'LL LEARN IN THIS HOUR:

- What CSS breakpoints are
- How to define breakpoints
- Deciding on the best breakpoints for your site
- Recommended breakpoints
- How to define breakpoints for Retina displays

Breakpoints are a great tool for making your web pages responsive. Even if you have only one breakpoint on a web page, the page will respond to the presence of that breakpoint and respond appropriately to user agents that match. In this hour you will learn what breakpoints are and how to use them. Plus, you'll learn what makes good breakpoints and how to support a wide variety of devices.

What Is a Breakpoint?

A CSS breakpoint is a device feature with a media query declaration assigned to it. Most media queries are based on the browser widths, so most designers think of breakpoints as the widths of their design where it changes to accommodate different devices.

To be responsive, a web design must have at least one breakpoint that changes the look of the design.

Before you decide you're going to have 10 breakpoints or some other arbitrary number, you need to remember that each additional breakpoint adds to the cost of building (and, to some extent, maintaining) the website. I'll talk more about the drawbacks of RWD in Hour 20, "Problems with Responsive Web Design."

NOTE

Most Best Practices Recommend Using at Least Two Breakpoints

Most experts recommend using at least two breakpoints so that your site has three versions: one for small mobile devices, one for midsized tablets, and one for desktop computer screens. But for best results, you should use breakpoints as appropriate for your particular website.

For each breakpoint in your design, you add on one more version of the page to style. In other words, you have to style the page, even if you have no breakpoints. When you add one breakpoint, you then have a second version of the page to style, and so on.

How to Define Breakpoints in CSS

You define breakpoints by using CSS media queries, which are discussed in Hour 10, "CSS Media Queries." The most common type of breakpoint is based on the width of the device. Listing 11.1 shows the CSS file for a site that has three designs and two breakpoints: one for every browser (in other words, the smallest widths), one for widths between 480px and 800px (in other words, larger smartphones and smaller tablets), and one for widths larger than 800px.

LISTING 11.1 A Page with Two Breakpoints

```
<!doctype html>
<html>
<head>
<meta charset="UTF-8">
<title>Listing 11.1</title>
<style type="text/css">
body {
  color: blue;
  font-family: "Handwriting - Dakota", "Lucida Calligraphy Italic",
    Papyrus;
}
@media all and (min-width:480px) and (max-width:800px) {
  body { color: red; }
}
@media screen and (min-width:801px) {
  body { color: green; }
}
</style>
</head>

<body>
<p>Lorem ipsum dolor sit amet, consectetur adipiscing elit. Etiam id
eros semper luctus. Proin nisl lectus, ullamcorper ultrices leo in,
rutrum risus. Morbi congue diam tempor lorem semper, congue tempor turpis
pretium. Nunc eget dui ut lorem auctor ornare. Vivamus lectus purus,
velit eu, iaculis ultrices dui. Aliquam consectetur risus non ligula
gravida lectus bibendum. Etiam laoreet luctus nibh. Nulla sit amet
arcu accumsan mollis.</p>
</body>
</html>
```

Listing 11.1 uses very simple styles that change the color of the text, depending on the size of the browser—blue for small screens and red for larger screens. You can see this in Figure 11.1.

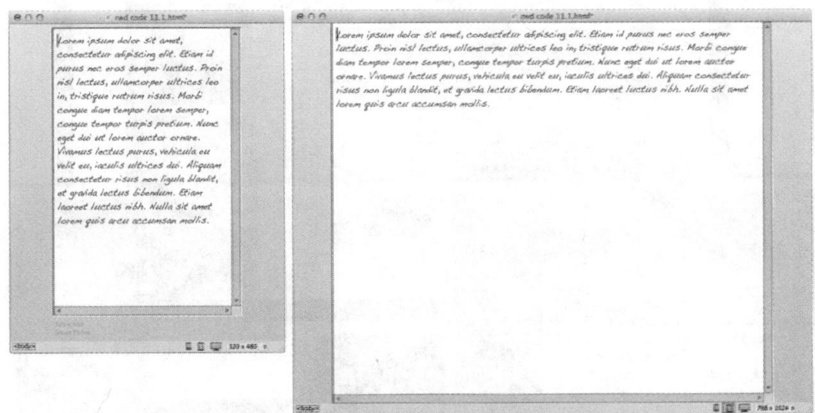

FIGURE 11.1
The same page previewed in Dreamweaver at 320x480 and 768x1024.

Defining the Styles That Remain the Same for Every Device

When you're writing a style sheet for a responsive website, the first styles you want to define are those that are the same no matter what device views them. The following are examples of these types of things:

- Reset styles
- Colors
- Font families
- Background images

While it's certainly possible that you could have designs that use different colors, font families, resets, and background images, depending on the device, most websites keep a consistent branding. By keeping these things the same, you reassure your customers that they are on the same page no matter what device they are using.

Back in Hour 2, "Alternatives to Responsive Web Design," I shared with you my Dandylions web page that I want to make responsive. Figure 11.2 shows three mockups of the page, for smartphones, tablets, and desktop computers.

FIGURE 11.2
The same design mocked up for smartphone, tablet, and desktop browsers.

In these mockups, you can see that the font family for the headlines and navigation remains the same, and the colors do, too. The header background image could be the same image, just clipped for smaller screens.

Listing 11.2 shows how this portion of the CSS might look. I have removed the reset styles for brevity.

LISTING 11.2 Initial CSS for the Dandylions Page

```
@charset "UTF-8";

@font-face {
  font-family: 'bitstream_vera_serifbold';
  src: url('fonts/VeraSerif-Bold-webfont.eot');
  src: url('fonts/VeraSerif-Bold-webfont.eot?#iefix')
      format('embedded-opentype'),
        url('fonts/VeraSerif-Bold-webfont.woff') format('woff'),
        url('fonts/VeraSerif-Bold-webfont.ttf') format('truetype'),
        url('fonts/VeraSerif-Bold-webfont.svg#bitstream_vera_serifbold')
          format('svg');
  font-weight: normal;
  font-style: normal;
}

/* reset styles here */

/* standard colors */
body { background-color: #fff; color: #000; }
```

```
h1, h2 { color: #fbd91f;  /* yellow */ }
h3, h4, h5 { color #000; }

/* standard fonts */
h1, h2, h3 {
  font-family: bitstream_vera_serifbold, Baskerville, "Times New Roman",
    serif;
}
h1 {
  text-shadow:2px 3px 3px #000000;
  -webkit-text-stroke: 1px black;
  margin-bottom: 0.5em;
}
h2 {
  text-shadow: 2px 2px 0 rgba(0,0,0,.5);
  margin-bottom: 0.5em;
}

/* background images */
header {
  width: 100%;
  padding: 0.5em 0 3em 0.25em;
  background-image: url(images/dandy-header-bg.png);
  background-repeat: no-repeat;
  background-size: cover;
  background-position: 0% 100%;
}
```

While some of the styles I've set may be changed for specific devices, this is a good baseline. I set a base font family for my headlines by using the `@font-face` rule. I gave the document black text and a white background. And I defined a background image for my header. As with any other design, there is more to do, but this is a start.

Adding Specific Styles for Small Screens

Once you've got your basic styles for any device in the style sheet, you need to add styles that are specific to the smallest screens. You should put them below your styles for all devices but *not inside a media query*. These styles will be overwritten by the styles in the media queries because of the CSS cascade.

I will go over specific styles you should consider in later hours, but in general, you want to add styles that make your pages as mobile friendly as possible. Here are a few rules of thumb:

- The width of every content element should be 100% to fill the screen.
- You should use just one column of content.

- Lists, especially lists of links, should have a lot of space between them, to make them easy to read and click.

Listing 11.3 shows some of the styles I added, and Figure 11.3 shows how it now looks on a small-screen phone.

LISTING 11.3 CSS Added for Small Screens

```
/* ######## mobile specific styles ######## */
/* headlines */
h1 { font-size: 2em; }
h2 { font-size: 1.5em; }

/* navigation bar */
nav { width: 100%; background-color: #000; }
nav ul { padding-top: 0.15em; padding-bottom: 0.15em; }
nav ul li { margin: 0 0 0.5em 0.2em; }

/* article */
article { width: 100%; padding: 0.25em; }
article img { width: 100%; height: auto; }

/* aside */
aside { width: 100%; }
aside img { width: 100%; height: auto; }
```

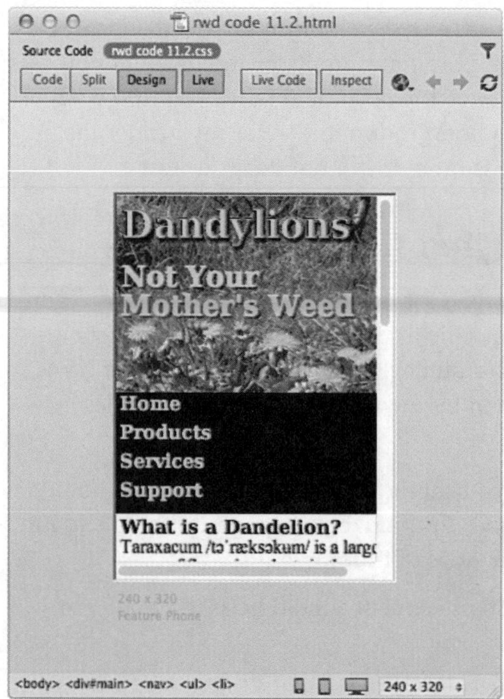

FIGURE 11.3
Web page in mobile preview in Dreamweaver CC.

Adding Media Queries for Larger Screens

The last thing to add in your style sheet is the media queries with the styles specific to those devices. You add the media queries as discussed in Hour 10. For my Dandylions page, I have two breakpoints: one for medium-sized devices between 481px and 800px wide and one for large devices with a width bigger than 801px. Listing 11.4 shows you how to write the CSS for this.

LISTING 11.4 The Media Queries in the CSS

```
/* ######## medium sized devices ######## */
@media only screen and (min-width: 481px) and (max-width: 800px) { }

/* ######## large sized devices ######## */
@media only screen and (min-width: 801px) { }
```

You need to remember the order of your CSS file. Because of the cascade, whatever styles come last will take precedence over styles that come before. So if I style the `article` element to have 100% width in the first section and then change that to 80% or something else in the medium- or large-sized device media queries, that is the style that will display.

CAUTION

Make Sure You Style Everything

Remember that RWD style sheets use the cascade to set initial styles and then overwrite them with styles for other devices later in the document. But if you aren't using a WYSIWYG editor or previewing your styles regularly, it can be easy to forget what already has a style. For example, I set the width of the `article` element to 100%, but in larger screens, I won't want that because it will make the text too long to read. But if I forget to preview the styles in many different browser widths, I could be surprised by the result.

Optimal Breakpoints

One of the most common questions those new to RWD ask is "What are the best breakpoint numbers?" The correct answer to this question is that it depends on your customers and your design. But Table 11.1 shows some popular devices and their widths in portrait and landscape modes.

You can use the widths in Table 11.1 to come up with a breakpoint plan that works for your site, but a better solution is to choose breakpoints based on customers and your design. Use your analytics software to find the most common resolutions that visit your site. Then decide where the design breaks down and put a breakpoint at that width to fix the breakdown.

CAUTION

Apple Devices Always Use Portrait for `device-width`

Apple recommends always using the `viewport` meta tag, like this: `<meta name="viewport" content="width=device-width">`. This ensures that the content is not blown up and made blurry or hard to read. But Apple defines `device-width` as the width in portrait mode, even if the device is rotated to landscape mode. Most Android devices assign `device-width` as the width of the device screen as the customer views it—the long value in landscape mode and the short value in portrait mode.

TABLE 11.1 Popular Devices and Their Widths

Device	Portrait Width	Landscape Width
Amazon Kindle Fire HDX 8.9	1600px	2560px
Samsung Galaxy NotePRO		
Apple iPad Air	1536px	2048px
Apple iPad Mini 2		
Apple iPhone 5s/5c	720px	1136px
Asus MeMO Pad HD7	600px	1024px
Blackberry Z30	720px	1280px
HTC One		
Dell Venue 8	800px	1280px
Google Nexus 7	1200px	1920px
Google Nexus 5	1080px	1920px
Microsoft Surface		
Nokia Lumia		
Samsung Galaxy S5	1440px	2560px

Best Practices for Breakpoints

At the end of this hour, I will give you the breakpoints I use most often, but before that, you should know some of the best practices for choosing the breakpoints you use:

- It's tempting to choose breakpoints for exactly the resolution of the devices you want to support, such as a `min-width` of 720px to target iPhone 5S devices. But doing this is a mistake. It's better to choose a width based on where your design starts getting difficult to read or use.
- When you use more than one breakpoint, make sure that the second one is for screens exactly 1px wider or narrower than the first. In other words, if your smallest breakpoint is for browsers with a width of 480px or smaller, then the next breakpoint should have a minimum width of 481px. If you use the same number for each, this can cause browsers that match that width to use the wrong styles.
- If you have the time and resources to do so, you should consider changing your design based on the orientation of the device and not just the width.
- Don't forget Retina displays.

Breakpoints for Retina Devices

This heading is a little misleading, as there isn't a specific width or breakpoint that will detect Retina devices. But there is a media query feature that you can use to define styles for Retina devices: `-webkit-device-pixel-ratio`. You use this just like other features, adding the `min-` or `max-` prefixes in your media query.

Retina displays have a 2x pixel ratio. So you can define styles for Retina devices with this media query:

```
@media (-webkit-min-device-pixel-ratio: 2) { }
```

You can also look at the resolution and detect devices with a minimum resolution of 192dpi. But the best media queries use both, like this:

```
@media (-webkit-min-device-pixel-ratio: 2), (min-resolution: 192dpi) { }
```

My Recommended Breakpoints

I can't stress enough how important it is to choose your breakpoints based on your design and your customers, but if you must have a starting point, these are the breakpoints I typically start with:

- I start with devices 300px wide or smaller and create a simple, cell phone–friendly design.
- For smartphones between 301px and 500px, I make the designs slightly more complex but still fairly simple, with a single column and simplified navigation.
- Bigger phones and tablets between 501px and 1200px get a more complex design, with a few columns and fancier navigation.
- Finally, big tablets and desktops with 1201px or wider screens get full complexity, with lots of columns and fancy navigation.

Listing 11.5 shows my starting breakpoints written as media queries. When the project requires less time or lower cost, I first remove the smallest query (300px wide and smaller) and then remove the mid-range tablets query (501px to 1200px).

LISTING 11.5 My Starting Breakpoints

```
@charset "UTF-8";
/* ###### styles for all devices ###### */

/* ###### styles for devices <300px wide ###### */
```

```
/* ###### styles for devices 301-500px wide ###### */
@media screen and (min-width:301px) and (max-width:500px) { }

/* ###### styles for devices 501-1200px wide ###### */
@media screen and (min-width:501px) and (max-width:1200px) { }

/* ###### styles for devices >1201px wide ###### */
@media screen and (min-width:1201px) { }
```

As you saw in Table 11.1, there are many devices that have screens much wider than 1200px, and when you throw in landscape mode, there are even more. Right now I think that treating these large tablets (and smartphones) the same as desktop computers works well. But I continue to test and evaluate all the designs I work on to make sure they still look good and are usable.

Summary

In this hour you've learned what a breakpoint is and how to choose good breakpoints for a responsive design. You've learned the CSS to create media queries to back up those breakpoints. And you've also learned how to create media queries to detect Retina devices. Finally, I shared with you some of the breakpoints I often use when starting to build a new website design.

Workshop

The workshop contains quiz questions to help you process what you've learned in this lesson. Try to answer all the questions before you read the answers.

Q&A

Q. Why is it important to design for the smallest devices first?

A. You can find a complete answer in Hour 9, "Mobile First." In a nutshell, it's because most of the smallest devices are also the least feature filled. In order to build a site using progressive enhancement, you should focus on the minimum you need for the site to work. And that is what you should display to all customers, even the small-screen devices.

Q. Is it possible for me to create a desktop layout first and then design down?

A. Of course, it's possible, but it ends up being a lot more work because you have to remove all the complex styles rather than simply add on to a simple design.

Q. Can I use media features other than just `width` to set my breakpoints? Why does everyone only seem to use device widths?

A. Width is the easiest type of breakpoint to understand and test. When you use a minimum or maximum width, you can use your web browser to test your designs by simply resizing the browser window. As long as you're browsing on a fairly large screen, you can test nearly any device width. It's a lot harder to test orientation on a desktop computer monitor. But you can use any media feature you need to create the breakpoints that are best for your design.

Quiz

1. How many breakpoints do you need in order to create a responsive design?

2. What do best practices say is the minimum recommended number of breakpoints?

3. Write the CSS for a breakpoint that catches devices 400px and smaller.

4. Write the CSS for a breakpoint that catches all devices between 800 and 1600px wide.

5. What is the media query to detect Retina devices?

Answers

1. A responsive design needs at least one breakpoint.

2. Best practices recommend that you have at least two breakpoints to catch small, midsized, and large screens.

3. This is the CSS for a breakpoint to catch all devices 400px and smaller:

```
@media screen and (max-width:400px) { }
```

4. This is the CSS to catch all devices between 800 and 1600px wide:

```
@media screen and (min-width:800px) and (max-width:1600px) { }
```

5. This is the media query to detect Retina devices:

```
@media (-webkit-min-device-pixel-ratio: 2), (min-resolution: 192dpi)
{ }
```

Exercises

1. Look at the analytics for the site you are working on and decide what breakpoints you want to use for your design. Then create a CSS style sheet with a media query structure to support those breakpoints.

2. Add to your style sheet the CSS styles that apply to all devices, regardless of device size.

HOUR 12
Layout

In this hour you will learn all about layout. Many web designers think that layout is all that RWD is about: You just add more columns for wider screens. And on many websites, that is all that the media queries do. But there is more to layout than just how many columns a page has.

WHAT YOU'LL LEARN IN THIS HOUR:

- The different types of layouts and which are best for RWD
- Layout standards and when you should use them
- How to use CSS3 columns in RWD layouts
- How to build a responsive navigation system

What Is Web Layout?

When you are working on a web page design, you need to be aware of the placement and position of every element on the page. Web layout includes the white space on the page, the position of graphics and blocks of text, and even how wide the text blocks are.

Many web designers start with a wireframe to design their layout without worrying about the images and text that are going to make up the page. But when you're doing RWD, you need to create more than one layout, so you need more than one wireframe. Figure 12.1 shows a wireframe for the same page at three different widths.

Headline
Subhead
Main Content
Navigation
Sidebar 1
Sidebar 2
Sidebar 3

Headline
Subhead
Sidebar 1
Navigation
Sidebar 2
Main Content
Sidebar 3

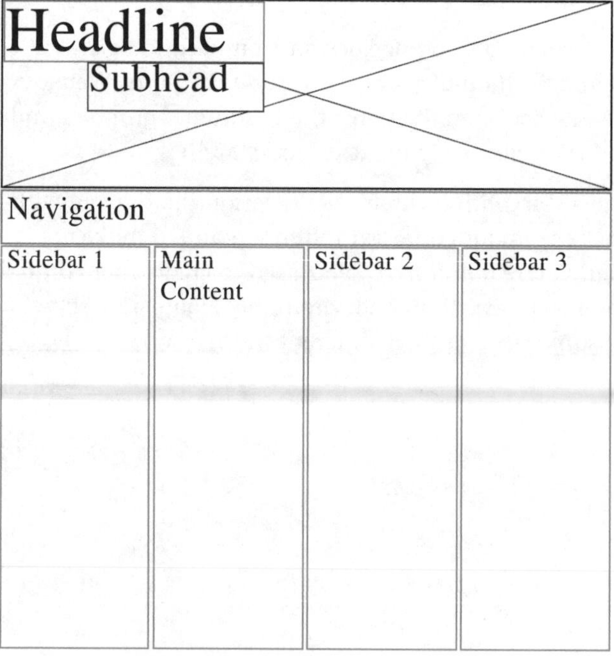

FIGURE 12.1
Three different wireframes for the same website: cell phone, tablet, and desktop.

Types of Layouts

There are many ways to do web layout. But the most common types are fixed-width layout, fluid (also called liquid) layout, and elastic layout. There are also hybrid layouts that use aspects of fixed and liquid or elastic layouts.

It is possible to create a responsive design using any of these layout types, and each presents unique challenges and opportunities.

Fixed-Width Layouts

Many web designers gravitate to fixed-width layouts because they make it crystal clear what is going to happen. Every element on the design has a predefined width (and sometimes height), and any content that varies, such as text blocks, will flow within the predefined width.

To create a fixed-width layout, you start by defining the width of the entire page. Most designers choose 960px wide because that number is divisible by 2, 3, 4, 5, 6, 8, 10, 12, and 15. So you can create a grid and place all your elements on that grid, and as long as their widths are also multiples of 2, 3, 4, 5, etc., you know they will line up correctly in the layout.

TRY IT YOURSELF ▼

Give a Page a Fixed-Width Layout

It's easy to get started with fixed-width layouts. In the following steps, you will take some basic HTML and add the CSS to make it a fixed-width layout:

1. Open the HTML shown in Listing 12.1 in a web page editor.

LISTING 12.1 Basic HTML

```
<!doctype html>
<html>
  <head>
    <meta charset="UTF-8">
    <title>Dandylions</title>
    <link href="styles.css" rel="stylesheet">
  </head>
  <body>
    <div id="main">
      <header>
        <h1>Dandylions</h1>
```

▼ TRY IT YOURSELF

Give a Page a Fixed-Width Layout

continued

```
      <h2>Not Your Mother's Weed</h2>
    </header>
    <nav>
      <ul>
        <li>Home</li>
        <li>Products</li>
        <li>Services</li>
        <li>Support</li>
      </ul>
    </nav>
    <article>
    <h3>What is a Dandelion?</h3>
    <p><span
      class="pronounce"><strong><em>Taraxacum</em></strong>
    <em>/tə'ræksəkʉm/</em></span> is a large genus of flowering
    plants in the family Asteraceae. They are native to Eurasia
    and North and South America, and two species, T. officinale
    and T. erythrospermum, are found as weeds worldwide. Both
    species are edible in their entirety. The common name
    <span class="pronounce"><strong>dandelion</strong>
    <em>/'dændɨlaɪ.ən/</em></span> (dan-di-ly-ən, from French
    dent-de-lion, meaning "lion's tooth") is given to members of
    the genus, and like other members of the Asteraceae family,
    they have very small flowers collected together into a
    composite flower head. Each single flower in a head is called
    a floret. Many <em>Taraxacum</em> species produce seeds
    asexually by apomixis, where the seeds are produced without
    pollination, resulting in offspring that are genetically
    identical to the parent plant.</p>
</article>
    <aside>
      <img src="images/dandy.jpg" width="400" height="300"
        alt=""/>
    </aside>
    <footer>
      <p>Text from
      <a href="http://en.wikipedia.org/wiki/Dandelion">
        Wikipedia</a></p>
    </footer>
  </div>
 </body>
</html>
```

2. Create the blank style sheet file `styles.css` and put it in the same directory as the HTML.

3. For a fixed-width layout, the first thing you need to set is the width of the body, so open the `styles.css` file and add this:

```
#main { width: 960px; }
```

TRY IT YOURSELF ▼

Give a Page a Fixed-Width Layout

continued

4. To make this show up better, add some background colors to your body and the main area, like this:

```
body { background-color: #dfdfdf; }
#main { background-color: #fff; }
```

5. Finally, in really large screens, this will be very close to the left margin, and these layouts often look better when they are centered, so add the following to the `#main` style:

```
margin: 0 auto;
```

Listing 12.2 shows the entire CSS document that results from these changes.

LISTING 12.2 CSS for a Simple Fixed-Width Layout

```
body { background-color: #dfdfdf; }
#main {
  width: 960px;
  background-color: #fff;
  margin: 0 auto;
}
```

If you open the page in a browser and resize the window, you see that the design stays the same width no matter how large or small the window is. This means that on small browsers, there will be a horizontal scrollbar.

Fixed-width layouts have some important benefits: They are easy to create and manage. The widths don't change, so doing the page design is a bit like creating a design on static media like print. Plus, most advertising is already a fixed width that can't easily be changed, so advertising can be added to fixed-width layouts very easily.

You can use fixed-width layouts in RWD, but you need to reset the width for each breakpoint. I recommend coming up with a minimum width you will support (for instance, 320px) and starting your mobile design there. Then at each breakpoint, you can change the width of your page to be slightly smaller than the minimum width for that breakpoint. So, for a design with breakpoints at 480px and 960px, you could set fixed widths of 320px for the smallest browsers, 480px for the medium-size browsers, and 960px for the largest browsers. And since those widths all fit in the 960px grid mentioned earlier, they will still be easy to manage.

But the drawbacks to fixed-width layouts should be pretty obvious, too: If you don't use media queries, smaller screens will have to scroll horizontally, which is at best difficult and at worst impossible to do on some phones. But the problem isn't just with small screens. Fixed-width layouts can look pretty strange on wide-screen monitors as well. Figure 12.2 shows what my website —which has a centered fixed-width layout—looks like on my wide-screen monitor. There is a huge amount of white space on the sides of the screen, and it can be distracting.

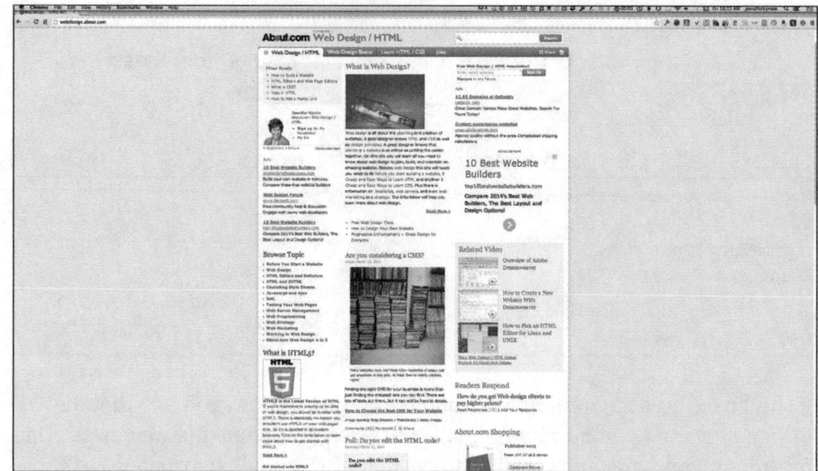

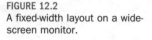

FIGURE 12.2
A fixed-width layout on a wide-screen monitor.

But before you throw out fixed-width layouts completely, remember that with media queries, you can do some really interesting things. I've seen sites that have hidden "Easter eggs" for people who view their pages on extremely wide browsers. I saw one site add additional advertising in some of the white space created by the fixed-width layout. (Be careful with this, though: You don't want your site to appear spammy.) And as long as you keep scan length (discussed later in this hour) in mind, you can always add another breakpoint at 1920px and build another, even wider, version of the design.

Fluid or Liquid Layouts

Most web designers start with fluid layouts simply because they don't specify a width on the body content. When no width is specified, browsers display the content filling up all the width available without showing a scrollbar.

You can also create fluid layouts with percentage widths. Instead of using a static number like 960px, you can use a percentage, like 90%, to make the page fill up most of the browser window but not all of it. When you set the width of an element to a percentage, you are setting it to a percentage of the parent element's width.

For example, if you look back at Listing 12.1, in that HTML, you'll see that there is a `<div id="main">` container that contains the rest of the elements. If you don't give that `<div>` or the `<body>` element a width, the whole page will fill 100% of the screen. But you can then set the `<article>` element to have a 50% width with this line in the CSS:

```
article { width: 50%; }
```

The article will then fill up half of the screen. But if you change `<div id="main">` to have an 80% width, `<article>` will take up 50% of that `<div>`, but that is less than half of the full browser window. Listing 12.3 shows the CSS you can use to change your style sheet and see this in action.

LISTING 12.3 CSS for a Fluid Layout with Fluid Internal Elements

```
body { background-color: #dfdfdf; }
#main {
  width: 80%;
  background-color: #fff;
  margin: 0 auto;
}
article {
  width: 50%;
}
```

Figure 12.3 shows what this looks like in a narrow browser.

A benefit of fluid layouts is that they adapt better to different sizes of viewports. In fact, with a fluid layout, you don't always need media queries because the browsers do the resizing for you. Plus, fluid layouts can readily make use of all the available space in the browser window.

NOTE

Just Remove the Widths to Make a Design Fluid

If you did the Try It Yourself in the previous section, you can see what a fluid layout looks like by simply commenting out `width: 960px;` (surround it with `/*` and `*/`) in the CSS. Then, if you resize your browser, the content will resize to continue to fit on the screen, like water—so you can see why they are called fluid, or liquid, layouts.

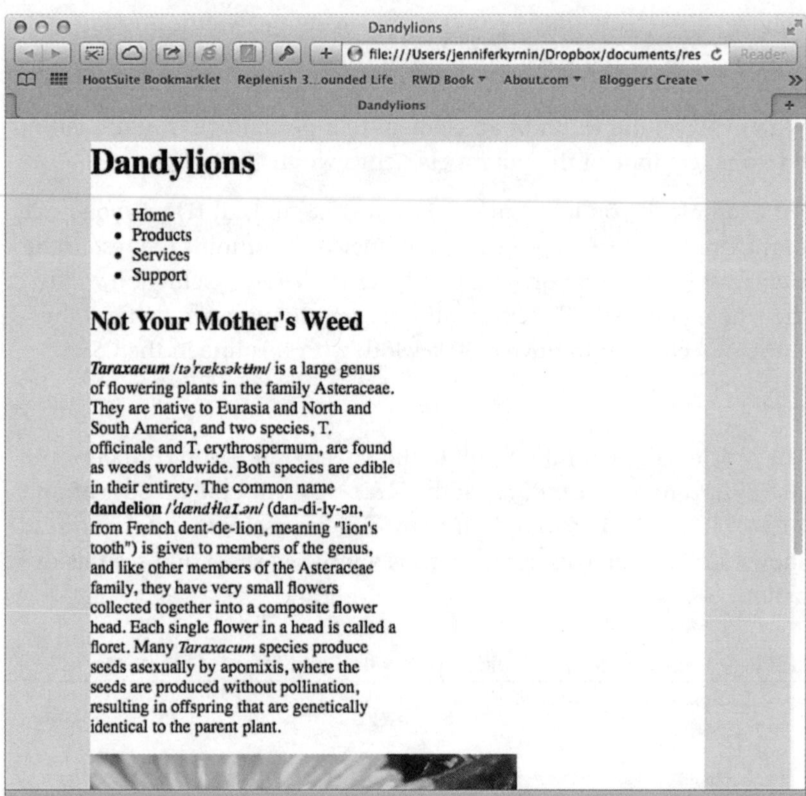
Dandylions
file:///Users/jenniferkyrnin/Dropbox/documents/res
HootSuite Bookmarklet
Replenish 3...ounded Life
RWD Book
About.com
Bloggers Create
Dandylions
Dandylions
Home
Products
Services
Support
Not Your Mother's Weed
Taraxacum /təˈræksəkʉm/ is a large genus of flowering plants in the family Asteraceae. They are native to Eurasia and North and South America, and two species, T. officinale and T. erythrospermum, are found as weeds worldwide. Both species are edible in their entirety. The common name dandelion /ˈdændɨlaɪ.ən/ (dan-di-ly-ən, from French dent-de-lion, meaning "lion's tooth") is given to members of the genus, and like other members of the Asteraceae family, they have very small flowers collected together into a composite flower head. Each single flower in a head is called a floret. Many Taraxacum species produce seeds asexually by apomixis, where the seeds are produced without pollination, resulting in offspring that are genetically identical to the parent plant.

FIGURE 12.3
A fluid layout in a narrow browser window.

CAUTION

Fixed Widths Inside a Fluid Layout Can Break the Layout

Most web designers who use a fluid layout make it a hybrid layout without realizing it because they use fixed widths for some of the elements within the layout. For example, they typically define images with explicit pixel widths rather than percentage widths. But that means when a fluid container gets too small for the fixed width, the image breaks the container. Figure 12.4 shows how this can look.

But fluid layouts, as you can see in Figure 12.4, have some drawbacks as well. As the Caution says, if you have fixed-width elements in a fluid design, they can break the container.

Another big problem with fluid layouts is that many people get the urge to fill all the space. While it's true that fluid layouts can give you a lot more space to put things (because the layout will stretch to fit in any size browser), there is a reason that design includes white space. And white space needs to be empty. If it's filled with stuff, it's no longer white space, and your design can look cluttered or hard to read.

Dandylions
file:///Users/jenniferkyrnin/Dropbox
Reader
HootSuite Bookmarklet
Dandylions
flower in a head is called a floret. Many Taraxacum species produce seeds asexually by apomixis, where the seeds are produced without pollination, resulting in offspring that are genetically identical to the parent plant.
Text from Wikipedia

FIGURE 12.4
A fluid layout with an image that is fixed width and too big.

As you have seen, fluid layouts can break on small screens, and while they don't necessarily break on wide screens, they can become very difficult to read. This is because the scan length of the text gets too long. A good rule of thumb for readable text is to keep the scan length between 7 and 14 words. Lines longer than this make it hard to find the beginning of the next line as you scan to read it. Lines shorter than this are hard to read because they are too choppy. The width to get a good scan length ultimately depends on what font family and font size you're using.

You can use RWD with fluid layouts to address some of these problems. For narrow browsers, you can set the width of the elements to 100% (or remove the widths), and then in larger media queries you can reduce the percentage of real estate you give to the entire page. Listing 12.4 shows a CSS document with two breakpoints and a fluid layout.

NOTE

You Can Continue to Use the Cascade in Your Media Queries

If you look closely at the CSS in Listing 12.4, you will see that there are three media queries, even though the document has only two breakpoints. This is because the first breakpoint defines all the points of similarity between the medium- and large-width devices, just as the first CSS block does to define all the styles that are the same across all browsers. The first query has just `min-width: 481px` to catch all larger browsers and give them a horizontal navigation and two-column layout. The second media query defines the width for medium-size screens and the third is for large-size screens.

LISTING 12.4 A Fluid Layout with Media Queries

```
html, body { margin: 0; padding: 0; border: 0; }
body { background-color: #dfdfdf; }
#main {
  width: 100%;
  background-color: #fff;
  margin: 0 auto;
}
header, article, aside, footer, nav {
  width: 100%;
}
nav ul, nav ul li {
  display: block;
  list-style-type: none;
  padding: 0;
  margin: 0;
}
nav ul li {
  background-color: black;
  color: white;
  padding: 2% 1%;
  border: 1px solid #DFDFDF;
}

@media screen and (min-width: 481px) {
  nav ul {
    background-color: #000;
    padding: 2% 1%;
  }
  nav ul li {
    width: 20%;
    display: inline;
    border: none;
    border-right: 1px solid #dfdfdf;
    padding-right: 2%;
  }
  article { width: 48%; float: left; }
  aside { width: 48%; float: right;  }
  aside img { width: 100%; height: auto; }
  footer { clear: both; }
}

@media screen and (min-width:481px) and  (max-width: 800px){
  #main { width: 90%; }
}

@media screen and (min-width: 801px){
  #main { width: 70%; }
}
```

Elastic Layouts

Elastic layouts are measured in ems rather than pixels or percentages. This means that the layout is compared to the font size. Elastic layouts work very similarly to fluid layouts, but they can often look much better in RWD because as the font size changes (more on this in Hour 14, "Responsive Fonts and Typography"), the layout changes as well. You can also tell an elastic layout if you use the browser Ctrl++ (Ctrl and the + key) and Ctrl+- (Ctrl and the - key) commands to resize the text, and the whole layout adjusts along with the text.

These layouts work best when *everything* is sized in ems—including images, fonts, multimedia, and the layout. And it can be challenging to size fixed-width items like videos and advertising with a more fluid measure like ems.

The biggest problem with elastic layouts is that they can get huge very quickly, and while the container may not break, the design can still be very hard to read.

Hybrid Layouts

To solve this problem, and many of the problems that are caused by the other layout types, most designers use what is called a *hybrid layout*. This means that they use a combination of fixed, fluid, and elastic measurements to define their layouts.

The best way to do this is to use the CSS `max-width` and `min-width` properties. You simply add a maximum width to any layout element where the design could get too large to read effectively and a minimum width to any element where the design could get too small. Be careful with using `min-width` on smaller devices, however, as you don't want a horizontal scroll bar.

For instance, to cause the fluid layout in Listing 12.4 to stop getting wider when browsers are more than 1200px wide, you add `max-width: 1200px;` to the `#main` style rule, like this:

```
#main {
  max-width: 1200px;
  width: 100%;
  background-color: #fff;
  margin: 0 auto;
}
```

Columns in Layout

As mentioned earlier, most people think of the layout of a web design as the number of columns it has. And while RWD is more than just one column for small screens, two for medium, and three or more for large, there is something to be said for that form of layout design. There are a few ways to create columns in a web design:

- Use CSS floats or positioning
- Use CSS3 columns
- Use layout tables—but I strongly recommend that you avoid this method

Using CSS floats and positioning allows you to create columns with your HTML elements based on where you position them on the page. Listing 12.4 creates a two-column layout in medium- and large-screen devices, using CSS floats to place the elements side-by-side. I call this the "old style" for creating columns. There is nothing wrong with this method; it's just older than the next method I mention: using CSS3 columns.

CSS3 columns use new CSS3 properties to allow the browser to define the columns. This allows your web page to flow more like a newspaper, with the text filling in the columns as it can. This is a more modern method of creating columns on web pages.

I mention layout tables only for posterity. While they are valid in HTML5, I do not recommend that you use them because many small-screen phones don't handle tables very well. Plus, layout tables can make your designs very rigid. If you insist on using layout tables for columns, you can do it, but this is the last time I will mention them.

Old-Style Columns

With old-style CSS columns, you use the `float` property or positioning properties to place the elements on the design where you want them. By using CSS and the `float` property, you can create very interesting column layouts.

To create any column layout, you need to do at least a little math. For example, to create a two-column layout, you give each of the two column elements a width that is less than the total space available. If you're using a fixed-width layout type, this is easy: You simply subtract the width of the first column from the total and make sure the second column is slightly narrower than that. For example, if the whole layout is 960px wide, and the main column is 720px wide, the second column can be 960px – 720px, or 240px, wide.

It works the same in fluid layouts but can seem a little trickier. You need to remember that the default width is always 100% of the parent container. So any percentage widths you set are also percentages of that parent.

Three-column layouts can be a little trickier with the `float` property because you need a bit more markup in your HTML to accomplish it. Listing 12.5 adjusts the HTML from Listing 12.1 so that the `<article>`, `<aside>`, and `<footer>` fall in three columns.

LISTING 12.5 Adding an Extra `<div>` for Three Columns

```
<!doctype html>
<html>
  <head>
    <meta charset="UTF-8">
    <title>Dandylions</title>
    <link href="rwd code 12.5.css" rel="stylesheet">
  </head>
  <body>
    <div id="main">
      <header>
        <h1>Dandylions</h1>
        <h2>Not Your Mother's Weed</h2>
      </header>
      <nav>
        <ul>
          <li>Home</li>
          <li>Products</li>
          <li>Services</li>
          <li>Support</li>
        </ul>
      </nav>
      <article>
      <h3>What is a Dandelion?</h3>
      <p><span class="pronounce"><strong><em>Taraxacum</em></strong>
      <em>/tə'ræksəkʉm/</em></span> is a large genus of flowering plants
      in the family Asteraceae. They are native to Eurasia and North and
      South America, and two species, T. officinale and T.
      erythrospermum, are found as weeds worldwide. Both species are
      edible in their entirety. The common name
      <span class="pronounce"><strong>dandelion</strong>
      <em>/'dændɨlaɪ.ən/</em></span> (dan-di-ly-ən, from French
      dent-de-lion, meaning "lion's tooth") is given to members of the
```

CAUTION

Watch for Borders and Paddings

If any of your elements are assigned borders, margins, or paddings, this can affect the width they take up in the layout. The traditional box model adds on the border and padding to the width of the element. So if an element has a 5px padding and a 2px border, that would add 14px (for both sides) to the width of the element. CSS3 provides a solution for this. You can define the `box-sizing` of an element to be `border-box`, which will make the final rendered box the declared width and include any border and padding inside that width. You just use `box-sizing: border-box;`. You can apply this to all your elements at the top of your CSS file by using this:

```
* {
  -webkit-box-sizing: border-
box;
  -moz-box-sizing: border-box;
  box-sizing: border-box;
}
```

```
      genus, and like other members of the Asteraceae family, they have
      very small flowers collected together into a composite flower head.
      Each single flower in a head is called a floret. Many
      <em>Taraxacum</em> species produce seeds asexually by apomixis,
      where the seeds are produced without pollination, resulting in
      offspring that are genetically identical to the parent plant.</p>
      </article>
      <div id="col2">
        <aside>
          <img src="images/dandy.jpg" width="400" height="300" alt=""/>
        </aside>
        <footer>
          <p>Text from
          <a href="http://en.wikipedia.org/wiki/Dandelion">Wikipedia</a></p>
        </footer>
      </div>
    </div>
  </body>
</html>
```

As you can see, in this listing you just add another `<div>` container (with the ID `col2`) surrounding the `<aside>` and the `<footer>`. Then you treat that `<div>` as a two-column layout and the `<article>` and the `<div>` as a two-column layout. Listing 12.6 shows how you do it.

LISTING 12.6 CSS for Three Columns

```
html, body { margin: 0; padding: 0; border: 0; }
body { background-color: #dfdfdf; }
#main {
  width: 100%;
  background-color: #fff;
  margin: 0 auto;
}
header, article, aside, footer, nav {
  width: 100%;
}
nav ul, nav ul li {
  display: block;
  list-style-type: none;
  padding: 0;
  margin: 0;
}

nav ul li {
  background-color: black;
  color: white;
  padding: 2% 1%;
  border: 1px solid #DFDFDF;
}
```

```
@media screen and (min-width: 481px) {
  nav ul {
    background-color: #000;
    padding: 2% 1%;
  }
  nav ul li {
    width: 20%;
    display: inline;
    border: none;
    border-right: 1px solid #dfdfdf;
    padding-right: 2%;
  }
  article, aside { width: 48%; float: left; }
  #col2, footer { width: 48%; float: right;  }
  aside img { width: 100%; height: auto; }
}
@media screen and (min-width:481px) and  (max-width: 800px){
  #main { width: 90%; }
}
@media screen and (min-width: 801px){
  #main { width: 70%; }
}
```

If you want more information on how to create columns in the old style, you should check out the many resources online, including the book *Sams Teach Yourself HTML and CSS in 24 Hours* by Julie C. Meloni.

CSS3 Columns

CSS3 brings in a whole new way to create columns in your designs: multicolumn layout properties. There are 13 new properties in CSS3 to create column layouts:

- **`column-width`**—Defines the width of each column
- **`column-count`**—Defines the number of columns
- **`columns`**—A shorthand property that defines both the column width and count
- **`column-gap`**—Defines the length of the gap between columns
- **`column-rule-color`**—Defines the color of the line between columns
- **`column-rule-style`**—Defines the style (for example, solid, dashed, or dotted) of the line between the columns
- **`column-rule-width`**—Defines the width of the line between columns

- **`column-rule`**—A shorthand property that defines the width, style, and color of the line between columns
- **`break-before`**, **`break-after`**, and **`break-inside`**—Define the page or column break behavior before, after, and inside the box, respectively
- **`column-span`**—Defines how many columns the element should span
- **`column-fill`**—Defines how to fill the columns either balanced between the columns (`balance`) or filled sequentially (`auto`)

Most of these properties are supported in modern browsers, as long as you use the browser prefixes. Listing 12.7 shows the CSS to make the `<article>` element in the HTML from Listing 12.1 into two columns.

LISTING 12.7 CSS for a Two-Column Article

```
article {
  -moz-column-count: 2;
  -webkit-column-count: 2;
  column-count: 2;
}
```

You can use multiple columns in RWD really easily: Just change the column count or column width for each breakpoint.

Summary

In this hour you've learned how layout works on web pages and how to do several different types of layouts. You've learned the differences between fluid, fixed, elastic, and hybrid layouts. And you've learned how to use these layouts in responsive web designs.

This hour also covers how to create columns in your layouts using standard CSS and using the new CSS3 multicolumn properties described in Table 12.1, which make it much easier to create columns in your web designs.

TABLE 12.1 CSS3 Column Properties

Property	Description
break-before, break-after, and break-inside	Defines the page or column break behavior before, after, and inside the box, respectively
column-count	Defines the number of columns
column-fill	Defines how to fill the columns either balanced between the columns (balance) or filled sequentially (auto)
column-gap	Defines the length of the gap between columns
column-rule	A shorthand property that defines the width, style, and color of the line between columns
column-rule-color	Defines the color of the line between columns
column-rule-style	Defines the style (for example: solid, dashed, or dotted) of the line between the columns
column-rule-width	Defines the width of the line between columns
column-span	Defines how many columns the element should span
column-width	Defines the width of each column
columns	A shorthand property that defines both the column width and count

Workshop

The workshop contains quiz questions to help you process what you've learned in this lesson. Try to answer all the questions before you read the answers.

Q&A

Q. You mentioned grids when you talked about the fixed-width layout type, but can you use grids in the other layout types?

A. Using grids is a useful layout technique no matter what layout type you use. Ethan Marcotte wrote about fluid grids in 2009 on A List Apart (see `http://alistapart.com/article/fluidgrids`).

Q. I've been told that CSS3 multicolumn properties aren't well supported. Is that true? If they aren't, why should I consider using them?

A. Right now, according to Can I Use... (`http://caniuse.com/#feat=multicolumn`), all the major browsers support most of the multi-column properties if you use the browser prefixes (`-webkit-` and `-moz-`). And that includes the most recent versions of Internet Explorer.

Quiz

1. What are two aspects of layout?
2. What are two types of layout?
3. What is a good length for a text block for readability?
4. What does the `column-rule` property do?

Answers

1. Layout includes white space, the position of block elements and images, and the width of text blocks.
2. There are four different types of layout: fixed width, fluid (or liquid), elastic, and hybrid.
3. For readability, the scan length of text blocks should be between 7 and 14 words.
4. The `column-rule` property defines the width, color, and style of any lines between columns.

Exercise

Take a look at the site design for the website you've been working with. Does the layout work for the breakpoints you've chosen? Decide whether to use fixed-width layout or fluid, and then add those styles to your style sheet.

HOUR 13
Navigation

WHAT YOU'LL LEARN IN THIS HOUR:

- What navigation is and how to create it on web pages
- How mobile navigation should differ from desktop navigation
- How to use progressive enhancement with your navigation

Navigation is a critical part of web design, including responsive web design. Navigation is how your customers get around on your site, so if your design changes depending on the size of the device viewing it, the navigation should change as well.

In this hour you will learn how to create navigation schemes that work for all the devices you want to support. You'll learn what makes navigation mobile friendly and how to add styles to your media queries to make sure the navigation doesn't ruin your site.

Why Responsive Navigation Is Important

Navigation on all web pages is important because it helps users move around on the site. But it's especially important to think about navigation when designing a responsive site because it could end up being all your customers see before they click away. There are some common problems with navigation in responsive web designs, including the following:

- Navigation that is too small
- Navigation that takes up the entire screen
- Navigation that disappears or doesn't work on mobile devices
- Navigation that is hard to use on mobile devices

Figure 13.1 shows two ways a navigation system might fail in your designs. The first failure is navigation that is smashed so small that it's not readable. And the second failure is navigation that, while readable, is the only thing that appears on a smartphone. None of the content is visible in either case. Customers will be annoyed by the first, and they might not scroll past the second to see what's on your page.

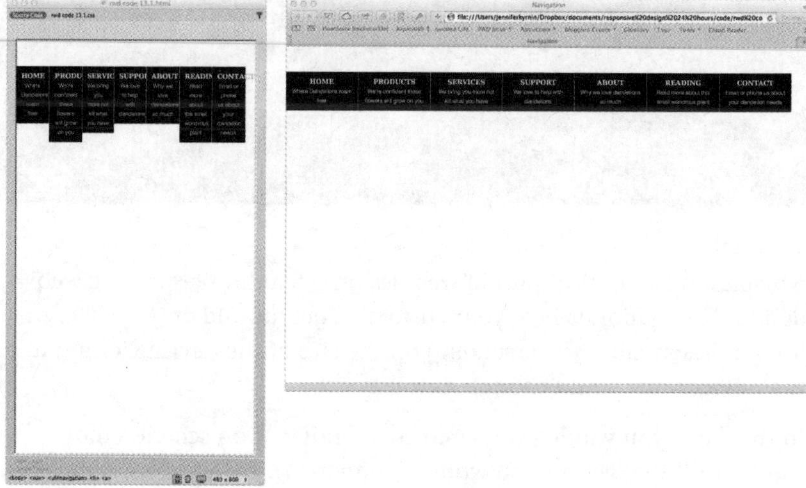

FIGURE 13.1
Navigation failures in responsive web design.

The point of navigation is to allow readers to find their way around your site. If they can't figure it out, they will simply leave your site and go to one that is more user friendly. This is especially true for mobile device users. By making sure your navigation works for even the smallest devices, you will keep more customers on your site.

What Makes Navigation Mobile Friendly?

Navigation needs to be easy to use and contain all the elements you want your customers to find. But there are a few specific requirements of a mobile-friendly navigation system:

- The links need to be big enough to be tapped with a finger.
- The text needs to be large and readable, even on small screens.
- You should avoid hover navigation.
- You should limit your menu to five links or fewer.

- If you have multilevel navigation, you shouldn't go more than two levels deep.
- You should never use horizontal scrolling menus.

The first two requirements should be self-explanatory. Most mobile devices are touch screens, and if users can't tap on the links because they are too small or too close together, they will get frustrated. This problem commonly happens in a list of links, where each item is a clickable link, but it's difficult to click the correct one on a small device.

Another link problem occurs when a single word, especially a small word, like *in* or *a*, is a link. Such small links can be virtually impossible to click on. Listing 13.1 shows a basic list of links, with a few difficult-to-tap portions.

LISTING 13.1 Basic List of Links

```
<ul>
  <li><a href="#a">test can you click on this?</a></li>
  <li><a href="#b">test can you click on this?</a></li>
  <li>test can you click <a href="#c">on</a> this? </li>
  <li><a href="#e">test can you click on this? </a></li>
  <li><a href="#d">test</a> <a href="#j">can</a> you
    <a href="#h">click</a>
  <a href="#i">on</a> <a href="#k">this</a>?</li>
  <li><a href="#f">test can you click on this? </a></li>
  <li><a href="#g">test can you click on this? </a></li>
</ul>
```

Figure 13.2 shows how this HTML might look on an iPhone. You can see how difficult it would be to tap on the various links and be sure you're clicking the one you want to click.

Hover navigation is tricky, and many sites use it by default. But you can't hover on a touch screen; you can only tap or not. Although this may change in the future as the new Apple Watch has tap-and-touch sensitivity to detect when a user presses on the device versus just tapping. It's not that you can't use multilevel navigation, but if the only way to access that navigation is by hovering over the links, you've made it impossible for touch screen users to use it.

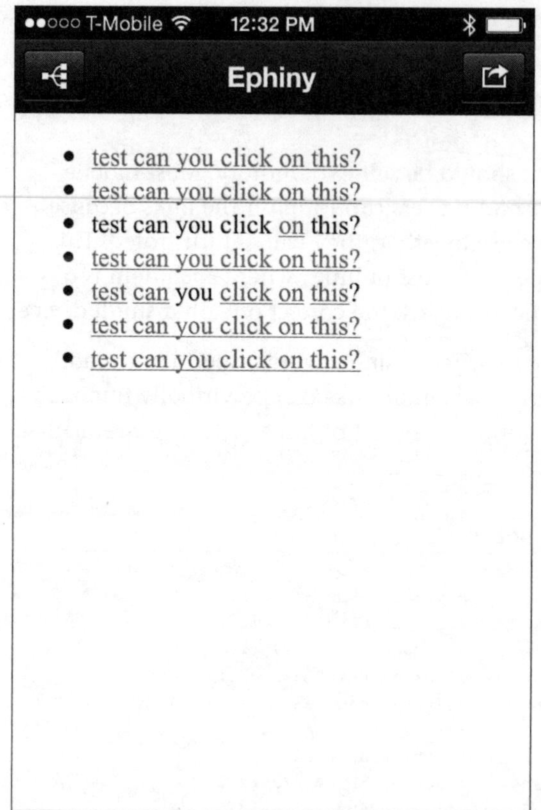

FIGURE 13.2
A list of links as viewed on an iPhone.

As you saw in Figure 13.1, having a lot of links in your navigation can cause your navigation to take over the entire screen. And as important as navigation is, your customers aren't coming to your page to view it. They are coming for the content. If you need a lot of links in your navigation, the best solution is to create multilevel navigation and make it accessible on click for your mobile customers.

Finally, as with all other design elements, your navigation should not slide off the right or left sides of the screen. Many mobile devices don't have the ability to scroll horizontally, and even when they can, most users don't realize that's possible.

Basic RWD Navigation Patterns

Design patterns are documented and reusable solutions to a problem. Patterns are created by looking at different designs and finding the things that work consistently. There are a number of popular patterns for RWD navigation, including the following:

- Basic navigation that resizes and repositions
- Select menus
- Hidden navigation
- Links added in other locations

In the next few sections you will learn how to work with each of these navigation patterns. For all these patterns, I use the HTML shown in Listing 13.2, which is just a list of links inside the `<nav>` element.

LISTING 13.2 HTML for Navigation

```
<nav>
  <ul id="navigation">
    <li><a href="#">Home<br>
    <small>Where Dandelions roam free</small></a></li>
    <li><a href="#">Products<br>
    <small>These flowers will grow on you</small></a></li>
    <li><a href="#">Services<br>
    <small>We care for the flowers you have</small></a></li>
    <li><a href="#">Support<br>
    <small>We love to help with dandelions</small></a></li>
    <li><a href="#">About<br>
    <small>Why we love dandelions so much</small></a></li>
    <li><a href="#">Reading<br>
    <small>Read more about this wondrous plant</small></a></li>
    <li><a href="#">Contact<br>
    <small>Ask us about your dandelion needs</small></a></li>
  </ul>
</nav>
```

As you can see, each list item has a link that also contains some descriptive text surrounded by the `<small>` tag. This gives you some flexibility in how to display the navigation. In the next few sections, you will see how to adjust the design by using this navigation.

Basic Navigation That Resizes and Repositions

Basic navigation that resizes and repositions is the most common pattern, as it requires the least amount of effort. In fact, in some designs, it can be considered a "do nothing" design because you use a basic navigation menu that is sized with percentages or ems so that it flexes with the size of the browser window. Listing 13.3 shows CSS for a navigation bar that resizes depending on the window size, and Listing 13.4 shows CSS for a navigation bar that repositions depending on the window size.

LISTING 13.3 CSS for a Resizing Navigation Bar

```
/* font family */
@font-face {
  font-family: 'bitstream_vera_serifbold';
  src:
url('fonts/bitstreamveraserif_bold_macroman/VeraSerif-Bold-webfont.eot');
  /* note: other font sources removed for clarity */
  font-weight: normal;
  font-style: normal;
}
/* basic reset */
*, *:before, *:after {
  padding: 0;
  margin: 0;
  -webkit-box-sizing: border-box;
  -moz-box-sizing: border-box;
  box-sizing: border-box;
}
/* nav bar */
nav {
  width: 100%;
  margin: auto;
}
nav ul {
  list-style: none;
  overflow: hidden;
  background: #000;
}
nav li a {
  display: block;
  float: left;
  width: 14.28%;
  padding: 10px;
  background: #000;
  border-right: 1px solid #fff;
  color: #fbd91f;
  font: 400 13px/1.4 bitstream_vera_serifbold, Baskerville,
    "Palatino Linotype", Palatino, "Times New Roman", serif;
  text-align: center;
  text-decoration: none;
  text-transform: uppercase;
}
/* small text */
nav small {
  color: #aaa;
  font: 100 11px/1 Helvetica, Verdana, Arial, sans-serif;
  text-transform: none;
}
```

Figure 13.3 shows how Listing 13.3 would look in a narrow browser window. Notice that the navigation stays all on one line, but the space for each button gets smaller.

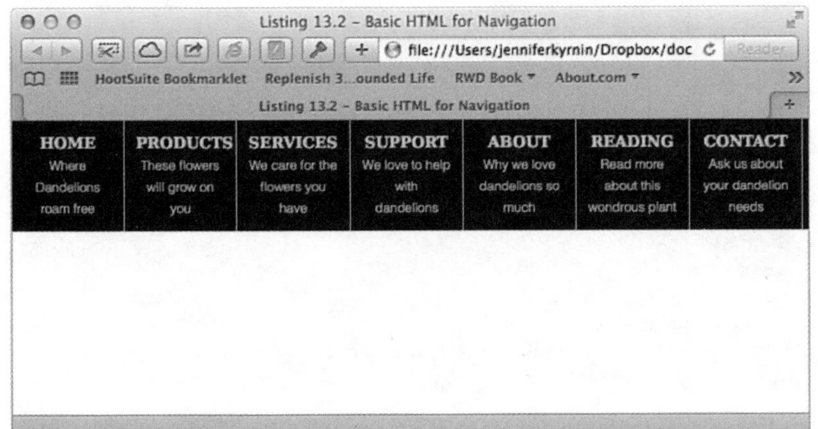

FIGURE 13.3
A navigation bar that resizes each element.

LISTING 13.4 CSS for a Repositioning Navigation Bar

```
/* font family */
@font-face {
  font-family: 'bitstream_vera_serifbold';
  src:
url('fonts/bitstreamveraserif_bold_macroman/VeraSerif-Bold-webfont.eot');
  /* note: other font sources removed for clarity */
  font-weight: normal;
  font-style: normal;
}
/* basic reset */
*, *:before, *:after {
  padding: 0;
  margin: 0;
  -webkit-box-sizing: border-box;
  -moz-box-sizing: border-box;
  box-sizing: border-box;
}
/* nav bar */
nav {
  width: 100%;
  margin: auto;
}
nav ul {
  list-style: none;
  overflow: hidden;
  background: #000;
}
```

```
nav li a {
  display: block;
  float: left;
  width: 12em;
  min-height: 8em;
  padding: 1.2em;
  background: #000;
  border-right: 1px solid #fff;
  color: #fbd91f;
  font: 400 0.8em/1.4 bitstream_vera_serifbold, Baskerville,
    "Palatino Linotype", Palatino, "Times New Roman", serif;
  text-align: center;
  text-decoration: none;
  text-transform: uppercase;
}
/* small text */
nav small {
  color: #aaa;
  font: 100 0.85em/1 Helvetica, Verdana, Arial, sans-serif;
  text-transform: none;
}
```

Figure 13.4 shows how Listing 13.4 would look in a narrow browser window. Instead of resizing the width of the elements, they reposition down below one another.

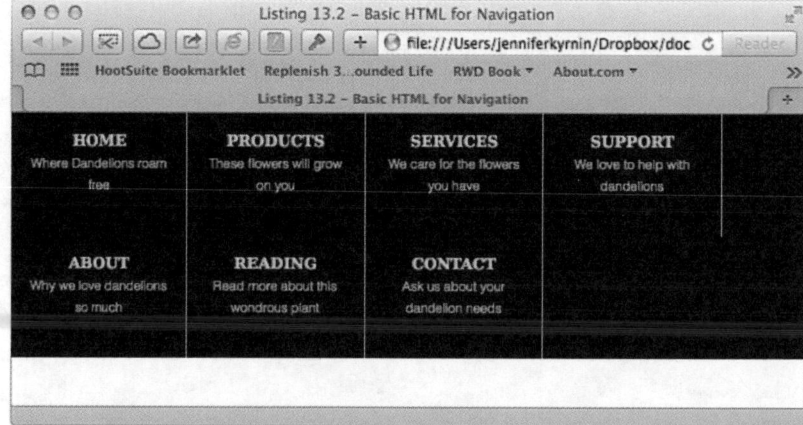

FIGURE 13.4
A navigation bar that repositions each element.

At first glance, Listings 13.3 and 13.4 look very similar. The only difference is in the `nav li a` rule. The width of these elements is changed from a percentage width to a width based on the size of the fonts (em). Listing 13.4 also includes `min-height` to keep the boxes around the same size, so they will float correctly. Finally, Listing 13.4 has changed the `font-size` values for both the links and the small text to ems so that they will flex correctly as well.

NOTE

What's Up with the `box-sizing` Styles?

In Listings 13.3 and 13.4 there is a simple reset at the top that changes `box-sizing` to `border-box`. This is a new feature in CSS that makes the sizing of boxes on your web designs a breeze. If you set the width to 100px and then add padding of 10px, you don't have to worry about whether the width will expand to 120px in some browsers. If you are designing for modern browsers, including Internet Explorer 8 and up, this technique (with the prefixes in the code listings) will make your life a lot easier. Find out more from Paul Irish, at `paulirish.com/2012/box-sizing-border-box-ftw/`.

Select Menus

A select menu is a form element that creates a drop-down menu. Some designers are reluctant to use them because most people don't seem to see them in large-screen designs, but they are a great alternative design for small screens such as cell phones because they are easy to use and no less visible than any other design element. In order to use a select menu, you have to add it to the HTML and then show and hide it, depending on the browser size using media queries.

TRY IT YOURSELF ▼

Add a Select Menu as a Navigation Option for Small Screens

In this Try It Yourself, you will start with the HTML used for the previous examples and add a select menu to it. Then you will add media queries to show and hide that menu, depending on the browser size.

1. Open the HTML in Listing 13.2 in your favorite web page editor.
2. Add the following HTML inside the `<nav>` element, below the unordered list:

```
<select id="mobileNav">
  <option value="">Go to...</option>
  <option value="/">Home</option>
  <option value="/products">Products</option>
  <option value="/services">Services</option>
  <option value="/support">Support</option>
  <option value="/about">About</option>
  <option value="/articles">Reading</option>
  <option value="/contact">Contact</option>
</select>
```

3. Add the following media queries to the CSS:

```
/* default to smallest browser size */
nav ul { display: none; }
nav select { display: inline-block; }
```

▼ TRY IT YOURSELF

Add a Select Menu as a Navigation Option for Small Screens
continued

```
/* change to full nav for larger screens */
@media screen and (min-width: 481px) {
  nav ul { display: block; }
  nav select { display: none; }
}
```

4. Go back to the HTML and add some jQuery to make it work. Add a script link to jQuery in the `<head>` of the document:

```
<script
src="http://ajax.googleapis.com/ajax/libs/jquery/1.6.2/jquery.min.
js"></script>
```

5. Add a script at the bottom of the document:

```
<script>
$(function() {
  $("nav select").change(function() {
    window.location = $(this).find("option:selected").val();
  });
});
</script>
```

LISTING 13.5 HTML for Navigation with a Select Menu

```
<!doctype html>
<html>
<head>
<meta charset="UTF-8">
<title>Listing 13.5 - Basic HTML with Select List for
Navigation</title>
<link href="rwd code 13.6.css" rel="stylesheet">
<script
  src="http://ajax.googleapis.com/ajax/libs/jquery/1.6.2/jquery.min.js">
</script>
</head>

<body>
<nav>
  <ul id="navigation">
    <li><a href="#">Home<br>
    <small>Where Dandelions roam free</small></a></li>
    <li><a href="#">Products<br>
    <small>These flowers will grow on you</small></a></li>
    <li><a href="#">Services<br>
    <small>We care for the flowers you have</small></a></li>
    <li><a href="#">Support<br>
    <small>We love to help with dandelions</small></a></li>
    <li><a href="#">About<br>
    <small>Why we love dandelions so much</small></a></li>
    <li><a href="#">Reading<br>
```

```
    <small>Read more about this wondrous plant</small></a></li>
    <li><a href="#">Contact<br>
    <small>Ask us about your dandelion needs</small></a></li>
  </ul>
  <select id="mobileNav">
    <option value="">Go to...</option>
    <option value="/home">Home</option>
    <option value="/products">Products</option>
    <option value="/services">Services</option>
    <option value="/support">Support</option>
    <option value="/about">About</option>
    <option value="/articles">Reading</option>
    <option value="/contact">Contact</option>
  </select>
</nav>

<script>
$(function() {
  $("nav select").change(function() {
    window.location = $(this).find("option:selected").val();
  });
});
</script>
</body>
</html>
```

TRY IT YOURSELF ▼

Add a Select Menu as a Navigation Option for Small Screens

continued

LISTING 13.6 CSS for Navigation with a Select Menu

```
/* font family */
@font-face {
  font-family: 'bitstream_vera_serifbold';
  src: url('fonts/VeraSerif-Bold-webfont.eot');
  src: url('fonts/ VeraSerif-Bold-webfont.eot?#iefix')
      format('embedded-opentype'),
    url('fonts/VeraSerif-Bold-webfont.woff')
    format('woff'),
    url('fonts/VeraSerif-Bold-webfont.ttf')
    format('truetype'),
    url('fonts/VeraSerif-Bold-webfont.svg#bitstream_vera_serifbold')
      format('svg');
  font-weight: normal;
  font-style: normal;

}
/* basic reset */
*, *:before, *:after {
    padding: 0;
    margin: 0;
    -webkit-box-sizing: border-box;
    -moz-box-sizing: border-box;
```

▼ TRY IT YOURSELF

Add a Select Menu as a Navigation Option for Small Screens

continued

```
    box-sizing: border-box;
}
/* nav bar */
nav {
  width: 100%;
  margin: auto;
}

nav ul {
  list-style: none;
  overflow: hidden;
    background: #000;
}
nav li a {
  display: block;
  float: left;
  width: 14.28%;
  padding: 10px;
  background: #000;
  border-right: 1px solid #fff;
  color: #fbd91f;
  font: 400 13px/1.4 bitstream_vera_serifbold, Baskerville,
    "Palatino Linotype", Palatino, "Times New Roman", serif;
  text-align: center;
  text-decoration: none;
  text-transform: uppercase;
}
/* small text */
nav small {
  color: #aaa;
  font: 100 11px/1 Helvetica, Verdana, Arial, sans-serif;
  text-transform: none;
}

/* default to smallest browser size */
nav ul { display: none; }
nav select { display: inline-block; }

/* change to full nav for larger screens */
@media screen and (min-width: 481px) {
  nav ul { display: block; }
  nav select { display: none; }
}
```

Verify the font URLs above to make sure you're pointing to the correct files.

Hidden Navigation

There are several ways you can hide menus but make them available to your users when they need them. These are some of the popular ways of doing this:

- ▶ Pushing the menu to the bottom
- ▶ Toggling the menu on and off with a button
- ▶ Creating fly-out menus
- ▶ Building multilevel menus
- ▶ Removing parts (or all) of the navigation completely

Moving your navigation menu to the bottom of the page is a good solution for pages where the content is the most important element of the page. This is especially true for sites where traffic comes directly from search engines to exactly the page the customer wants. By moving the navigation to the bottom of the page, you make the content more visible while providing the navigation when users want it—after they've read the content and want more.

When you move your navigation to the bottom of the page, you should add a button at the top of the page that takes readers down to the navigation with one click. This is as simple as writing `<a href="#navigation"> Click to go to navigation</a>` at the top of your web pages and showing it only to the devices that get that bottom navigation.

NOTE

Don't Forget "Back to Top" Links

If you are going to use anchor links to bounce your readers around your page, you should also include "back to top" links so they can get back where they were. If you're feeling especially ambitious, you could code those links to return users to the part of the page where they were most recently.

You can also take up less space with your navigation by creating a toggle button that turns the navigation on and off when the customer wants it. You see this often with a little icon to tap and get the navigation.

Fly-out menus are becoming more and more popular for navigation solutions. These are similar to toggle menus, but they usually have an icon or graphic on the right or left side of the screen. When the customer taps on the icon, the menu flies out from the side to cover the content.

As mentioned earlier in this hour, one problem with navigation menus on small screens is that they often contain too many options. But if you create a multilevel menu that appears with a tap, you can move some of the elements to a second level when the screen gets too small. As long as you make the menus accessible on touch screens, you can have several levels of navigation.

The last way to hide your navigation menus is to simply remove elements as the screen gets smaller. Some people refer to this as the "hide-

and-cry" navigation pattern because it assumes that people on a cell phone won't need or want the same content they want on a desktop. Since more and more people are browsing the web with mobile devices, this is a risky technique because customers might never realize that your site has more content than what they can find on their cell phones. One way to solve this problem is to provide the links inside your content, but that is just a stop-gap measure. It is best to avoid this pattern unless you have a very specific use case in mind.

Links Added in Other Locations

The final design pattern discussed in this lesson is including links to various parts of the site in alternate locations rather than just in the navigation menu. The most common location is the page footer. You will often see sites that include lots of links in the footer, even when they have an extensive navigation menu. Figure 13.5 shows an example of this from my site `html5in24hours.com`. The site responds to browser size by moving the columns in the footer into a single column in the smallest browser windows, but all the links are still there.

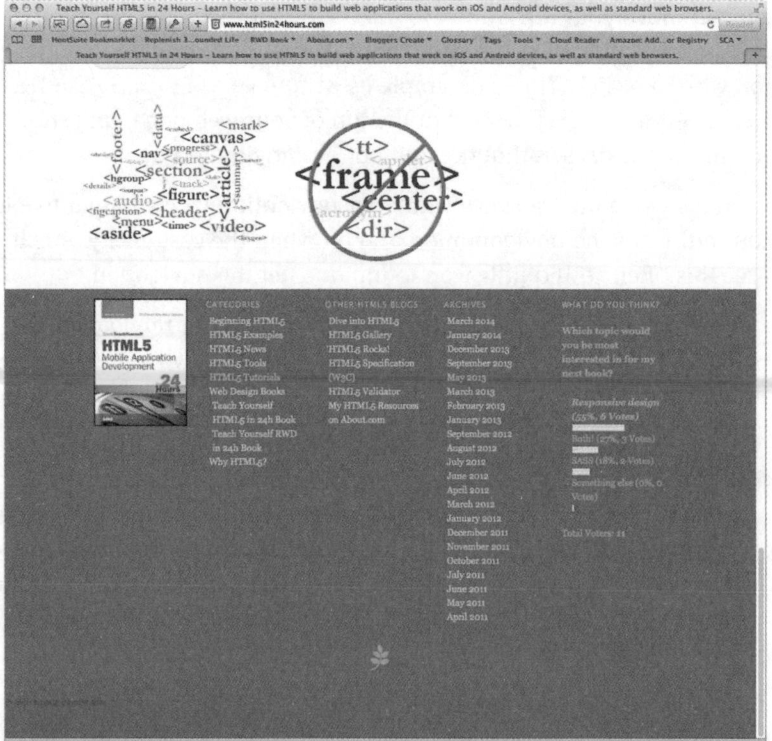

FIGURE 13.5
Lots of links in the footer.

But the footer isn't the only place you can add additional links. You can include sidebars that include additional links as well. This is especially effective if the links are related to the content on the page, but they can provide a way to get readers around your site beyond the standard navigation.

Remember when you're designing a responsive website that you need to think about what mobile customers need and want and then enhance the design for customers on larger devices. This is true for your navigation as well as for the rest of your design. Adding links throughout your pages helps your customers get around even if they don't use the standard navigation menu.

Summary

This hour you've taken a look at navigation through the lens of responsive design. When you're designing navigation, you need to be aware of how it's going to work on smaller devices. You also need to be aware of how customers respond to your site, so that you can make sure your navigation is unobtrusive yet helpful.

This hour you've learned how to make navigation more mobile friendly as well as why focusing on navigation design is so important. You've also learned about several navigation patterns you can use to create a responsive navigation system.

Workshop

The workshop contains quiz questions to help you process what you've learned in this lesson. Try to answer all the questions before you read the answers.

Q&A

Q. Aren't there any set-it-and-forget-it website navigation solutions?

A. If you really don't want to worry about your navigation, the best solution is to use the basic navigation that resizes and repositions pattern described in this lesson. This pattern doesn't typically need CSS media queries and doesn't require that you have any scripting or extra navigation elements. But you should test your navigation on the smallest screens you can to make sure it is still usable at those small sizes.

Q. I have thousands of pages I want to link to, but you said I shouldn't have too many levels in my navigation. What should I do?

A. There are lots of options you can try, but for sites with hundreds or thousands of content pages, you should consider more than just primary navigation for getting your pages noticed. Instead, you should include things like related links at the ends of articles, inline links to content, and sidebars. It's very tempting to use lists of links, but most people glaze over after just a few lines. Instead, try to create hubs of content that you can then link to in your navigation.

Q. You mentioned that touch screen devices don't support hover, but mine does. Can I use hover menus?

A. While some of the newer smartphones are generating apps and features to allow you to hover over parts of the screen, this hasn't been built into all web browsers or mobile devices. Your navigation should use progressive enhancement just like every other part of your site. This means that your navigation should provide what your customers need whether their device supports hovering or not.

Quiz

1. Which of the following is not a problem for mobile navigation?

- **a.** Navigation that doesn't work
- **b.** Navigation that takes up a fraction of the screen
- **c.** Navigation that is too small
- **d.** Navigation that is hard to use

2. Why should you not use lists of links?
3. How many links is too many in primary navigation?
4. What is a design pattern?
5. What is "hide-and-cry" navigation?

Answers

1. b. Mobile devices often have limited screen space, so navigation that is minimalistic is better than navigation that takes up the entire window.
2. When there are multiple links right next to one another, they can be very difficult to tap on small screen devices without zooming in on the text you should tap. Many customers don't think to zoom in, and so they get frustrated when they try to tap one link and get sent somewhere else.
3. You shouldn't use more than seven links in your primary navigation.
4. A design pattern is a documented and reusable solution to a problem. Design patterns are used to help make websites and other designs easier to use because they use familiar techniques and conventions.
5. With "hide-and-cry" navigation, you remove parts of the navigation for some layouts. It is called "hide-and-cry" because it can frustrate customers when they can't find parts of the site.

Exercises

1. Evaluate the site you are working on converting to RWD. What navigation pattern would work best for this site?
2. Start to rebuild the site's navigation for RWD by first making sure that the HTML for the primary navigation area is as clean and minimal as possible. Then create a small-screen version in your CSS. If you're not using the pattern to resize or reposition your navigation, you need to adjust the CSS in your media queries so that it still looks good in larger screens.

HOUR 14
Responsive Fonts and Typography

In this hour you will learn how to make your fonts and typography responsive. There is more to responsive fonts than just resizing text. You'll learn how to use web fonts to get exactly the typeface you want and how to choose sizes for your fonts so that they look good on any device. You'll learn the difference between three measurement values (pixels, ems, and percentages) and how the rem unit works.

WHAT YOU'LL LEARN IN THIS HOUR:

- What web fonts are and how to use them
- How to size web fonts in RWD
- The difference between pixels, ems, and percentages
- How to use new CSS3 measurement units

Using Web Fonts

Web fonts are font faces that are stored online, either on a server or on a content delivery network (CDN). Using web fonts ensures that the fonts you want to use in your designs are available to your customers. I cover web fonts in more detail in Hour 11 of my book *Sams Teach Yourself HTML5 Mobile Application Development in 24 Hours*, but here is a quick overview:

1. Find a font on Google Fonts (`http://www.google.com/fonts`) that you want to use. Figure 14.1 shows how Google Fonts looks.
2. Once you've found a font you like, click on the Quick Use icon (a right-pointing arrow in a box).
3. Select the font styles and character sets you want to use. Using only the minimum number of styles and characters will help your pages load as quickly as possible.
4. Switch to the @import tab and copy the code to your clipboard (by using Ctrl+C or Cmd+C). Figure 14.2 shows this step circled.

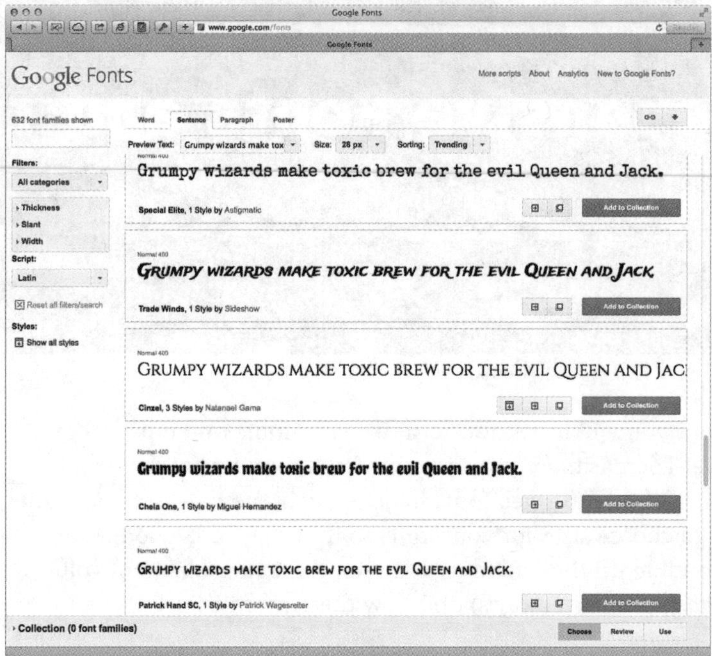

FIGURE 14.1
Choosing a font in Google Fonts.

FIGURE 14.2
Using the `@import` method.

5. Open your CSS file in an HTML or text editor.
6. Add the `@import` line to the top of the CSS file.
7. Add the `font-family` listed on the Google Fonts page to the style rules that you want to use the web font.

As you can see, web fonts are fairly easy to use, and using them is a great way to dress up your web pages. But they have some drawbacks as well. The biggest drawback is that they have to be downloaded from the web, just like images and other media. This means that the page takes longer to load. Since browsing on cell phone networks makes pages take longer to load anyway, it can be a good idea to not even download web fonts for the smallest screens. To block them from small screens, you use media queries.

CAUTION

Don't Forget a Fallback Font Family

Many web designers who are new to web fonts forget to include a fallback font in the web font stack. A *font stack* is a group of fonts listed in the order in which the web designer would prefer them to be used on a web page element. But it is tempting to assume that if you're using web fonts, you never need a fallback. While web fonts do lessen the urgency of this requirement, it is possible that a web font might not load, and if you don't have a fallback font in your font stack, the web browser will decide for you. It can be very disappointing to design a page with a beautiful blackletter font only to have the browser display the text in Helvetica or Comic Sans.

TRY IT YOURSELF ▼

Use Media Queries to Load Web Fonts

Media queries make it easy for you to use web fonts on only the devices where you want to use them. You can place your web font rules under your existing media queries, or you can add them to the `@import` line that imports the fonts directly. In the following steps, you'll learn how to add a media query to the `@import` line:

1. Open your HTML editor and paste in the HTML from Listing 14.1.

LISTING 14.1 Basic HTML

```
<!doctype html>
<html>
  <head>
    <meta charset="UTF-8">
    <title>Dandylions</title>
    <link href="styles.css" rel="stylesheet">
  </head>
  <body>
    <div id="main">
    <header>
      <h1>Dandylions</h1>
      <h2>Not Your Mother's Weed</h2>
```

▼ TRY IT YOURSELF

Use Media Queries to Load Web Fonts

continued

```
        </header>
        <nav>
          <ul>
            <li>Home</li>
            <li>Products</li>
            <li>Services</li>
            <li>Support</li>
          </ul>
        </nav>
        <article>
          <h3>What is a Dandelion?</h3>
          <p><span class="pronounce"><strong><em>
          Taraxacum</em></strong> <em>/tə'ræksəkʉm/</em></span> is a
          large genus of flowering plants in the family Asteraceae.
          They are native to Eurasia and North and South America, and
          two species, T. officinale and T. erythrospermum, are found
          as weeds worldwide. Both species are edible in their
          entirety. The common name <span class="pronounce"><strong>
          dandelion</strong> <em>/'dændɨlaɪ.ən/</em></span>
          (dan-di-ly-ən, from French dent-de-lion, meaning "lion's
          tooth") is given to members of the genus, and like other
          members of the Asteraceae family, they have very small
          flowers collected together into a composite flower head. Each
          single flower in a head is called a floret. Many
          <em>Taraxacum</em> species produce seeds asexually by
          apomixis, where the seeds are produced without pollination,
          resulting in offspring that are genetically identical to the
          parent plant.</p>
        </article>
        <aside>
          <img src="images/dandy.jpg" width="400" height="300" alt=""/>
        </aside>
        <footer>
          <p>Text from
          <a href="http://en.wikipedia.org/wiki/Dandelion">
          Wikipedia</a></p>
        </footer>
        </div>
      </body>
    </html>
```

2. Open a CSS file and name it `styles.css`.

3. Paste in the `@import` line from Google Fonts. For example:

```
@import url(
http://fonts.googleapis.com/css?family=Playfair+Display+SC:900
);
```

4. Add a rule for using the fonts, like this:

```
h1, h2, h3 { font-family: 'Playfair Display SC', serif; }
```

TRY IT YOURSELF ▼

Use Media Queries to Load Web Fonts

continued

This sets the font family for `h1`, `h2`, and `h3` tags in every browser. In the next step, you will add the media queries.

5. Go back to the `@import` line and add `screen and (min-width: 500px)` just before the semicolon, so the code looks like this:

```
@import url(
http://fonts.googleapis.com/css?family=Playfair+Display+SC:900
)
screen and (min-width: 500px);
```

You can change `min-width: 500px` value to whatever value works with your design.

6. Test your page in a browser that is smaller than 500px and in another browser that is larger. The web font should be visible only on the larger browsers.

Listing 14.2 shows the CSS file.

LISTING 14.2 A Simple CSS File with Fonts Imported

```
@import url(
http://fonts.googleapis.com/css?family=Playfair+Display+SC:900
)
  screen and (min-width: 500px);
h1, h2, h3 { font-family: 'Playfair Display SC', serif; }
```

You add media queries to `@import` by placing them after the URL you're importing. If you need more help using media queries, refer to Hour 10, "CSS Media Queries."

Sizing Typography

Giving your fonts a size is as easy as writing this:

```
p { font-size: 16px; }
```

But there is more to responsive typography than just setting a font size. If you set your fonts to a specific size, like 16px, they will never scale with the rest of the document. No matter what kind of device is displaying your content, the text will always be 16 pixels tall, for better or for worse.

CAUTION

Always Put `@import` Lines First

You should always put any `@import` lines in your style sheets at the very top of the document, before any styles. If you put any styles above the `@import` lines, the imported file will not load. So, when I say to put the `* {font-size: 100%; }` line at the top of your style sheet, what I really mean is to put it above the rest of your style rules, but not above any imported style sheets.

NOTE

Customers Control the Browser Font Size

Many people don't know this, but it is really easy to change the font size your browser displays. I do this all the time when a page uses a painfully small font or my eyes are tired from a lot of computer use. All you need to do in most browsers is press Ctrl++ (Cmd++ on a Mac) to increase the font size and Ctrl+- (Cmd+- on a Mac) to decrease it. Then, when you want to switch back to the default font size, you press Ctrl+0 (Cmd+0 on a Mac).

Relative Font Sizing

You should size your text relative to something else on the page, so that your font sizes can flex with the layout as much as your layout does. This means you should use a relative font size measurement. I go over this in more detail in the following section, but for now, just know that you can use the em unit.

The em unit is a measure that is relative to the font size of the element. So, when you use this measure, it's a good idea to first set the base font size of your entire document with the CSS style at the top of your style sheet:

```
* { font-size: 100%; }
```

This tells the browser to set all elements (*) to 100%. It may seem redundant to do this, but it ensures that the browser first uses the font size that your customers choose. Then, when you use the em font measure, it will be relative to the font size that your customers chose.

Once you have your base font size set, you can then set all the rest of your font sizes by using ems. Listing 14.3 shows some CSS with web fonts imported and the three headlines given using em sizes.

LISTING 14.3 CSS with Em Sizes

```
@import url(
http://fonts.googleapis.com/css?family=Playfair+Display+SC:900
)
  screen and (min-width: 500px);
* { font-size: 100%; }
h1, h2, h3 { font-family: 'Playfair Display SC', serif; }
h1 { font-size: 2.5em; }
h2 { font-size: 1.75em; }
h3 { font-size: 1.2em; }
```

To make your font sizes responsive, you simply change the font sizes to look good in the various breakpoints of your design. Listing 14.4 shows an example of how this might look.

LISTING 14.4 CSS with Fonts Sized for Different Browser Widths

```
/* CSS Document */
@import url(
http://fonts.googleapis.com/css?family=Playfair+Display+SC:900
)
screen and (min-device-width: 400px);
/* styles for all browser widths */
```

```
* { font-size: 100%; }

h1, h2, h3 { font-family: 'Playfair Display SC', serif; }

h1 { font-size: 2.2em; }
h2 { font-size: 1.75em; }
h3 { font-size: 1.3em; }
p, ul, ol, dl { font-size: 1em; }

/* styles for smartphones and tablets */
@media screen and (min-device-width: 400px) {
  h1 { font-size: 3em; }
  h2 { font-size: 2em; }
  h3 { font-size: 1.5em; }
}
```

Sizing Text

There is more to responsive font sizes than just the size of the fonts. You also have to think about text blocks and how readable they are. So you should look at `line-height` and the scan length of the text lines.

The `line-height` property defines the distance between lines of text. Figure 14.3 shows a web page in two windows; the only difference between the two versions is the line height of the headlines. In the first image, the line height is 0.75, and in the second the line height is 1.

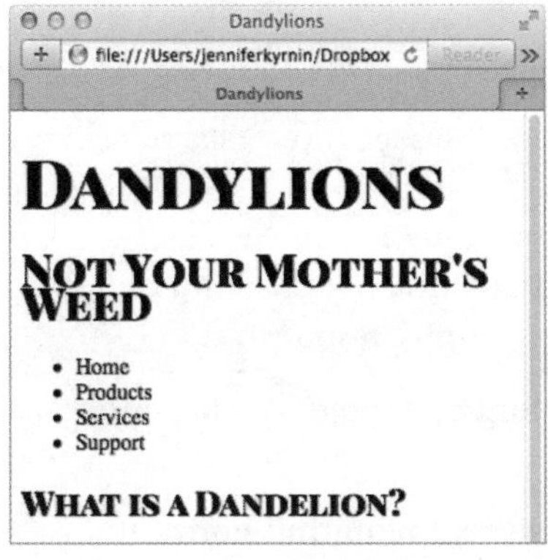

FIGURE 14.3
Line height of .75 on the left and line height of 1 on the right.

Other CSS properties that affect the distance between lines of text are the `margin` properties, especially `margin-top` and `margin-bottom`. If you

NOTE

CSS Resets Make Your CSS Easier to Work With

CSS resets are styles that make sure that every browser is starting with the same style formats. The first time you use CSS resets, you might find them difficult because they do things like remove all the bullets and numbers from your unordered and ordered lists. But resets make your CSS easier in the long run because you know every browser is starting from the same place. One popular and long-standing reset is Chris Meyer's CSS reset at `http://meyerweb.com/eric/tools/css/reset/`.

aren't using CSS resets, these values might be much larger than you want them to be. So it's a good idea to set them in your CSS and media queries, too.

Remember that small devices don't have as much room on the screen as larger ones, so you should adjust the font size, line height, and margins so that more fits on the screen. Figure 14.4 shows how a cell phone only 240px wide might interpret the basic design shown earlier in this chapter. As you can see, the font size is so large that the entire headline does not display on the screen. In order to make the page responsive, you need to make sure the font size is small enough to fit.

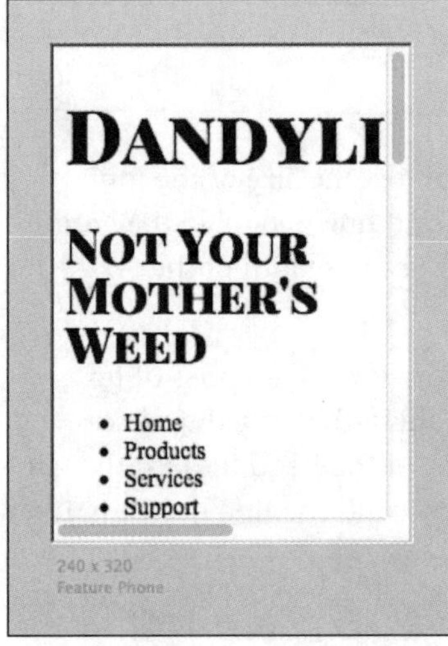

FIGURE 14.4
A Dreamweaver emulation of a small cell phone with fonts too large for the screen.

Once your fonts fit on a small screen, they may be too small on a larger screen, so you should adjust the sizes, line heights, and margins in your media queries to make your typography responsive.

Here are some general guidelines I use for checking and adjusting fonts and text:

- The text should fit on the screen without requiring horizontal scrolling. To adjust this, change the width of your layout elements and the font size.
- Spacing between lines of text should not feel cramped. To adjust this, change `line-height` or `margin-bottom` or `margin-top`.

- Body text lines should be no shorter than 7 words long and no more than 10 words long, or around 45 to 75 characters. To adjust this, change `font-size`. You can also change the `width` setting of the container element, but on small screens, this is usually already 100%, so making the font size slightly smaller often works better.

Listing 14.5 shows some CSS with only a minimal reset where I've adjusted the typography so that the text looks better in smaller screens and larger. Figure 14.5 shows how it might look at different size emulations.

LISTING 14.5 CSS for Adjusted Typography Sizes

```
@import url(
http://fonts.googleapis.com/css?family=Playfair+Display+SC:900
)
screen and (min-width: 400px);
/* styles for all browser widths */
/* very basic reset */
* { font-size: 100%; }
*, *:before, *:after {
  padding: 0;
  margin: 0;
  -webkit-box-sizing: border-box;
  -moz-box-sizing: border-box;
  box-sizing: border-box;
}

body { margin: 0 0.2em; }
h1, h2, h3 {
  font-family: 'Playfair Display SC', serif; line-height: 1.2;
}

h1 { font-size: 2em; }
h2 { font-size: 1.7em; }
h3 { font-size: 1.3em; }
p, ul, ol, dl { font-size: 1em; line-height: 1.275; }

/* nav bar */
nav {
  width: 100%;
  margin: auto;
}
nav ul {
  list-style: none;
  overflow: hidden;
  background: #000;
}
nav li a {
```

```
  display: block;
  float: left;
  width: 14.28%;
  padding: 10px;
  background: #000;
  border-right: 1px solid #fff;
  color: #fbd91f;
  font: 400 13px/1.4 bitstream_vera_serifbold, Baskerville,
    "Palatino Linotype", Palatino, "Times New Roman", serif;
  text-align: center;
  text-decoration: none;
  text-transform: uppercase;
}
/* small text */
nav small {
  color: #aaa;
  font: 100 11px/1 Helvetica, Verdana, Arial, sans-serif;
  text-transform: none;
}
/* default to smallest browser size */
nav ul { display: none; }
nav select { display: inline-block; margin: 0.5em 0; }

/* styles for smartphones and tablets */
@media screen and (min-width: 400px) {
  h1 { font-size: 3em; }
  h2 { font-size: 2em; }
  h3 { font-size: 1.5em; }
}

/* change to full nav for larger screens */
@media screen and (min-width: 481px) {
  nav ul { display: block; }
  nav select { display: none; }
}
```

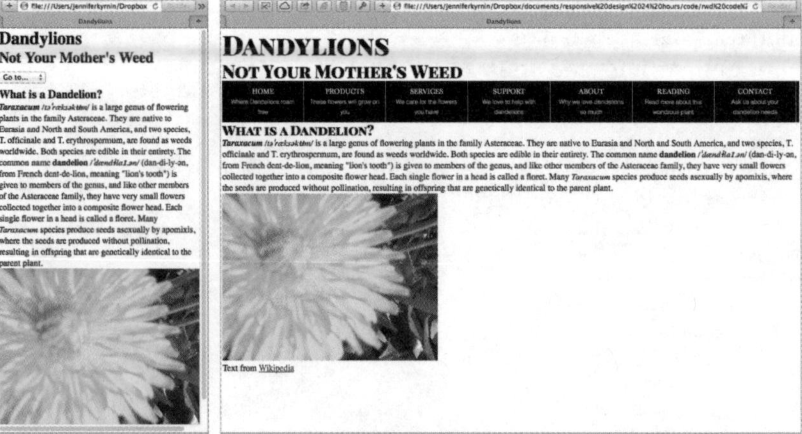

FIGURE 14.5
Safari displaying the same web page in a narrow width and wide width, with differing typography.

Relative Versus Absolute Font Sizes

In the previous section you learned how to adjust the typography of your pages to reflect different browser sizes, and I showed you how to use ems to define your fonts. As mentioned earlier, the em is a relative measure, where each value is relative to the base font size of the element. There are two relative font sizes in CSS level 2: em and ex. Ems are relative to the height of the font, and exes are relative to the font's *x* height.

Most web designers use em as their relative size for both fonts and layout. This allows the design to flex when the customer adjusts the font size so that images and layout stay consistent.

The problem with using relative measures like ems is that the displayed size of an em can change if what the em is relative to changes. Most web designers have come upon this problem at least once in their careers, and it can be incredibly frustrating. Let's look at an example.

Say that you have the following styles:

```
* { font-size: 100%; }
body { font-size: 1.5em; }
article { font-size: 1.3em; }
div { font-size: 1.2em; }
p { font-size: 1.1em; }
```

Which element will have the largest font? The logical answer is that since paragraphs have a size of 1.1 em and that is the smallest number, paragraphs must be the smallest. But as you can see in Figure 14.6, that isn't necessarily the case.

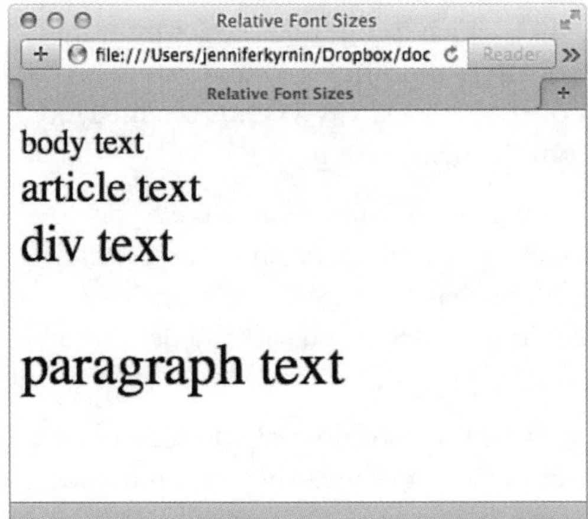

FIGURE 14.6
Safari showing that the body text is the smallest and paragraph text is the largest.

This happens because the font size is set *relative to the current element's font size*. In other words, if the elements are nested within one another, the font size changes relative to the parent element's font size. Listing 14.6 shows the HTML responsible for this problem.

LISTING 14.6 HTML That Generates Confusing Font Sizes

```
<!doctype html>
<html>
  <head>
    <meta charset="UTF-8">
    <title>Relative Font Sizes</title>
    <style>
    * { font-size: 100%; }
    body { font-size: 1.5em; }
    article { font-size: 1.3em; }
    div { font-size: 1.2em; }
    p { font-size: 1.1em; }
    </style>
  </head>

  <body>
    body text
    <article>
      article text
      <div>
        div text
        <p>paragraph text</p>
      </div>
    </article>
  </body>
</html>
```

As you can see, the paragraph is inside the `div` tag, which is inside the `article` tag, which is inside the `body` tag. So the paragraph text will be 1.1 times larger than the `div` text, which is 1.2 times larger than the `article` text, which is 1.3 times larger than the `body` text, which is 1.5 times larger than the default of 100%. Luckily, CSS3 has a remedy for this, and you'll learn about it in the next section.

An absolute size is a size that has a more explicit value based on something concrete, such as example centimeters (cm), millimeters (mm), and inches (in), which all have a concrete value in the real world. If you set your font sizes in millimeters, you should get those actual sizes on the screen.

The problem with using absolute sizes is that not only do they not adjust to the size of a device that's viewing them, they also may not display correctly on screens and other non-fixed media. In other words, an inch might be an inch on one monitor and might be significantly larger or smaller on another monitor. It's better to use absolute sizes for fixed media like print or slides.

New CSS3 Measurement Units

CSS3 added a bunch of new relative measurement units to make it easier for designers to set sizes that are relative to various parts of a document. Table 14.1 shows the new relative measurement units.

TABLE 14.1 New Relative Measurement Units in CSS3

Unit	Relative To
`ch`	The width of the 0 (zero) glyph in the element's font.
`rem`	The font size of the root element
`vw`	1% of the viewport's width
`vh`	1% of the viewport's height
`vmin`	1% of the viewport's smaller dimension
`vmax`	1% of the viewport's larger dimension

These new measures are perfect for RWD designers because they allow you to define the size of your elements based on the viewport size itself (with `vh`, `vw`, `vmin`, and `vmax`) or based on a single font size of the root element (rem).

You can start using rems today with some assurance that it will be understandable by most modern browsers. According to Can I Use (`http://caniuse.com/rem`), the rem unit currently has more than 85% support, including Internet Explorer 9 and up, Safari 5 and up, and Opera Mobile 12 and up.

You use rems the same way you use ems, just with the assumption that the size will always be relative to the root element's size. Figure 14.7 shows the result of the following CSS, which uses rem rather than em:

```
* { font-size: 100%; }
body { font-size: 1.5rem; }
article { font-size: 1.3rem; }
div { font-size: 1.2rem; }
p { font-size: 1.1rem; }
```

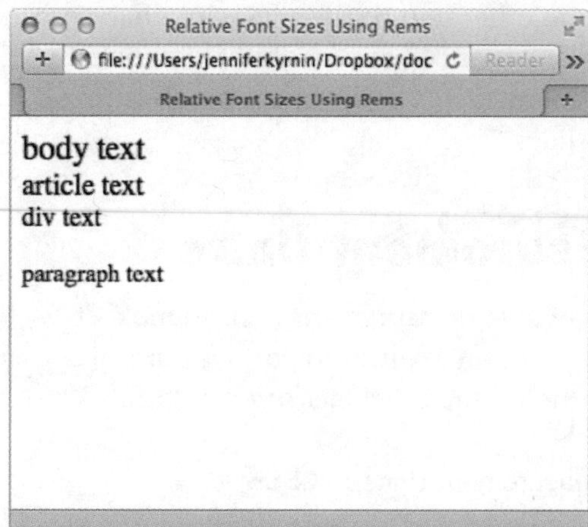

FIGURE 14.7
Safari showing the same page using rems instead of ems.

To be progressive in your support, you should continue to use ems as a fallback option. Simply place two `font-size` properties in your style sheet, with the em value first followed by the rem value. Browsers that support rem will overwrite the em value because of the cascade, and browsers that don't will ignore it and use the em value. But remember that you may have the compounding issue I mentioned in the previous section.

Summary

In this hour you've learned how to add web fonts and make sure they don't overwhelm mobile devices. You've also learned how to adjust font sizes and typography so that your text is legible on both small and large devices. Finally, you've learned about relative and absolute measurement units and how to use the new rem units.

Workshop

The workshop contains quiz questions to help you process what you've learned in this lesson. Try to answer all the questions before you read the answers.

Q&A

Q. Is there a specific font size or line height that you recommend for different screen sizes?

A. No. The challenge with font sizing is that it really depends on the font family you choose as well as the screen sizes. Thick, heavy blackletter fonts need more space between them and a larger font size to be legible than do thin, wispy sans serif fonts. You should adjust the values until you are satisfied, and if you're still not sure, you should show mockups to a few other people and get their thoughts on how readable your designs are.

Q. You didn't include percentage lengths in your list of relative units. Why not?

A. While it's true that percentages are a relative length, what they are relative to depends on the property the percentage is defined on. The W3C considers percentages to be a numeric data type. You can learn more about this at the W3C page `www.w3.org/TR/css3-values/#percentages`.

Q. Are pixels an absolute or relative length unit?

A. This is a tricky question because it changed from CSS level 2 to CSS3. CSS level 2 defines pixels as relative to the device they are viewed on, while CSS3 defines pixels as 1/96 inch. Learn more at the W3C site: `http://www.w3.org/TR/css3-values/#absolute-lengths`.

Quiz

1. How is an inch different from an em?
2. Why should you include a font stack with web fonts?
3. How do you add media queries to an `@import` tag?
4. True or False: The following style sheet will work:

```
* { font-size: 62.5%; }
@import url(fonts.css) all and (min-width:300px);
body { font-size: 1.6rem; }
h1 {font-size: 3in; }
```

5. How wide should a line of text be?

6. Name three relative measurement units in CSS3.
7. Name three absolute measurement units in CSS3.
8. What is `ch` relative to?
9. If a point (`pt`) is 1/72 of an inch, what type of unit is it?
10. If a pica (`pc`) is 12 points, what type of unit is it?

Answers

1. An inch is an absolute unit of measure, while an em is a relative unit.
2. You should always include a font stack that specifies at least one font other than the web font so that if there is a problem loading the web font, the browser uses a font you prefer.
3. You add media queries to the end of the `@import` tag before the semicolon. You add them in the same way you add them to `@media` tags.
4. False. This style sheet will not yield the results you expect because the `@import` rule is not listed first.
5. A line of text should be between 7 and 10 words long, or between 45 and 75 characters.
6. The relative measurement units in CSS3 are `em`, `ex`, `ch`, `rem`, `vw`, `vh`, `vmin`, and `vmax`.
7. The absolute measurement units in CSS3 are `cm`, `mm`, `in`, `pt`, `pc`, and `px`.
8. The `ch` unit is relative to the 0 glyph width in the current element's font.
9. A point is an absolute unit of measure.
10. A pica is an absolute unit of measure.

Exercises

1. Find a web font on Google Fonts or another free web font source (my favorite is Font Squirrel, at `http://www.fontsquirrel.com`) that works well with the web page you're adjusting for this book. Open that page and add the font to it. Convert the font sizes to rems and use em as a fallback.
2. Evaluate the design in a small window like a cell phone and adjust your typography to suit that.
3. Finally, check your other breakpoints and adjust the typography so that it all looks good and is legible.

HOUR 15
Creating and Using Images in RWD

WHAT YOU'LL LEARN IN THIS HOUR:

- What makes an image responsive
- How to change what images different devices see
- Tips for building images that download quickly
- Working with images for Retina devices

In this hour you will start working with a problem that most web designers starting to work with RWD come across sooner or later: what to do about images. Images in responsive designs can be frustrating because they can take up too much space in small screens while being barely visible in larger screens. And they also can cause pages to be really slow when they take a long time to download.

Making Images Responsive

If you are like most other web designers, you learned to write images by using HTML like this:

```
<img src="my-image.jpg" alt="my image" width="100" height="50">
```

The `<img>` tag has a `src` that defines the location of the image, an `alt` that provides alternative text if the image can't display for some reason, and `width` and `height` to define how much space the image would take up in the design. This might result in a page that looks like Figure 15.1, with some fairly large images decorating the page.

But even though this website is responsive and will change based on browser features, the images still remain the same. And in smaller windows, as you can see in Figure 15.2, the large images don't work as well.

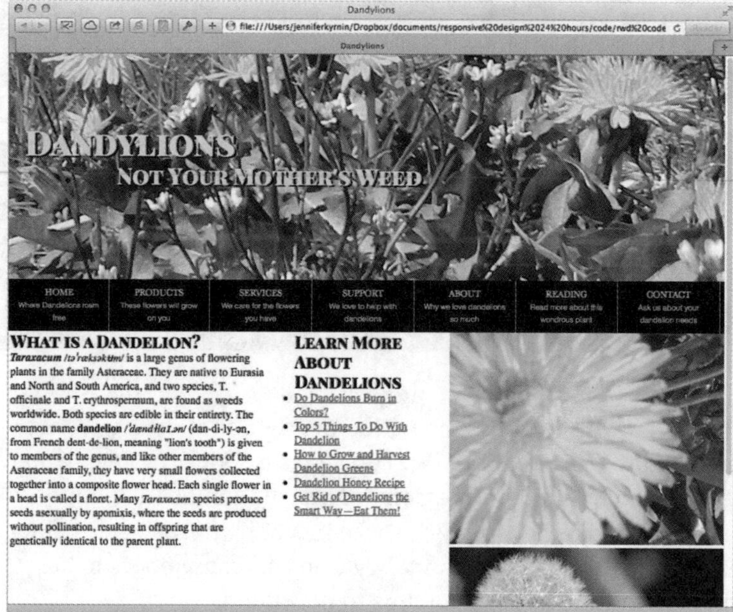
Dandylions
file:///Users/jenniferkyrnin/Dropbox/documents/responsive%20design%2024%20hours/code/rwd%20code
Dandylions
DANDYLIONS
NOT YOUR MOTHER'S WEED
HOME
Where Dandelions roam free
PRODUCTS
These flowers will grow on you
SERVICES
We care for the flowers you have
SUPPORT
We love to help with dandelions
ABOUT
Why we love dandelions so much
READING
Read more about this wondrous plant
CONTACT
Ask us about your dandelion needs
WHAT IS A DANDELION?
Taraxacum /tə'rækəkʉm/ is a large genus of flowering plants in the family Asteraceae. They are native to Eurasia and North and South America, and two species, T. officinale and T. erythrospermum, are found as weeds worldwide. Both species are edible in their entirety. The common name dandelion /'dændɨlaɪ.ən/ (dan-di-ly-ən, from French dent-de-lion, meaning "lion's tooth") is given to members of the genus, and like other members of the Asteraceae family, they have very small flowers collected together into a composite flower head. Each single flower in a head is called a floret. Many Taraxacum species produce seeds asexually by apomixis, where the seeds are produced without pollination, resulting in offspring that are genetically identical to the parent plant.
LEARN MORE ABOUT DANDELIONS
Do Dandelions Burn in Colors?
Top 5 Things To Do With Dandelion
How to Grow and Harvest Dandelion Greens
Dandelion Honey Recipe
Get Rid of Dandelions the Smart Way—Eat Them!

FIGURE 15.1
The Dandylions website with fairly large images.

Dandylions
file:///Users/jenniferkyrnin/Dropbox/documents/responsive%20
Dandylions
DANDYLIONS
NOT YOUR MOTHER'S WEED
HOME
Where Dandelions roam free
PRODUCTS
These flowers will grow on you
SERVICES
We care for the flowers you have
SUPPORT
We love to help with dandelions
ABOUT
Why we love dandelions so much
READING
Read more about this wondrous plant
CONTACT
Ask us about your dandelion needs
WHAT IS A DANDELION?
Taraxacum /tə'rækəkʉm/ is a large genus of flowering plants in the family Asteraceae. They are native to Eurasia and North and South America, and two species, T. officinale and T. erythrospermum, are found as weeds worldwide. Both species are edible in their entirety. The common name dandelion /'dændɨlaɪ.ən/ (dan-di-ly-ən, from French dent-de-lion, meaning "lion's tooth") is given to members of the genus, and like other members of the Asteraceae family, they have very small flowers collected together into a composite flower head. Each single flower in a head is called a floret. Many Taraxacum species produce seeds asexually by apomixis, where the seeds are produced without pollination, resulting in offspring that are genetically identical to the parent plant.
LEARN MORE ABOUT DANDELIONS
Do Dandelions Burn in Colors?
Top 5 Things To Do With Dandelion
How to Grow and Harvest Dandelion Greens
Dandelion Honey Recipe
Get Rid of Dandelions the Smart Way—Eat Them!

FIGURE 15.2
The Dandylions website in a smaller browser window.

The main problem with the images in Figure 15.2 is that they are too big for the screen. The images don't flex with the design. In fact, they are not responsive at all. There are three ways you can deal with the images in a responsive web design:

- Use the images as you always would.
- Set the image width to something flexible.
- Change what images are displayed, depending on device properties.

The only advantage of the first solution is that it's easy. The other two solutions are much better because they allow the images to be responsive.

Using Flexible-Width Images

Using flexible-width images is often the best solution because it's almost as easy as doing nothing and results in images flexing with the browser width. All you need to do is set the `width` and `max-width` of images to `100%` and the `height` to `auto`:

```
img { width: 100%; max-width: 100%; height: auto; }
```

You set the `img` rule in your global style sheet before you set any media queries, so that the rule applies to all devices. Then you test your design in several browser widths and see what happens. Chances are you'll need to add some container width information so that the images don't blow out the entire browser window in some sizes. Figure 15.3 shows how my yellow dandelion image ended up as wide as the browser window by mistake.

Listing 15.1 shows the HTML for the page in Figure 15.3. As you can see, some container `<div>` tags surround various portions of the page so that they can be styled separately. These are `<div id="bodyContent">`, `<div class="sidebars">`, and `<div id="main">`. Of course, other tags act as containers for the images, including the `<article>`, `<aside>`, and `<p>` tags.

CAUTION

Always Set the Height to Auto

When you add an image, most web page editors automatically include the `width` and `height` attributes on the `<img>` tag. CSS overrides these values, but if you don't set a height for your images, you will end up with some really ugly images. Setting the height to `auto` tells the browser to use a height that has the same ratio as the original image.

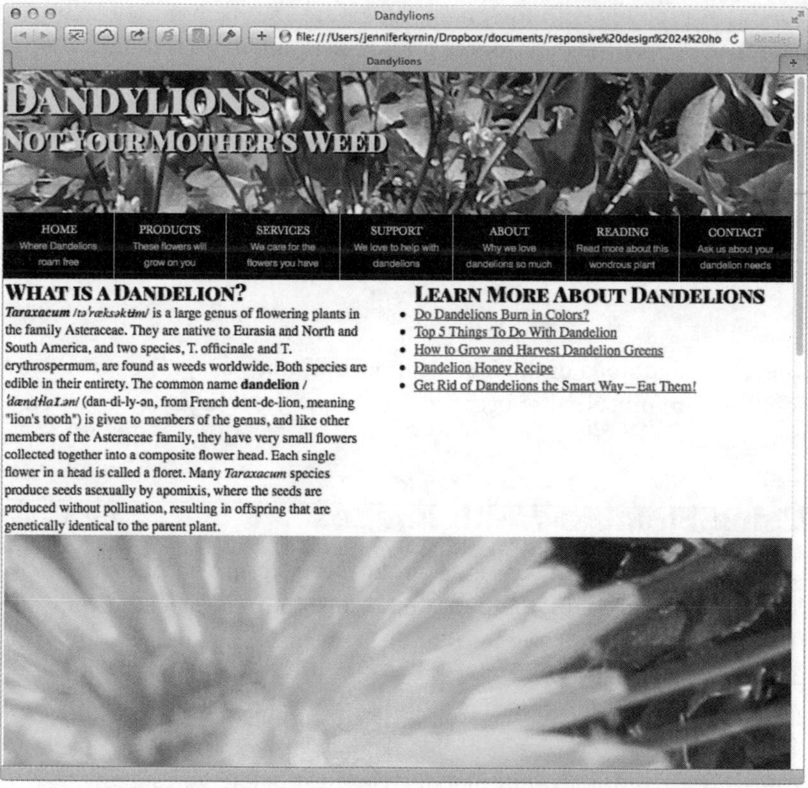
Dandylions
file:///Users/jenniferkyrnin/Dropbox/documents/responsive%20design%2024%20ho
Dandylions
DANDYLIONS
NOT YOUR MOTHER'S WEED
HOME
Where Dandelions roam free
PRODUCTS
These flowers will grow on you
SERVICES
We care for the flowers you have
SUPPORT
We love to help with dandelions
ABOUT
Why we love dandelions so much
READING
Read more about this wondrous plant
CONTACT
Ask us about your dandelion needs
WHAT IS A DANDELION?
Taraxacum /tə'ræksəkʉm/ is a large genus of flowering plants in the family Asteraceae. They are native to Eurasia and North and South America, and two species, T. officinale and T. erythrospermum, are found as weeds worldwide. Both species are edible in their entirety. The common name dandelion / 'dændɨlaɪ.ən/ (dan-di-ly-ən, from French dent-de-lion, meaning "lion's tooth") is given to members of the genus, and like other members of the Asteraceae family, they have very small flowers collected together into a composite flower head. Each single flower in a head is called a floret. Many Taraxacum species produce seeds asexually by apomixis, where the seeds are produced without pollination, resulting in offspring that are genetically identical to the parent plant.
LEARN MORE ABOUT DANDELIONS
Do Dandelions Burn in Colors?
Top 5 Things To Do With Dandelion
How to Grow and Harvest Dandelion Greens
Dandelion Honey Recipe
Get Rid of Dandelions the Smart Way—Eat Them!

FIGURE 15.3
The image at the bottom needs a container width.

LISTING 15.1 HTML with Containers for Images

```
<!doctype html>
<html>
  <head>
    <meta charset="UTF-8">
    <title>Dandylions</title>
    <link href="rwd code 15.1.css" rel="stylesheet">
    <script
src="http://ajax.googleapis.com/ajax/libs/jquery/1.6.2/jquery.min.js">
    </script>
  </head>
  <body>
    <div id="main">
      <header>
        <h1>Dandylions</h1>
        <h2>Not Your Mother's Weed</h2>
      </header>
      <nav>
        <ul id="navigation">
          <li><a href="#">Home<br>
          <small>Where Dandelions roam free</small></a></li>
```

```
    <li><a href="#">Products<br>
    <small>These flowers will grow on you</small></a></li>
    <li><a href="#">Services<br>
    <small>We care for the flowers you have</small></a></li>
    <li><a href="#">Support<br>
    <small>We love to help with dandelions</small></a></li>
    <li><a href="#">About<br>
    <small>Why we love dandelions so much</small></a></li>
    <li><a href="#">Reading<br>
    <small>Read more about this wondrous plant</small></a></li>
    <li><a href="#">Contact<br>
    <small>Ask us about your dandelion needs</small></a></li>
  </ul>
  <select id="mobileNav">
    <option value="">Go to...</option>
    <option value="/home">Home</option>
    <option value="/products">Products</option>
    <option value="/services">Services</option>
    <option value="/support">Support</option>
    <option value="/about">About</option>
    <option value="/articles">Reading</option>
    <option value="/contact">Contact</option>
  </select>
</nav>
<div id="bodyContent" class="clearfix">
  <article id="mainarticle">
    <h3>What is a Dandelion?</h3>
    <p><span class="pronounce"><strong><em>Taraxacum</em></strong>
    <em>/tə'ræksəkʉm/</em></span> is a large genus of flowering
    plants in the family Asteraceae. They are native to Eurasia and
    North and South America, and two species, T. officinale and T.
    erythrospermum, are found as weeds worldwide. Both species are
    edible in their entirety. The common name <span
    class="pronounce"><strong>dandelion</strong>
    <em>/'dændɨlaɪ.ən/</em></span> (dan-di-ly-ən, from French
    dent-de-lion, meaning "lion's tooth") is given to members of
    the genus, and like other members of the Asteraceae family,
    they have very small flowers collected together into a
    composite flower head. Each single flower in a head is called a
    floret. Many <em>Taraxacum</em> species produce seeds asexually
    by apomixis, where the seeds are produced without pollination,
    resulting in offspring that are genetically identical to the
    parent plant.</p>
  </article>
  <div class="sidebars">
    <aside id="links">
      <h3>Learn More About Dandelions</h3>
      <ul>
      <li><a href="do-dandelions-burn-in-colors.htm">Do Dandelions
      Burn in Colors?</a></li>
      <li><a href="10-uses-for-dandelions.htm">Top 5 Things To Do
      With Dandelion</a></li>
      <li><a href="How-To-Grow-Dandelion-Greens.htm">How to Grow
```

```
            and Harvest Dandelion Greens</a></li>
            <li><a href="bljelly9.htm">Dandelion Honey Recipe</a></li>
            <li><a href="kill_dandelions_2.htm">Get Rid of Dandelions the
            Smart Way&#8212;Eat Them!</a></li>
            </ul>
          </aside>
          <aside id="sidebar">
            <p><img src="images/dandy.jpg" width="400" height="300"
            alt=""></p>
            <p><img src="images/seeded.jpg" width="400" height="300"
            alt=""></p>
          </aside>
        </div><!-- end sidebars -->
      </div> <!-- end bodyContent -->
      <footer>
        <p>Text from
        <a href="http://en.wikipedia.org/wiki/Dandelion">
        Wikipedia</a></p>
      </footer>
    </div><!-- end main -->
    <script>
    $(function() {
      $("nav select").change(function() {
        window.location = $(this).find("option:selected").val();
      });
    });
    </script>
  </body>
</html>
```

Setting the width so that the images flex with their containers works well, but you need to upload images that are large so that they look good on large-screen monitors. But remember that the larger you make the images, the longer they will take to download.

Changing the Images Displayed

In order to create a site that has responsive images that aren't too big for small devices to download, you need to change which images are displayed for various devices. This is especially true for images sent to mobile devices on mobile networks. Even the fastest cell phone networks are not as fast as cable and other high-speed Internet connections to homes and businesses, and large images slow pages significantly on these networks.

One of the most common ways that many designers handle loading images is to not put them in the HTML but rather use some other

HTML element, give it specific dimensions, and then put the image on the background. This works best for design elements like headers and decorations, but it doesn't work as well for content images.

When you have an area that needs a background image, you need to decide how many versions of that background you want. I like to use a small, low-resolution version for small devices and a larger, high-resolution image for tablets and computers. Listing 15.2 shows a portion of the CSS that would show a small image for the dandelions header for small-screen devices and a large image for large-screen devices.

LISTING 15.2 CSS for Adjusting Background Images

```
/* CSS Document */

/*header */
header {
  background: url(images/dandy-header-bg-small.png) bottom left
no-repeat;
  color: #EDEE6A;
  text-shadow: 3px 2px #000000;
}

/* styles for smartphones and tablets and desktops */
@media screen and (min-width: 400px)  {
  header {
    background: url(images/dandy-header-bg.png) bottom left
no-repeat;
  }
}
```

As you can see, I put the big image inside a media query for screens at least 400 pixels wide (`@media screen and (min-width: 400px)`). The default image is in the global styles for all devices.

Another way to change how the images display is to hide either entire images or portions of images in smaller screens. While I don't recommend removing images that are part of the content, if you have images that are design elements, you can hide them with the `display: none;` style property so that they don't take up the design space on smaller screens.

You can also crop images by using CSS so that only a portion of each image displays. Figure 15.4 shows the same image twice on the page. The first one is just in a paragraph tag, and the second is in a paragraph that is cropped and positioned to get the seed floret better centered. Listing 15.3 shows the HTML for this page.

CAUTION

Hide the Parent Element, Not the Image

When you're building a responsive website, it can be tempting to set large images to not display in smaller screens by using the style `display: none`. But *they still download* to the device. So if the reason you were turning off the display was so that smaller screens don't have to download them, that doesn't work.

What does work is hiding the parent element that contains the image. In other words, say that you have the following HTML:

```
<div class="largeImage">
<img src="largeImage.jpg"
alt="large image">
</div>
```

If you set the container element `<div class="largeImage">` to `display: none;`, that will stop the image from downloading in most mobile browsers.

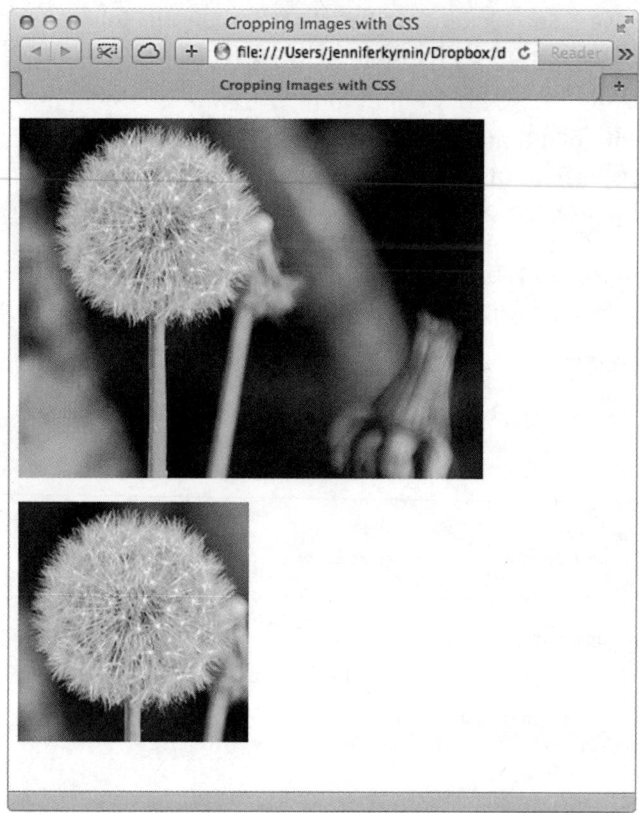

FIGURE 15.4
An image shown full size and cropped with CSS.

LISTING 15.3 HTML and CSS for Cropping an Image

```
<!doctype html>
<html>
<head>
  <meta charset="UTF-8">
  <title>Cropping Images with CSS</title>
  <style>
  .cropped {
    width: 200px;
    height: 200px;
    overflow: hidden;
  }
  .cropped img {
    position: relative;
    right: 20px;
  }
  </style>
</head>
<body>
  <p>
```

```
  <img src="images/seeded.jpg" width="400" height="300" alt=""/>
  </p>
  <p class="cropped">
  <img src="images/seeded.jpg" width="400" height="300" alt=""/>
  </p>
</body>
</html>
```

As you can see, the cropped image is in a small paragraph with the `width` and `height` settings defined smaller than the image. The important part is that `overflow` is set to `hidden`. This hides any bits of image that are larger. Then, with CSS positioning, you can move the image around inside the paragraph to show just the part of the image you want to display.

There are also tools that will help you display specific images to specific devices. I discuss these in more detail in Hour 21, "Tools for Creating Responsive Web Designs."

Improving Download Speeds

Even with all the methods already discussed for showing different images, the images are still being downloaded to every device that sees them. So it's a good idea to make sure your images are as small as possible.

These are a few rules of thumb for creating images that will download quickly:

- Use PNG or JPG for photographs.
- Use PNG or GIF for flat color images (clip art and illustrations).
- Crop images to keep the dimensions as small as possible.
- Use as few colors (in GIF and PNG images) as possible.
- Use the "save for web" option that's available in most image-editing programs.

Building and Using Retina-Ready Images

When Apple announced its Retina screens, it caused a lot of consternation among web designers because suddenly images that had looked fine before became grainy and ugly on the Retina screens. But while it's tempting to just switch all your images to high-resolution, Retina-ready images, doing so is a mistake.

Most devices, including desktop computers, don't have Retina or high-resolution screens, so instead you should focus first on the smallest, least capable screens and then progressively enhance the pages for more capable devices.

Here are some good rules for dealing with Retina devices:

- **Start with CSS and avoid images as much as possible.** Replace everything you can with CSS, including rounded corners, gradients, borders, and so on.
- **Optimize your images.** Just because an image is high resolution doesn't mean it should be gigabytes in size. Use standard image optimization techniques to keep your images as small as possible.
- **Use low-resolution images as your first choice.** As mentioned earlier, there are a lot more non-Retina screens than Retina screens, so you should save the high-resolution images for the screens that can display them.
- **Use resolution-independent solutions as your second choice.** Methods like using scalable vector graphics (SVG) and using special characters and fonts with `@font-face` can give you visual imagery that is resolution independent.
- **Use tools to update images on-the-fly.** Hour 21 describes some tools you can use to detect and download only the images that a viewing device can handle.

What Makes an Image "Retina Ready"?

Retina images have a higher resolution than normal images because there are more pixels in the same amount of space in a Retina image as in a normal image.

When you create a Retina image, you don't create the same image with a higher resolution. Instead, you double the size of the original image; for example, you would resize a 100×100 image to 200×200. Then when the image is displayed on a Retina device, it is shown at the original 100×100 dimensions.

TRY IT YOURSELF ▼

Convert an Image to a Retina Image

For the following steps, you need an image that you'd like to convert into a Retina image. You will also need a recent version of Photoshop. When you have these things, follow these steps:

1. Open your image in Photoshop.
2. Open the Image Size dialog by pressing Ctrl+Alt+I or Cmd+Opt+I.
3. Change the width to 200% in the drop-down box.
4. Change the resample drop-down to Nearest Neighbor and make sure it stays checked.
5. Save the file with @2x in the file name right before the extension. For example, you would save `header.jpg` as `header@2x.jpg`.

This method doesn't produce the best results, but it's faster than going back to your vector art program and redrawing all your images.

Using Media Queries to Serve Retina Images

Once you have all your images created as Retina versions, you'll want to get them on your web pages, but you should display them only to devices that can see them. An easy way to do this is with CSS media queries. Webkit offers the browser-prefixed media query `min-device-pixel-ratio`. Here is an example:

```
@media only screen and (-webkit-min-device-pixel-ratio: 2),
  only screen and (min-device-pixel-ratio: 2) {
  header {
    background-image: url(images/header@2x.png);
    background-size: 2000px 1000px;
  }
}
```

This tells the browser that if this is a Retina display (`min-device-pixel-ratio: 2`), it should use the `header@2x.png` file resized down to the original dimensions of 2000×1000px.

Don't forget to use the `background-size` property so that the image displays at the original size; otherwise, you'll get the same fuzziness you see in non-Retina images, but the image will be twice as large.

Using Retina.js

Another way you can automate using Retina images is with a simple JavaScript script called Retina.js (http://imulus.github.io/retinajs/). Download the file and install it on your web server. Then include this line of JavaScript at the bottom of your document:

```
<script type="text/javascript" src="/scripts/retina.js"></script>
```

Now, when someone on a Retina device visits your page, the script will automatically swap out all images to the Retina versions. Just make sure that both your Retina images and your normal images are saved in the same directory.

Creating Images in SVG

Scalable vector graphics (SVG) make great Retina-ready images because they are not bitmaps and so can scale up and down without any loss of quality.

You can create SVG images in vector image programs like Illustrator and then include them in HTML5 documents just as you would any other image, like this:

```
<img src="myImage.svg" width="100" height="200" alt="my SVG image">
```

This method works in all modern browsers. The only browsers you might have trouble with are Internet Explorer 8 and lower and Android 2.3 and lower.

Using `@font-face` for Custom Icons

One of the great things about web fonts is that they don't limit you to alphabetic glyphs. People have made font sets out of all sorts of things, and if you have a web font version of a font set, you can use its characters as scalable images on your web pages.

Using icon fonts as images on a site is a great solution for Retina devices because the fonts scale without blurring, you can change colors with CSS, and you can add other styles to them (like borders, background colors, shadows, gradients, and so on) just as you can to text.

There are lots of icon fonts available on the web. CSS-Tricks has a great list of free and inexpensive icon fonts; see http://css-tricks.com/flat-icons-icon-fonts/. See Hour 14, "Responsive Fonts and Typography," for more information on using web fonts.

Summary

In this hour you've learned more about making your images responsive and how to optimize your images so that they display both clearly and quickly on all devices.

You've learned about Retina images and how to make them from your existing images. You've also learned of a number of alternative solutions to getting images to work well for Retina devices and non-Retina devices.

Workshop

The workshop contains quiz questions to help you process what you've learned in this lesson. Try to answer all the questions before you read the answers.

Q&A

Q. What is the optimal size for images on the web?

A. There is no good answer to this question because there are so many variables. When you're deciding how big to make an image, you need to take into account things like how many images are already on the page, whether you have mostly mobile customers, and how important an image is to the page.

Q. I was taught never to let the browser resize images. Why is it okay to do this now?

A. The reality is that you can still end up with some horrendous-looking images when you let the browser do the scaling. This is most common when the browser increases the size of the image beyond the original dimensions. The best way to deal with this is to set `max-width` so that it's no larger than the actual width of the image. To do this on a site-wide scale, you should re-create all your images with the same large width (for example, 1500px or wider). Then you can set `max-width` on your image style rule to `max-width: 1500px;`. Then, even when someone views the page in a huge monitor, the image will not look distorted. And if you're starting with a small image, you'll need to resize it with care so that you don't end up with a low-quality image that web browsers will just make worse. You can find out more in the article "Increasing Image Resolution" by Sue Chastain at `http://graphics-soft.about.com/cs/resolution/a/increasingres.htm`.

Q. In the examples in this lesson, you made the images responsive by setting the width to 100%, but what if I want an image to be a specific width?

A. You don't have to set the width to 100%. You can leave it at the setting the browser determines for it or whatever the HTML attributes say the width should be. But for an image to remain responsive and not over-power a layout, you should always include the `max-width:100%;` and the `height: auto;` styles.

Q. I've heard a lot about the `<picture>` tag for responsive images. Why didn't you mention it in this hour?

A. The `<picture>` tag is an option that the W3C is evaluating for assisting web designers in creating images that are truly responsive. The idea is to use the `<picture>` tag similarly to how you use the `<video>` tag. You define a picture and then provide multiple `<source>` files with media queries embedded to define which source is for which devices. The problem is that no modern browsers have implemented the `<picture>` tag. While it is an interesting idea, it can't really be used just yet.

Quiz

1. Why should you use responsive images?
2. Name one way you can display images in a responsive design.
3. How do you make an image have a flexible width?
4. How can you make an image responsive but use a fixed width?
5. Why do you set `max-width`?
6. What should you set the `height` to?
7. Name two rules you should follow when adding Retina-ready images.
8. True or False: A Retina-ready image is just an image with a higher resolution.
9. What is the media query to select for Retina devices?
10. How do you use `@font-face` for images?

Answers

1. You should use responsive images so that your images flex with your designs and don't look bad on very large or very small screens.
2. When you're using responsive design, there are three options for displaying images: Use images as you always have, with no responsive aspects; make the images flexible to fit the layout; or change what images are displayed to fit the device.
3. To give an image a flexible width, you set `width:100%;` and `max-width:100%;`.
4. If you want your images to be responsive but have a fixed width, you can set `width` to a specific value and then set `max-width` to `100%`.

5. You should always set `max-width` to `100%` (or less) so that the images don't take up more room than they are allocated in the design.

6. You should always set `height` to `auto` so that the images remain proportional.

7. In order for your designs to use progressive enhancement, you should follow these rules: Start with CSS and avoid images as much as possible. Optimize your images. Use low-resolution images as your first choice. Use resolution-independent solutions as your second choice. Use tools to update images on-the-fly.

8. False. A Retina image is an image that has been resized up to create a larger version of the image, which is then displayed in the smaller dimensions.

9. The media query to select for Retina devices is `min-device-pixel-ratio: 2` with the browser-prefixed version `-webkit-min-device-pixel-ratio: 2` as a backup.

10. You get an icon font (sometimes called wingdings or dingbats) and use the glyphs as images on your site. Using fonts as images is useful because you can scale them as large or small as you need, and you can style them like text.

Exercises

1. Open the website you're working on in your web page editor. Add a line to your CSS for all devices to make your images flexible. Then test your pages and fix any issues you might find in the design by adding container elements where you need them in the HTML and giving them explicit widths.

2. Create Retina-ready images for each of the images on your site and use the `@2x` file-naming convention. Then use either media queries or the `retina.js` script to make your site Retina ready.

HOUR 16

Videos and Other Media in RWD

WHAT YOU'LL LEARN IN THIS HOUR:

- How to add video to a web page with HTML5
- How to make HTML5 video responsive
- How to display different videos to different devices
- How to create a video background for a page
- How to make an embedded YouTube video responsive

One challenge that responsive web designers face is how to make videos, which have fixed widths and heights, responsive. In this hour you'll learn that HTML5 makes this easy, but since many video services don't use HTML5, you need to know another way.

How to Make Videos Responsive

There are two ways you can embed videos in web pages. You can use the older method of embedding an `<object>` or `<iframe>` or you can use the HTML5 `<video>` tag.

Using HTML5 to Embed Videos in Web Pages

When you're adding video to web pages, the best way is to start with HTML5. To do this, you use the `<video>` tag. Here is the HTML for adding a video in HTML5:

```
<video controls>
    <source src="video.mp4">
</video>
```

You use the `<source>` tag for as many versions of the video as you have. Then if a browser can't play MP4 videos, but it can play WebM, you can have that version, too. In the book *Sams Teach Yourself HTML5 Mobile Application Development in 24 Hours*, I have an entire hour devoted to adding HTML5 video. There you can learn even more about fallback options, creating custom video controls, and other HTML5 video tags and attributes.

If you use the HTML above, you'll notice that the video is not responsive at all. Figure 16.1 shows how the video displays in a narrow browser window. It forces the user to scroll horizontally, and that's not feasible when watching a video.

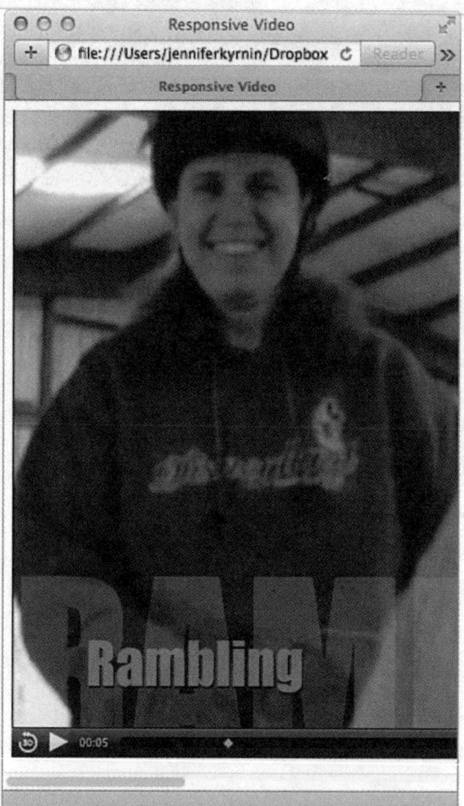

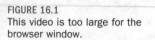

FIGURE 16.1
This video is too large for the browser window.

Adding CSS to Make HTML5 Video Responsive

The advantage of using HTML5 to add videos is that you can add CSS just as you do for images (see Hour 15, "Creating and Using Images in RWD"). Listing 16.1 shows some HTML and CSS to make a video responsive inside a simple web design. And Figure 16.2 shows how that listing will look in a browser the same width as Figure 16.1.

LISTING 16.1 HTML5 and CSS for Responsive Video

```
<!doctype html>
<html>
<head>
<meta charset="UTF-8">
<title>Responsive Video</title>
<style>
#main { width: 100%; }
video {
  max-width: 100%;
  height: auto;
}
@media screen and (min-width:401px) {
  #main {
    max-width: 900px;
  }
}
</style>
</head>

<body>
  <div id="main">
  <h1>Ramblin' Rambler</h1>
  <video controls>
    <source src="images/rambler2006.mp4">
  </video>
  </div>
</body>
</html>
```

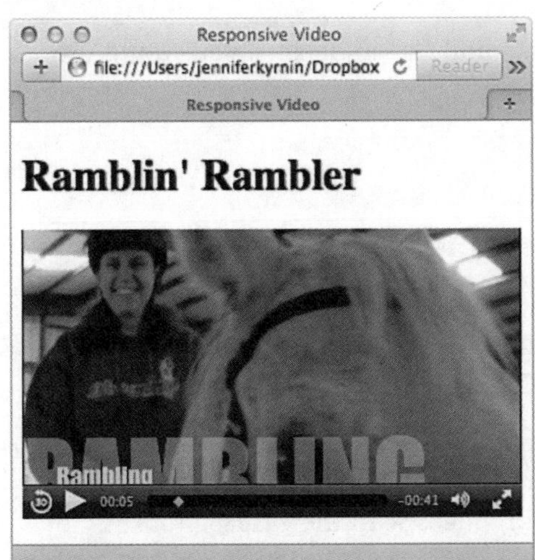

FIGURE 16.2
The video now responds to the browser size.

By adding the following CSS, you tell the browser to set all video tags to no more than 100% of the browser width, with the height following the proportions of the video:

```
video {
  max-width: 100%;
  height: auto;
}
```

The video will then display as big as it can within the container while staying in the correct proportion for viewing.

Using Media Queries to Display Different Sources

One great feature of using HTML5 videos is that you can display better source videos for different devices. You might want to display HD videos for Retina devices, and you might want to display smaller videos to smaller screens so they don't have to download as much.

All you need to do to determine what videos should display and where to use the `media` attribute on your `<source>` tags. Then you put the appropriate media query in that attribute. For example, to display an HD source file to Retina devices, you would use this:

```
<source src="videoHD.mp4" media="(-webkit-min-device-pixel-ratio: 2),
(min-resolution: 192dpi)">
```

Or to display a smaller video to small screen devices, you would use this:

```
<source src="video-small.mp4" media="(max-width: 400px)">
```

HTML5 Video Backgrounds

One other trick that HTML5 allows is using video files as backgrounds on your web pages. And all you need is your video files, the HTML5 `<video>` tag, and some simple CSS.

You should add your video with as many source files as you can so that it's supported widely. I recommend using at least MP4 and WebM source files. Then you insert your videos with the `<video>` tag:

```
<video id="videoBG" preload="auto" autoplay loop muted volume="0">
```

The important parts of this line are that the video is set to `autoplay` so that it starts automatically when the page loads, `loop` is set so that the video starts over when it ends, and you have an ID on it that you'll remember for the CSS to attach to. I recommend setting the volume to zero and adding the `muted` attribute as well so that you don't annoy any visitors who are at work or another place where sound on a website would be annoying. Then you load your source files as you normally would.

Listing 16.2 shows the CSS you should add to your style sheet.

LISTING 16.2 CSS for Background Videos

```
#videoBG {
  position: absolute;
  top: 0;
  left: 0;
  min-width: 100%;
  min-height: 100%;
  width: auto;
  height: auto;
  z-index: -1000;
  overflow: hidden;
}
```

By setting the video to an absolute position at the bottom-right corner of the screen with the minimum width and height both set to 100%, you stretch the video across the screen. Then `z-index:-1000;` ensures that the video will be below everything else on the screen. Finally, using `overflow:hidden` ensures that the video is clipped to the space on the screen.

Making YouTube Videos Responsive

The problem with using HTML5 is that not all videos that are available for use on the web use HTML5. And you might not have access to the MP4 files to upload to your website. Most people, instead of using HTML5 videos, use a video service like YouTube to host and play their videos because it's both easier and takes up less bandwidth on their web hosting server.

▼ TRY IT YOURSELF

Embed a YouTube Video in Your Web Page

When you find a YouTube video you want to share on your website, you need to follow the instructions on YouTube to embed it. Here is how you do it:

1. Find a video on YouTube that you want to embed in your site.
2. Below the video, look for the gray link that says Share. Click on it. YouTube opens a section with a bunch of social media links.
3. Because you want to put this video on a web page, click on the Embed link.
4. Choose your options and then select the HTML code and copy it onto your web page. It will look something like this:

```
<iframe width="560" height="315"
src="http://www.youtube.com/embed/eGFGG-xKT_A?rel=0"
frameborder="0" allowfullscreen></iframe>
```

As you can see, this video is in an `<iframe>` tag rather than an HTML5 `<video>` tag. It might also be in an `<object>` or `<embed>` tag, depending on the options you chose.

If you try to set the same CSS for the `<iframe>` (or `<object>` or `<embed>`) as you did for the HTML5 video, it won't work. That's because these elements essentially have a fixed width and height that can't be adjusted. But with a few simple CSS styles, you can make these video elements responsive as well.

The trick is to use a container around the embedded video. Then you give that container a bottom padding between 50% and 60% and hide the overflow. It's a good idea to explicitly set the position to `relative` so that the browser doesn't get confused.

Then, any `<iframe>`, `<object>`, or `<embed>` tag inside the container element should be given a position of `absolute`, set to the top-left part of the container. You set the width and height to 100%, and the video will then flex responsively. Listing 16.3 shows the HTML and CSS in action.

LISTING 16.3 HTML and CSS for Responsive YouTube Videos

```
<!doctype html>
<html>
<head>
<meta charset="UTF-8">
<title>Responsive YouTube Embedded Video</title>
<style>
#main { width: 100%; }
.videoContainer {
  position: relative;
  padding-bottom: 55%;
```

```
  height: 0;
  overflow: hidden;
}
.videoContainer iframe,
.videoContainer object,
.videoContainer embed {
  position: absolute;
  top: 0;
  left: 0;
  width: 100%;
  height: 100%;
}

@media screen and (min-width:401px) {
  #main {
    max-width: 900px;
  }
}
</style>
</head>

<body>
  <div id="main">
  <h1>Cruising with a Drone</h1>
    <div class="videoContainer">
      <iframe width="853" height="480"
      src="http://www.youtube-nocookie.com/embed/eGFGG-xKT_A"
      frameborder="0" allowfullscreen></iframe>
    </div>
  </div>
</body>
</html>
```

If you have other objects on your web pages that use the `<object>` or `<embed>` or `<iframe>` tags, you can use this technique to make them responsive as well. Be sure to test things like Java applets to make sure they work as you expect at different sizes.

Summary

In this hour you've learned how to add fixed-dimension videos and objects into a responsive web design and have them be responsive. You've learned how easy the HTML5 `<video>` tag makes it to show responsive video. Plus you've learned how to use the HTML5 `<video>` tag as a background on your web designs.

You've also learned how to add videos in other elements, like `<iframe>`, to make embedded YouTube videos responsive. You no longer have to worry that your responsive web designs will be broken by a video breaking the layout container.

Workshop

The workshop contains quiz questions to help you process what you've learned in this lesson. Try to answer all the questions before you read the answers.

Q&A

Q. I noticed that you positioned the background video at the top left of the container. Can I position a video at the bottom or right side of the page?

A. Yes. Where you position it affects how a video will display on the screen. If most of the interesting features are on the right side, then positioning a video from the right and bottom makes more sense. If the video is getting clipped in a strange location on some of your screens, you can adjust the positioning to be where you want it.

Q. What browsers support HTML5 video and the YouTube embedding you mention in this hour?

A. Both of these techniques are supported by all modern browsers except Internet Explorer 8 (and lower). You can check many aspects of HTML5 and CSS support, as well as other things, on the site `http://caniuse.com`.

Quiz

1. Name the two HTML5 tags you use to embed video on a web page.
2. What is the best way to embed video?
3. True or False: You can have many `<source>` tags inside a `<video>` tag.
4. True or False: You use the same CSS to make the `<video>` tag responsive as you do to make the `<img>` tag responsive.
5. True or False: You use the `media` attribute on the `<video>` tag to assign videos to different devices.
6. Why do you set video backgrounds to `autoplay`?
7. Name three of the four most important style rules for creating a background video.
8. True or False: You can use the same CSS for YouTube videos as you use for HTML5 videos to make them responsive.

9. What HTML tags can you use to embed videos?
10. What do you put around the YouTube `<iframe>` tag to allow the video to be responsive?

Answers

1. You use the `<video>` and `<source>` tags to embed HTML5 video.
2. The best way to embed video is with the HTML5 `<video>` tag.
3. True. You can have as many `<source>` tags as you have source video files.
4. True. You use the `max-width:100%;` and `height:auto;` properties on your `<video>` tags, which is the same way you make `<img>` tags responsive.
5. True. The `media` attribute lets you add media queries to your `<source>` tags.
6. You set video backgrounds to `autoplay` because then they will start when the browser loads. There are no user controls on these videos, so they need to start automatically.
7. The four most important styles for a background video are `min-width:100%;`, `min-height:100%;`, `z-index:-1000;`, and `overflow: hidden;`.
8. False. If you use the same CSS as for `<video>` tags, the YouTube videos will ignore it and will not be responsive.
9. You can use `<video>`, `<embed>`, `<object>`, and `<iframe>` to embed videos on web pages.
10. You use a container element, usually a `<div>` that you style with some bottom padding, zero height, and the overflow hidden.

Exercises

1. Create a page with a video background. Find a video that you think would be interesting as a background and generate at least an MP4 version of it. For best compatibility, you should also create a WebM copy.
2. If the website you are working on for this book contains any video pages, make them responsive. Add container elements around non-`<video>` elements and add the CSS to make them and HTML5 videos responsive.

HOUR 17
Tables in Responsive Web Design

Data tables are often very big and can thus be very difficult to handle in a responsive design, especially for small devices. If you are working in a mobile-first progressive enhancement mode, you may want to avoid data tables completely, but some sites really need them.

In this hour you will learn some of the techniques designers use to adjust their designs so that data tables can still be used with some effectiveness on small-screen as well as large-screen devices.

WHAT YOU'LL LEARN IN THIS HOUR:

- Why making tables responsive is difficult
- What you need to know to adjust your tables to make them responsive
- Three ways to make your tables responsive
- How to responsively use tables for layout
- A technique for creating tables out of HTML that is not a `<table>` tag

Tables on Small Devices

The problem with tables is that they can be very wide, and wide tables can be hard to read on small-screen devices. Figure 17.1 shows a simple three-column table that is nearly impossible to read when viewed on an iPhone.

As you can see, if you show the entire table in the window, the text is too small to read. To read the text you need to zoom in, but then you have to scroll horizontally and vertically.

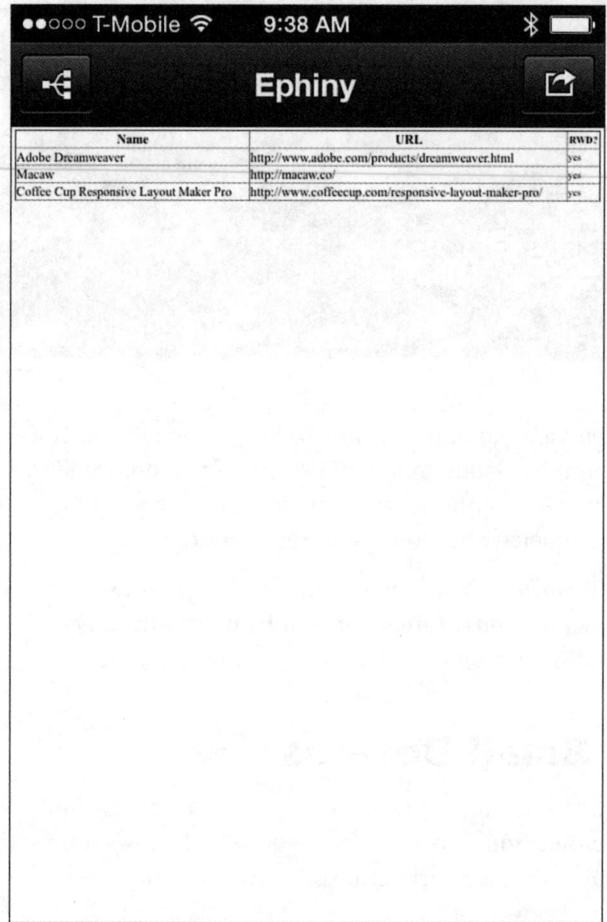

FIGURE 17.1
A three-column table viewed on an iPhone.

Can Tables Be Responsive?

When dealing with tables in RWD, you need to do more than just resize the element to get it to work better on your responsive web pages. In order to make tables responsive, you need to think about a few issues:

- **What data is essential to the table and must display on every device?** Mobile first dictates that you should include all the data in some fashion for even the most limited devices, but you can hide the less crucial information until users need it. So you need to know what information is most important.

- **How do customers use the data on the table?** If customers need to compare different rows or columns to each other, such as in a list of the web editor features, then your responsive design needs to reflect that. But if the data is in a table to make the information easier to digest, such as a table listing books with their publishing information, then the responsive design doesn't have to make comparing easy.
- **What are the breakpoints where the table no longer displays legibly on the screen?** These are the points where you will need to rethink how the table is displayed.

Once you have answers to these questions, you can make decisions about how you want to build your data tables so that they are responsive. In general, there are three typical ways web designers handle data tables in RWD:

- Resize the cells.
- Rearrange the table.
- Remove or hide content.

Resizing Cells in a Data Table

Resizing cells is the easiest way to handle data tables because it's the way that tables rearrange themselves by default. Listing 17.1 shows the HTML for a simple table. Because the `width` attribute is set to `100%`, it will automatically adjust to the width of the browser.

LISTING 17.1 Basic HTML Table

```
<table width="100%" border="1">
  <thead>
    <tr>
      <th>Name</th>
      <th>URL</th>
      <th>RWD?</th>
      <th>Windows</th>
      <th>Macintosh</th>
    </tr>
  </thead>
  <tbody>
    <tr>
      <td>Adobe Dreamweaver</td>
      <td>http://www.adobe.com/products/dreamweaver.html</td>
      <td>yes</td>
```

```
      <td>yes</td>
      <td>yes</td>
    </tr>
    <tr>
      <td>Macaw</td>
      <td>http://macaw.co/</td>
      <td>yes</td>
      <td>yes</td>
      <td>yes</td>
    </tr>
    <tr>
      <td>Coffee Cup Responsive Layout Maker Pro</td>
      <td>http://www.coffeecup.com/responsive-layout-maker-pro/</td>
      <td>yes</td>
      <td>yes</td>
      <td>yes</td>
    </tr>
    <tr>
      <td>Microsoft Notepad</td>
      <td>http://www.notepad.org/</td>
      <td>no</td>
      <td>yes</td>
      <td>no</td>
    </tr>
    <tr>
      <td>Tumult Hype</td>
      <td>http://tumult.com/hype/</td>
      <td>no</td>
      <td>no</td>
      <td>yes</td>
    </tr>
  </tbody>
</table>
```

The problem is that when the table gets down to really narrow widths, it becomes unreadable. But there are some things you can do with CSS media queries to improve this situation.

In browsers around 650px wide, this table grows too large for the screen and causes horizontal scrolling. If you reduce the font size from the default 16px to 14px in small screens, you don't see horizontal scrolling until around 480px. Listing 17.2 shows the CSS you can use to make this table fit without any adjustments to the HTML.

LISTING 17.2 CSS to Help a Table Fit with Font Size Changes

```
@charset "UTF-8";
/* styles for all devices */
table {
  border-collapse: collapse;
  font-size: 14px;
```

```
}
/* zebra stripe the table */
table tr:nth-child(2n+1)    {
  background-color: #dfdfdf;
}
/* styles for devices larger than 650px wide */
@media screen and (min-width:651px){
  table {
    font-size: 16px;
  }
}
```

While this CSS helps a table fit on the screen, it doesn't address the issue pointed out at the beginning of this hour: the table being simply too small to read when the whole thing is shown on the page.

Rearranging Tables in Response to Browsers

Another way to make tables responsive is to rearrange how the data is displayed in different devices. To do this, you need to understand how customers will use the data in the table. For example, a table of contacts can be displayed one contact after another, while a table of rated web page editors needs the rows and columns to be comparable to each other.

Whereas Listing 17.1 shows a table that needs to be comparable, Listing 17.3 shows a table where each row of data can stand alone.

LISTING 17.3 Contact Information Table

```
<table width="100%" border="1">
  <tr>
    <th>Name</th>
    <th>Title</th>
    <th>Home Page</th>
    <th>Email</th>
  </tr>
  <tr>
    <td>Jennifer Kyrnin</td>
    <td>Chief Dandylion Officer</td>
    <td>http://htmljenn.com/</td>
    <td>htmljenn@gmail.com</td>
  </tr>
  <tr>
    <td>McKinley</td>
    <td>Dandelion Observation Officer</td>
    <td>http://responsivewebdesignin24hours.com/mckinley</td>
    <td>mckinley@rwdin24hours.com</td>
```

```
  </tr>
  <tr>
    <td>Rambler</td>
    <td>Chief Taste Tester</td>
    <td>http://responsivewebdesignin24hours.com/rambler</td>
    <td>rambler@rwdin24hours.com</td>
  </tr>
</table>
```

Because of the URLs, this table breaks the container at around 720px, and because it includes contact information, you don't want to mess with the font size, so you need to adjust how the table displays.

One way to do that is to change the table from a horizontal list of items to a vertical list, with each item displayed individually. Listing 17.4 shows the CSS to get the table to do this, and Figure 17.2 shows the before and after.

LISTING 17.4 CSS to Rearrange a Table

```
@charset "UTF-8";
/* styles for all devices */
table {
  border-collapse: collapse;
}

/* styles for small devices */
@media (max-width:720px){
  table { border: none; }
  /* display the whole table as a block */
  table, thead, tbody, th, td, tr {
    display: block;
  }
  /* Hide the headers */
  thead tr {
    position: absolute;
    top: -9999px;
    left: -9999px;
  }

  tr { border: 1px solid #ccc; margin-bottom: 1em; }
  tr:nth-of-type(odd) {
    background: #eee;
  }

  td {
    /* Behave  like a "row" */
    border: none;
    border-bottom: 1px solid #eee;
    position: relative;
```

```
    padding-left: 20%;
  }

  td:before {
    /* Now like a table header */
    position: absolute;
    /* Top/left values mimic padding */
    top: 1px;
    left: 6px;
    width: 45%;
    padding-right: 10px;
    white-space: nowrap;
  }

  /* Label the data */
  td:nth-of-type(1):before { content: "Name"; }
  td:nth-of-type(2):before { content: "Title"; }
  td:nth-of-type(3):before { content: "Home Page"; }
  td:nth-of-type(4):before { content: "Email"; }
}

/* styles for larger devices */
@media (min-width:721px) {
  tr:nth-child(2n+1) {
    background-color: #80C5F5;
  }
  table thead tr:nth-child(n) {
    background-color: #3d447e;
    color: #dfdfdf;
  }
}
```

I found this example on Chris Coyier's CSS-Tricks site (`http://css-tricks.com/responsive-data-tables/`). With this technique, you turn the table elements (`<table>`, `<tr>`, `<td>`, etc.) into block elements, hide the `<th>` elements (but don't remove them with `display:none;` so that the table is still accessible), and add separate line headers for each row in the table.

You're not limited to rearranging the table but can also change how the data is displayed; for example, you can move from a horizontal table to a graphic or a chart at smaller screen sizes. As long as the data is still available to mobile customers, displaying a graphical chart instead of a table can work. And you might find that a chart is useful for larger-screen devices as well.

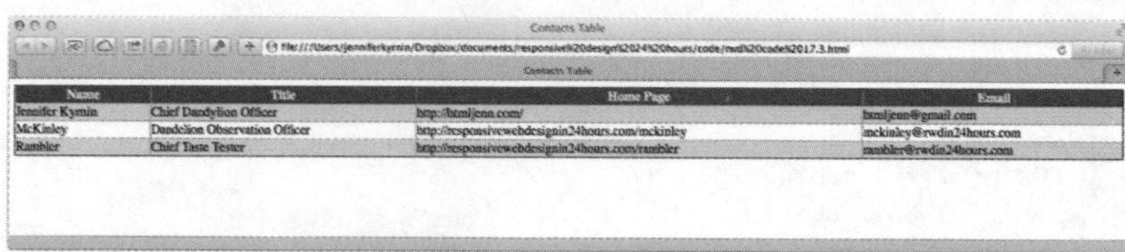

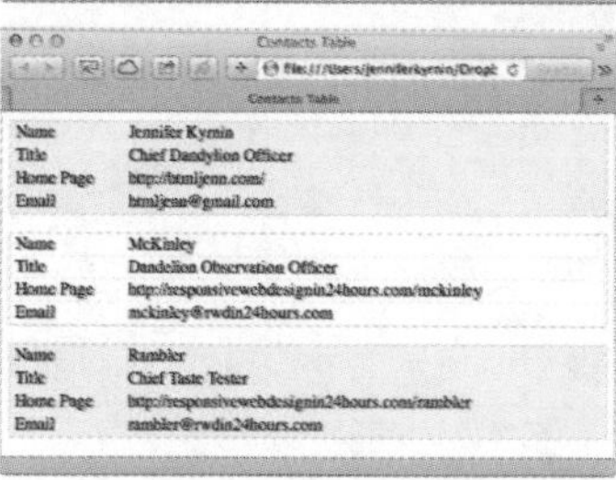

FIGURE 17.2
The same table in a wide browser window and in a narrow one.

Hiding Table Content

It's not a good idea to rearrange tables as described in the previous section when the columns or rows need to be easily compared. A solution to this problem is to hide some of the content in smaller screens. And to do this, you need to know which items on your table are the most important.

For the table created by Listing 17.1, you might prioritize the data in this way:

- The software name and RWD support are required.
- Operating systems are important but optional.
- The URL is least important.

In order to apply these rankings to the data, you can add three classes, one to each column:

- `required`
- `important`
- `optional`

Then you can create some CSS media queries to hide those columns on smaller screens. Listing 17.5 shows how it might look.

LISTING 17.5 HTML and CSS to Hide Columns on Smaller Screens

```
<!doctype html>
<html>
<head>
<meta charset="UTF-8">
<title>Responsive Tables</title>
<style>
/* styles for all devices */
table {
  border-collapse: collapse;
}
/* zebra stripe the table */
table tbody tr:nth-child(odd)    {
  background-color: #dfdfdf;
}
thead tr {
  background-color: #6E2B75;
  color: #efefef;
}

/* hide the important and optional columns from small screens */
@media screen and (max-width:480px) {
  .optional, .important,
  tr td:nth-child(2),
  tr td:nth-child(4),
  tr td:nth-child(5){
    display: none;
  }
}

/* hide the optional columns from medium width screens */
@media screen and (min-width:481px) and (max-width:780px) {
  .optional,
  tr td:nth-child(2) {
    display: none;
  }
}
</style>
</head>

<body>
<table width="100%" border="1">
  <thead>
    <tr>
      <th class="required">Name</th>
      <th class="optional">URL</th>
      <th class="required">RWD?</th>
      <th class="important">Windows</th>
      <th class="important">Macintosh</th>
    </tr>
  </thead>
  <tbody>
```

```
    <tr>
      <td>Adobe Dreamweaver</td>
      <td>http://www.adobe.com/products/dreamweaver.html</td>
      <td>yes</td>
      <td>yes</td>
      <td>yes</td>
    </tr>
    <tr>
      <td>Macaw</td>
      <td>http://macaw.co/</td>
      <td>yes</td>
      <td>yes</td>
      <td>yes</td>
    </tr>
    <tr>
      <td>Coffee Cup Responsive Layout Maker Pro</td>
      <td>http://www.coffeecup.com/responsive-layout-maker-pro/</td>
      <td>yes</td>
      <td>yes</td>
      <td>yes</td>
    </tr>
    <tr>
      <td>Microsoft Notepad</td>
      <td>http://www.notepad.org/</td>
      <td>no</td>
      <td>yes</td>
      <td>no</td>
    </tr>
    <tr>
      <td>Tumult Hype</td>
      <td>http://tumult.com/hype/</td>
      <td>no</td>
      <td>no</td>
      <td>yes</td>
    </tr>
  </tbody>
</table>
</body>
</html>
```

The problem with hiding the data is that customers still want to see the hidden data, even if it's harder to read on their devices. So you should always give your customers an option to see the data. Several tools listed in Hour 21, "Tools for Creating Responsive Web Designs," can help you automate hiding and showing table data.

But there is another option. Most tables break the design because the data is too wide for the layout, and so the entire design must scroll horizontally in order for the user to be able to see everything. But while horizontal scrolling of the entire page is bad, most smartphone users understand what they need to do when they see a scrollbar below a table, and they can easily scroll from right to left inside that table.

TRY IT YOURSELF ▼

Create a Scrolling Table

The trick to creating a scrolling table is to use a `<div>` tag around the table and put the scrollbars on it. The following steps show you how:

1. Open your web page editor and build a multicolumn and multirow table, like the one in Listing 17.1.
2. Surround the entire table with `<div>` tags:

```
<div>
<table width="100%" border="1">
  ...
</table>
</div>
```

3. Inside the `<div>` tags, set `class` to `responsive-table`:

```
<div class="responsive-table">
```

4. Then create a media query for around the size where your table breaks, like this:

```
@media only screen and (max-width: 480px) { }
```

   If you'd rather have all small tablets and smartphones see a scrolling table, to make it easier to read, use a `max-width: 767px` rule as your breakpoint.

5. Add the following CSS to that media query:

```
.responsive-table {
  width: 100%;
  margin-bottom: 15px;
  overflow-y: hidden;
  overflow-x: scroll;
  -ms-overflow-style: -ms-autohiding-scrollbar;
  border: 1px solid #ddd;
  -webkit-overflow-scrolling: touch;
}
```

This makes the table take up as much room as it needs to be legible, with any overflow on the `<div>` hidden by the scrollbar. Customers can then scroll left or right to see the entire table, even on small-screen devices.

A number of sites, including these, offer scripts to help you create even fancier responsive tables:

- Crafty Responsive Tables (`http://zurb.com/playground/responsive-tables`) uses both CSS and jQuery.
- Responsive Tables 2 by David Bushell (`http://dbushell.com/2012/01/05/responsive-tables-2/`) uses CSS.
- Filament Group (`http://filamentgroup.com/lab/responsive_design_approach_for_complex_multicolumn_data_tables/`) created a nice-looking responsive table that hides the non-essential columns and then uses jQuery to add them back in if the customer wants to see them.

Where Do Layout Tables Fit in RWD?

Only a few years ago, professional web designers were decrying the use of tables for layout. But with the advent of HTML5 and a few new CSS3 properties, it's now not only okay to use tables for layout, you can also take advantage of how tables work differently from block elements like paragraphs (`<p>`) and `<div>` elements.

Layout tables were frowned on for a number of reasons, including these:

- Tables are hard for cell phones, especially older ones, to render.
- Tables can be very difficult for screen readers and other accessibility devices to read correctly.
- Tables are for tabular data, as discussed earlier in this hour.
- Tables can slow down pages.

Many Designers Want Tables for Layout

The fact of the matter is that most designers who used tables for layout just didn't care about the drawbacks. They found layout tables easy to use and understand, and their designs were fast enough and easy enough for their customers to read and use that the objections just didn't matter. Luckily, HTML5 listened to the upsides, and using tables for layout is again a valid way to write HTML. Anyone who tells you differently is not up on current markup standards.

All you have to do is indicate in some fashion that a table is a layout table, and most screen readers will handle it correctly. The simplest and most common way to indicate this is by doing something you're probably already doing—setting `border` to `0`:

```
<table border="0">
```

Just this simple line of HTML is enough to indicate a presentation table. There are other methods you can use to indicate this as well, and I explain them in my article "HTML5 and Tables for Layout" (`http://www.html5in24hours.com/2014/09/html5-allows-tables-layout/`).

Using Layout Tables for Advertising

As I discuss in greater depth in Hour 20, "Problems with Responsive Web Design," advertising is a huge deal on many websites, and web designers can't just change the sizes of ads on their sites willy-nilly. Most advertisements have very specific dimensions. The Interactive Advertising Bureau (IAB) has specific sizes for all its ads, and these are the four basic sizes:

- Medium rectangle: 300×250
- Rectangle: 180×150
- Wide skyscraper: 160×600
- Leaderboard: 728×90

There are many more rules than just these. You can read all about them at `http://www.iab.net/guidelines/508676/508767/displayguidelines`.

When you build a responsive site that uses flexible layout blocks, you can run into problems with the advertising messing up the layout at smaller sizes. And unlike with images, you can't simply make the ads smaller to fit. With a table layout, you could simply put an ad in a table cell, and you would know that it would stay beside the content cell because that's how tables work.

But before you go and switch back to HTML tables for your layout, there is a solution that uses the CSS layout you already have but treats blocks as tables. Listing 17.6 shows the HTML you can use.

LISTING 17.6 Basic CSS Layout with Ads

```
<!doctype html>
<html>
  <head>
    <meta charset="utf-8">
    <title>HTML with Ad Block</title>
    <style>
    body { background-color: #EDEE6A; }
    section {
      width: 95%;
      margin: 0 auto;
      background-color: #fff;
    }
    article {
      background-color: #dfdfdf;
      overflow: auto;
      width: 60%;
      float: left;
    }
    aside {
      width: 300px;
      float: right;
    }
    img { max-width: 100%; width: 300px; height:200px;
      background-color: #F17A24; }
    </style>
  </head>
  <body>
  <section>
    <article>
      ... article copy ...
      blah blah blah
      blah blah blah
      blah blah blah
      blah blah blah
      blah blah blah
    </article>
    <aside class="ads">
      <img id="ad300">
    </aside>
   </section>
</html>
```

This layout works fine in browsers that are around 805px or wider. The advertisement floats to the right of the article copy. But with browsers smaller than that, the ad becomes too large for the space and ends up below the article. But because it's floated, it still hangs out to the right side, leaving a strange empty space above it and beside it. Figure 17.3 shows what this looks like.

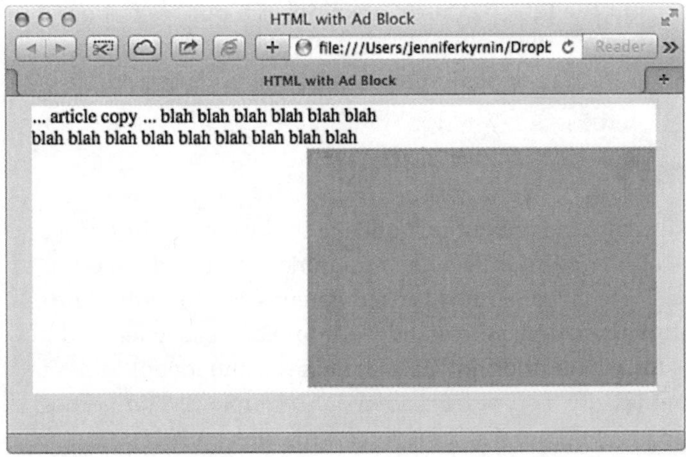

FIGURE 17.3
Safari showing an ad image that's too large for the layout.

But with a table, you could create the layout you want without encountering this problem, and CSS lets you define items as tables without including any new HTML. You just get rid of the `float` and `overflow` properties, as well as the `width` property on the `<article>` tag. Then you add a `display:table;` property to the `<section>` tag and make the `<article>` and `<aside>` table cells with the `display: table-cell;` property. Listing 17.7 shows the CSS to do this.

LISTING 17.7 CSS Creating Tables Out of Other Tags

```
/* CSS Document */

body { background-color: #dfdfdf; }
section {
  display: table;
  width: 95%;
  margin: 0 auto;
  background-color: #fff;
}
article {
  background-color: #fff;
  display: table-cell;
  vertical-align:top;
}
aside {
  width: 300px;
  display: table-cell;
  vertical-align:top;
}
img { max-width: 100%; width: 300px; height:200px;
  background-color: #F17A24; }
```

You'll want to put the table features in your media queries for larger screens so that you don't run into the same problems that you have with data tables. And then you'll have the best of both worlds.

Summary

This hour you've learned about a challenge that most responsive web designers encounter eventually when designing RWD: making data tables responsive. You've learned three different ways to make data tables responsive and why you would want to. You've also learned how to use tables for layout and that HTML5 makes using layout tables a good solution. Finally, you've learned about a couple CSS properties that can help you build table-like layouts with non-table HTML: `display: table;` and `display: table-cell;`.

Workshop

The workshop contains quiz questions to help you process what you've learned in this lesson. Try to answer all the questions before you read the answers.

Q&A

Q. I thought we were supposed to think mobile first in all situations, but most of the examples in this hour seem to focus on desktop designs first. Why is that?

A. Except for very small tables, most data tables don't look good on narrow devices. So as a designer, you need to think about the data itself and how to best present it in all scenarios. While you should consider mobile first in your design process, the fact is that most data tables are delivered as tables, either from spreadsheets or databases. So it's easier to work with them at the large screen sizes typical of computers and adjust them so that they still work for smaller screens.

Q. In Listing 17.4 you used `content` style properties to embed the titles for each row. But I thought that was considered bad form. Is there a better way to do it?

A. Yes, if you're truly trying to keep content separate from styles, you should not use the `content` styles to add content. Instead, you should use `data-*` properties to embed the titles into the cells. You would write your HTML table cells like this:

```
<tr>
  <td data-th="Name">Jennifer Kyrnin</td>
  <td data-th="Title">Chief Dandylion Officer</td>
  <td data-th="URL">http://htmljenn.com/</td>
  <td data-th="Email">htmljenn@gmail.com</td>
</tr>
```

Then, in the media query, you would replace the lines that call for `content` styles with this:

```
td:before { content: attr(data-th); }
```

Q. You explained how to create a table-like layout with CSS that has only one row. Is it possible to use CSS to make more rows and groupings?

A. Yes, it is. The `display` property now has multiple table values, including `table`, `table-cell`, `table-row`, `table-header-group`, and `table-footer-group`. These have very good browser support, including Internet Explorer 8 and up as well as all other modern desktop and mobile browsers.

Quiz

1. What is the main problem with most data tables on small-screen devices?
2. Why should you be concerned with which data cells are critical?
3. True or False: Knowing how customers compare the data in a table is not important.
4. What might cause you to consider adding a breakpoint to fix a table?
5. Name two ways you can make a table responsive.
6. What method of making a table responsive is the easiest?
7. Why should you avoid the easiest method of making a table responsive if possible?
8. What is one way you might rearrange a table to be responsive?
9. Why is hiding table content a less-than-ideal solution with responsive tables?
10. How can you address the problems that hiding table content, in a "hide-and-cry'' type of design, causes?

Answers

1. Most data tables are very wide, and on narrow screens, this can cause the design to scroll horizontally, which is hard for most cell phones to do. But often even if there is no horizontal scrolling, wide tables are nearly impossible to read on small-screen devices.
2. You should know the importance of all the data in a table so that if you need to hide some of it to make it legible in smaller browsers, you know you are keeping the critical data on the screen.
3. False. If you don't know how customers use your data tables, you might create a responsive design that makes the tables unusable for some of your users.
4. You might add a breakpoint when the table cells starts overwriting each other, or when the text is illegible, or when the table seems cramped.
5. You can make a table responsive by resizing the cells, rearranging the table, or hiding portions of the table.
6. Resizing the table cells is the easiest because tables do it automatically.

7. You should avoid that method because it doesn't address most of the problems associated with tables on smaller screens.
8. You might change a horizontal table to display vertically, with the headers displayed in a column on the left of each cell.
9. Hiding table content is similar to the "hide-and-cry" design method mentioned in Hour 13, "Navigation." By removing content from the view of mobile customers, you risk annoying them.
10. You can solve this problem by giving your customers ways to get the content back, such as using JavaScript to make the hidden columns reappear or putting scrollbars on the table so that users can scroll horizontally just on the table portion of the design.

Exercises

1. Find a data table that you need to display on the site you're updating. Then work on making it responsive. Decide how the table is best used and then provide a solution that makes it easier to get that data in smaller screens.
2. If you don't have a data table you need to edit, practice using one of the methods found on the CSS-Tricks "Responsive Data Table Roundup" article, at `http://css-tricks.com/responsive-data-table-roundup/`.

HOUR 18
Responsive Web Forms

Using web forms is the primary way that customers interact with web pages. But most web designers build their forms first on a computer and assume that most smartphone and tablet users will be able to use the form without much change.

But while most smartphones and tablets *can* use the forms built for desktop screens, it doesn't mean those forms are easy to use. In this hour, you will learn some of the mistakes designers commonly make when building web forms on responsive web pages and how to make those forms not only work on the smaller screens but make your customers want to fill them out because it's so pleasant and easy.

WHAT YOU'LL LEARN IN THIS HOUR:

- The new HTML5 input tags
- How to validate a form with HTML5 tags and attributes
- Rules for writing usable forms
- How to create a responsive web form

HTML5 Forms

The first thing you should do when building forms is use HTML5. It is amazing to me how many websites have beautifully designed mobile-first responsive sites and a form that uses only `<input type=text>`.

HTML5 offers a bunch of new features for web forms, and if you use only one of them, it should be the new `<input>` types:

- `color`
- `date`
- `datetime`
- `datetime-local`
- `email`
- `month`

- `number`
- `range`
- `search`
- `tel`
- `time`
- `url`
- `week`

These input fields help you help your customers give you the data in a format that is useful to you. For a form that gets a lot of responses, without HTML5 you have to wade through those responses and clean up the data. People might input text for phone numbers, numbers for email addresses, and random characters for URLs. If any of that data is critical to the functioning of the form, it could break the form. But with HTML5 input types, you can request an email address type, and with most browsers doing validation themselves, you can be reasonably sure that's what you'll get.

These types are widely supported across mobile and computer browsers, and even older browsers that don't support them directly will treat them as text input fields. So there is absolutely no reason not to use them. If you're not using them on your forms right now, you are being lazy and are annoying your mobile customers.

While these input types do sometimes do different things on desktop computers, they really shine on mobile screens. Figure 18.1 shows how easy these fields make forms on mobile devices.

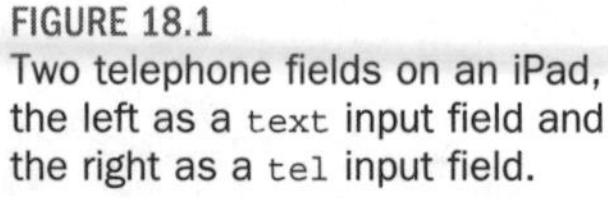

FIGURE 18.1
Two telephone fields on an iPad, the left as a `text` input field and the right as a `tel` input field.

You can see in Figure 18.1 that the telephone field with the `<input type=tel>` value (shown in the right image) is going to be much easier for a mobile customer to fill in because the device shows a different keyboard with numbers more prominent. All modern tablets and smartphones adjust the input fields to reflect the type of input requested.

I can't state this strongly enough: If you have customers visiting on mobile devices and you want them to fill out any type of form, you should use these input types. And this goes for login forms, too. Many sites expect people to use their email address as their login. Listing 18.1 shows a simple login form that will help your mobile customers log in more quickly while not affecting computer customers at all.

LISTING 18.1 A Simple Login Form

```
<!doctype html>
<html>
<head>
<meta charset="UTF-8">
<title>Simple Form</title>
<style>
fieldset {
  width: 50%;
  max-width: 400px;
  background-color: #EDEE6A;
  margin: 0 auto;
}
legend {
  font-size: 18px;
  font-family: sans-serif;
}
input {
  display: block;
  width: 80%;
  font-size: 18px;
  margin: 0 auto 1em auto;
}
input[type=submit] {
  width: 40%;
}
label {
  position: absolute;
  top: -9999px;
  left: -9999px;
}
</style>
</head>
<body>
<form id="loginForm" novalidate>
```

```
  <fieldset>
    <legend>Login</legend>
    <label for="username">Username:</label><input type="email"
      placeholder="Username or Email Address" id="username">
    <label for="password">Password:</label><input type="password"
      placeholder="Password" id="password">
    <input type="submit" value="Go!" id="submit">
  </fieldset>
</form>
</body>
</html>
```

CAUTION

Don't Validate `Email` **Types if They Can Accept Plain Text**

While you can build a login form by using `<input type=email>` to accept plain text as well as email addresses, you should make sure you set the form to `novalidate`—for example, `<form id="loginForm" novalidate>`. Otherwise, some browsers will attempt to validate the form automatically and may cause problems if a customer types in a login name that is not an email address.

As you can see in the HTML, the `email` input type can accept more than just email addresses.

To use any of the HTML5 input types, simply replace `text` in the `type` attribute with the type of data you want to collect from your customers. For example, to request a date, you use this:

```
<input type="date" id="date">
```

Browsers that support the type will show appropriate input controls, and those that don't will show a text field. You can learn more about HTML5 input controls in my book *Sams Teach Yourself HTML5 Mobile Application Development in 24 Hours*.

NOTE

Don't Leave Out the Labels

Listing 18.1 also includes text that identifies every form field with a `<label>` tag. This is not new in HTML5, but it is a way to keep the forms accessible. In the sample login screen, Listing 18.1 moves the labels far off the visible screen with this CSS:

```
label {
  position: absolute;
  top: -9999px;
  left: -9999px;
}
```

This ensures that screen readers will still see the labels, even if they don't read the placeholder text.

Other HTML5 Form Attributes

HTML5 offers a lot more for forms than just new `<input>` tag types. You can use a number of attributes on your form fields to make them easier for everyone to use:

- **Placeholder text**—You saw this in the login form in Listing 18.1. It is text that appears inside the form fields as a placeholder. Many designers now use the placeholder text as a field label, which makes forms look cleaner.
- **Autofocus**—You can place the `autofocus` attribute on any one form field on a page to have the page load with the cursor in that field (in non-touch screen devices). This makes it that much easier for people to start filling in the form.
- **Autocomplete and data lists**—HTML5 provides a way to build form fields with prepopulated answer choices. You use the `<datalist>` tag to define the different possible values for the field and then use the `autocomplete` attribute to have the form help customers choose a value from the list automatically. Figure 18.2 shows how a data list looks in a browser.

FIGURE 18.2
A <datalist> tag displaying in Chrome.

Using these HTML5 form elements makes your forms easier for all your customers, not just mobile customers.

Validating an HTML5 Form with No Scripting

HTML5 has several attributes to help validate forms:

- `novalidate`
- `required`
- `pattern`

The `novalidate` attribute goes on the `<form>` tag. It prevents modern browsers from automatically validating any form data they can.

The easiest type of form data to validate comes from using the new input types mentioned earlier. Not all web browsers validate against these fields, but most modern browsers do some type of check. For example, Chrome reports "Please include an '@' in the email address" when you try to submit a form with an invalid email address in an `<input type=email>` field .

HTML5 provides two other attributes to help validate forms: `required` and `pattern`. The `required` attribute is self-explanatory. Fields that have this attribute are required to submit the form, and validating browsers should display an error message if a customer tries to submit them empty.

The `pattern` field is a little bit trickier. You put a regular expression in this field, and the browser checks that that the text the customer submits matches that pattern. For example, here is a pattern that matches the standard format for U.S. telephone numbers:

```
pattern="\([0-9]{3}\) [0-9]{3}-[0-9]{4}"
```

This will match a phone number that looks like `(408) 555-1212` but not one that looks like `408-555-1212`. If you use patterns on your input fields, you should indicate the patterns somewhere on the page so that you don't annoy your customers too much.

CAUTION

Don't Hide Your Password Patterns

If you're setting up a signup form where a customer needs to create a user name and password, one of the first places customers drop off is at the password field. It's bad enough that the field is usually hidden with ****** characters so they can't see what they typed, but then most signup forms force the customers to fill it in twice. So if there's a mistake, they don't know which field is wrong. But the worst are the forms that have a pattern required for the password to be accepted. These are things like "must have at least one uppercase letter, one lowercase letter, and one numeral. No special characters allowed."

The problem is *not* with requiring special characters or numbers. Such requirements are good: They help make the passwords more secure. The problem is in how you validate passwords. Most validators check for one thing and then throw the password out. So your customer might have this happen:

She enters *password* as her password.

The system responds with "The password cannot be a word in the dictionary."

So the user enters *passw0rd* in the form.

The system responds with "There must be at least one uppercase letter."

She enters *passW0rd* in the form.

The system responds with "There must be at least one special character."

And the customer gets fed up and leaves.

You can avoid losing this customer by just posting the rules for passwords somewhere on the form page. Or having the validator respond with all the rules, not just one of the ones that was broken.

A good place to display patterns for form fields is in the `placeholder` attribute. For example, you might include the phone number pattern above in a tag like this:

```
<input type="tel" placeholder="(###) ###-####"
pattern="\([0-9]{3}\) [0-9]{3}-[0-9]{4}">
```

This way, the customer can see immediately how to fill out that form field.

Making Web Forms Usable

If you have switched over to HTML5 forms with the correct input types for each field, you will have gone a long way toward making your forms look and act better on mobile devices. But there are a few tricks you should be aware of to make your forms more responsive to small screens:

- Keep forms as simple as possible.
- Remove extraneous page elements.
- Remove or combine form fields, where possible.
- Avoid long drop-down menus.
- Allow customers to type answers.

Keeping Forms Simple

If you do nothing else for your customers, you should keep your forms as simple as possible. This is true for desktop customers as well as mobile. While you may find your 150-question in-depth form to be critical for the success of your business, chances are you are losing all but the most dedicated customers midstream.

If you can't keep a form simple, then you should make it as entertaining as possible. No one wants to go through a bland series of text fields, filling in text and ticking boxes. Add visual elements like pictures to help make the form more enjoyable. Some of the best forms I've ever seen used pictures as the form itself. For instance, instead of a check box for indicating your gender, one form offered a photo of a man and another of a woman to click or tap on.

Removing Extraneous Page Elements

The best forms are often the only elements on the page (except for maybe the site logo). This approach helps customers focus on the form and encourages them to fill it out.

This is especially true for mobile customers. You should make your forms take up the whole screen. Use vertically aligned labels above or in the placeholder text to keep the form looking tidy. And then stretch the fields so they take up the entire width of the device.

Remember that most mobile devices include a virtual keyboard that will pop up and take over as much as half of the bottom part of the screen. So, while you want your form fields to be big and easy to fill out, you need to make sure they can be seen above that virtual keyboard.

Removing or Combining Form Fields

Look at your forms and think about how a mobile customer might want to use them. Chances are if you have a bunch of fields that aren't required, your mobile customers are going to leave them blank. So you should remove them from the initial form. If they add value, you can give users the option to include them, but they should not be in the form you first display.

If you can't remove all the fields, you might be able to combine them or even fill them in automatically for your mobile customers. For example, if your form requires a zip code, you could have a script populate the state they live in automatically from that zip code. You can also combine fields that are typically seen together. For example, first and last name might be separate boxes on a large-screen version of the form, but for the small screen you could combine them into one "name" field.

Avoiding Long Drop-Down Menus

Drop-down menus are often hard to use on small-screen devices. They can be hard to scroll through, and tapping on one value might activate another by mistake.

If a drop-down menu is more than 7 to 10 items long, you should consider replacing it with a text field and asking the customers to simply type in an answer. This is much easier to do on a mobile device.

Allowing Customers to Type Answers

Many form designers love to use select lists, radio buttons, check boxes, and drop-down menus, but these options are often more difficult for a user to use than `<input>` fields, which require simply typing in an answer.

For example, a contact form might ask what state the customer lives in; a drop-down menu for states would have at least 50 options. This drop-down would likely come after the customer has filled in several other text fields, such as name and address. The user's hands are on the keyboard, not the mouse, but in order to easily navigate the drop-down menu, it's necessary to switch to the mouse and then scroll through possibly 40 or more states to the right one. (I live in Washington state, and I have to do this all the time.) And mobile customers have to scroll through long lists, which, as mentioned above, is difficult to do.

If instead you provided an `<input>` field for the two-letter abbreviation for the state, the customer can quickly type in the state abbreviation and move on.

This may seem like a minor usability issue, but web forms are so tedious and difficult to fill out that often the simplest issues can cause people to stop filling them out, which means one less lead for your company.

TRY IT YOURSELF ▼

Create a Data List to Make a Text Field Easier to Use

If you use the `<datalist>` tag mentioned earlier along with the `autocomplete` attribute, you can create a form field that gets consistent data but is easier to fill in for many customers. The following steps show you how to create a simple data list for a form:

1. Open your web page editor to a blank HTML document.
2. Add a `<form>` tag to the page:

```
<form>
</form>
```

3. Inside the `<form>` tag, add a labeled input field:

```
<label for="animal">My Favorite Animal</label>
<input type="text" id="animal">
```

4. Anywhere on the page add a data list:

```
<datalist id="animals">
</datalist>
```

5. Inside the data list, include the options you'd like to provide to your customers:

```
<option value="cat">
<option value="dog">
<option value="horse">
```

▼ TRY IT YOURSELF

Create a Data List to Make a Text Field Easier to Use

continued

6. Finally, link the data list to your input field by adding the `list` attribute to the field:

```
<input type="text" id="animal" list="animals">
```

Unfortunately, the `<datalist>` tag is only supported by Chrome for Android version 37 on mobile devices, and mobile devices are where this field would be most useful. It's also not supported by Safari and has only partial support in Internet Explorer 10. In my book *Sams Teach Yourself HTML5 Mobile Application Development in 24 Hours*, I explain how to use jQuery UI as a fallback option for browsers that don't yet support it.

Creating Responsive Forms

Creating responsive forms involves the same process as creating other responsive elements: You decide on your design for mobile and then enhance it for larger screens, using the rules and techniques specific to forms listed earlier this hour.

For my website `http://www.htmljenn.com`, I needed a contact form. Listing 18.2 shows the HTML for my form.

LISTING 18.2 My HTMLJenn.com Contact Form

```
<form>
  <article>
    <section id="mainform">
    <h2>Contact Information</h2>
    <label for="name" class="inputbox">Your Name</label>
    <input id="name" placeholder="Your Name" required
    class="inputbox" autofocus>

    <label for="email" class="inputbox">Your Email Address</label>
    <input id="email" type="email" placeholder="Your Email Address"
    required class="inputbox">

    <label for="url" class="inputbox">Your Website URL</label>
    <input id="url" type="url" placeholder="Your Website URL"
    class="inputbox">

    <label for="phone" class="inputbox">Your Phone Number</label>
    <input id="phone" type="tel" placeholder="Your Phone Number"
    class="inputbox">
    </section>
    <section id="messagearea">
    <h2>Share Your Thoughts</h2>
    <textarea id="message" placeholder="Your Thoughts" required
```

```
    class="inputbox"></textarea>
    </section>
  </article>
  <aside class="clearfix">
    <section id="messageabout">
    <h2> This Message Is About</h2>
    <select id="msgAbt" required class="inputbox">
    <option selected></option>
    <option>Writing Opportunity</option>
    <option>Web Design Opportunity</option>
    <option>Consulting Opportunity</option>
    <option>Collaboration Opportunity</option>
    <option value="article">Article Correction</option>
    <option value="other">Other</option>
    </select>

    <label for="article-url" class="inputbox hide">URL that needs
    correction</label>
    <input id="article-url" type="url"
    placeholder="URL that needs correction" class="inputbox hide">

    <label for="other" class="inputbox hide">What is this message
    about?</label>
    <input id="other"
    placeholder="what is this message about? (200 chars or less)"
    maxlength="200" class="inputbox hide">
    </section>
    <section id="messagepriority">
    <h2>Message Priority</h2>
    <p><input type="radio" name="priority" id="high" value="high">
    <label for="high" class="radio">High</label></p>
    <p><input type="radio" name="priority" id="medium"
    value="medium" checked>
    <label for="medium" class="radio">Medium</label></p>
    <p><input type="radio" name="priority" id="low" value="low">
    <label for="low" class="radio">Low</label></p>
    </section>
  </aside>
  <section id="submitmessage">
  <input type="reset" value="Reset">
  <input type="submit" value="Submit">
  </section>
</form>
```

To make this form responsive, I made the form and label elements take up the full width of the screen in the smallest browsers. I gave the form two sections, by using the `<article>` and `<aside>` tags, and then in the very smallest browsers, I removed the less important `<aside>`. In larger browsers I turned the form into a two-column layout to make it a little easier to view. Listing 18.3 show the CSS.

LISTING 18.3 CSS for a Responsive Form

```
/* very basic reset */
*, *:before, *:after {
  padding: 0;
  margin: 0;
  -webkit-box-sizing: border-box;
  -moz-box-sizing: border-box;
  box-sizing: border-box;
}
.clearfix:after {
  content: ".";
  visibility: hidden;
  display: block;
  height: 0;
  clear: both;
}

/* most form elements should take up the whole screen */
.inputbox, select, textarea {
  display: block;
  width: 100%;
}
form { max-width: 1000px; }
h1, h2, h3, label {
  font-family: Gotham, "Helvetica Neue", Helvetica, Arial,
    sans-serif;
}
section { margin-bottom: 1em; }
input, textarea, select {
  font-family: Gotham, "Helvetica Neue", Helvetica, Arial,
    sans-serif;
  font-size: 1em;
  font-size: 1rem;
  border: solid 0.25em #b4cebc;
  margin-bottom: 1em;
  padding: 0.2em;
  -webkit-box-shadow: 3px 3px 15px #B4CEBC;
  box-shadow: 3px 3px 15px #B4CEBC;
}
input, textarea { max-width: 600px; }
select { max-width: 300px; }
[required]:focus {
  border: 0.25em solid #026F23;
}
aside h2, aside select {
  font-size: medium;
}
/* hide aside from smallest browsers */
aside { display: none; }
@media (min-width: 480px) {
  aside { display: block; }
  form {
```

```
    padding: 0.5em;
  }
}
@media (min-width: 768px) {
  article {
    width: 60%;
    float: left;
  }
  aside {
    width: 35%;
    float: right;
  }
  label.inputbox {
    position: absolute;
    top: 9999px;
    left: 9999px;
  }
  #submitmessage { clear: both; }
}
```

Finally, because I wanted some of the form fields to appear only if they were needed, I added some jQuery (see Listing 18.4) to show and hide those elements when the customer chooses specific fields in the drop-down menu. This is just extra functionality; the form looks fine even if these fields display.

LISTING 18.4 jQuery for a Responsive Form

```
$( document ).ready(function() {
  $("#article-url").hide();
  $("#other").hide();
  $('#msgAbt').change(function() {
    var selected = $(this).val();
    if(selected == 'article'){
      $('#article-url').show();
      $('other').hide();
    }
    else if (selected == 'other') {
      $("#other").show();
      $("#article-url").hide();
    }
    else {
      $('#article-url').hide();
      $('#other').hide();
    }
  });
});
```

If you try putting together this form on your own site, you'll see that there are a lot of other styles I've added to make the form look nice. You can add and remove those features as you like for various browsers. But as long as you bear in mind the rules you've learned in this hour about web forms, you'll have a responsive form your customers will enjoy filling out.

Summary

This hour you've learned about the HTML5 tags and attributes that can help you build a web form that is much easier to use than older HTML 4 forms. You've also learned some of the rules for building usable web forms for mobile and non-mobile customers. Finally, you've seen how I went about designing a web form for one of my own sites, including why I made some design decisions and how I implemented them. Table 18.1 shows the new HTML5 form tags mentioned in this chapter.

TABLE 18.1 HTML5 Form Tags

Tag	Description
`<input type="color">`	Input a color using a color picker.
`<input type="date">`	Input a date in the format YYYY-MM-DD.
`<input type="datetime">`	Input a date in the format YYYY-MM-DDTHH:MMZ+00:00.
`<input type="datetime-local">`	Input a date in the format YYYY-MM-DDTHH:MM.
`<input type="email">`	Input an email address.
`<input type="month">`	Input a date in the format YYYY-MM.
`<input type="number">`	Input a number.
`<input type="range">`	Input a number without a precise value, within a range of numbers.
`<input type="search">`	Input a phrase to search for.
`<input type="tel">`	Input a telephone number.
`<input type="time">`	Input a time in the format HH:MM.
`<input type="url">`	Input a URL.
`<input type="week">`	Input a week in the format YYYY-W##.
`<datalist>`	Specify a list of items to be shown as data on the page.

Workshop

The workshop contains quiz questions to help you process what you've learned in this lesson. Try to answer all the questions before you read the answers.

Q&A

Q. I want to use the new HTML5 input types, but not all browsers give me the nice input controls, like a calendar for choosing the date. Is there some way I can force this?

A. You can use jQuery UI (`http://jqueryui.com`) and Modernizr (`http://modernizr.com`) to create a fallback option for your date (or other input types) fields. Here's how:

1. Get jQuery UI and Modernizr and insert them in your web pages (by following the instructions on the respective pages).

2. Add a `<script>` tag to the bottom of the form page:

```
<script>
</script>
```

3. Add the following jQuery script inside the `<script>` tag:

```
if (!Modernizr.inputtypes.date) {
  $(function() {
    $( "#date" ).datepicker({ dateFormat: 'yy-mm-dd' });
  });
}
```

4. Change the `#date` setting to the ID of your date input tag.

Q. I noticed that none of the form examples you gave included an `action` attribute. How do I get my forms to work?

A. There are lots of ways to get forms to work, from using jQuery to detect when a submit button is clicked, to including `mailto:emailaddress` in the `action`, to using PHP and CGI scripts on the server in the `action` attribute of the form. For help learning how to make your web forms work, check out some of the many resources online.

Q. You never used the `method` attribute this hour. Isn't that a required field?

A. While it's a good idea to use the `method` attribute on forms that are submitted to a web server, most jQuery and JavaScript forms use the `get` method, and that is the default for all forms. If you need to use the `post` method, then you should explicitly state that in your `<form>` tags. Otherwise, you can leave it off.

Quiz

1. Name two input types that let you collect date or time information.
2. What is the difference between `range` and `number` input types?
3. Why is using the HTML5 input types so important?
4. Name the three validation attributes described in this hour.
5. When would you use the `novalidate` attribute?
6. Where is a good place to describe the patterns required by a field?
7. Why should you keep forms simple?
8. What is one way to change a form to make it more responsive?
9. True or False: A 100-item-long drop-down menu is as easy to use as a text field.
10. What tag do you use with `<datalist>` to list items?

Answers

1. There are six new date and time types in HTML5: `date`, `datetime`, `datetime-local`, `time`, `month`, and `week`.
2. `number` is a specific number value, while `range` is nonspecific.
3. The new input types make it much easier for customers to provide the data you want in a format you want. But they are especially useful for mobile customers because the devices display different keyboard layouts for the different types.
4. We discussed `novalidate`, `required`, and `pattern` in this hour.
5. You would use the `novalidate` attribute on forms where you don't want the browser to do any validation. One example is on a login form where the most common user name is an email address but a user can instead choose a user name as well. By setting the form to `novalidate`, both types are allowed. By using the `email` type, mobile browsers will display an email-related keyboard.

6. A good place to mention required patterns is next to the field in which they are used. Another good place is in the `placeholder` attribute.
7. Forms can be difficult to fill out, and in order to get the most completed forms possible, you should remove distractions from the page and make filling out the form as easy as possible.
8. You can remove extra form elements, rearrange them on the screen, or resize them so they fit differently on different screen sizes.
9. False. Most people find a text box much easier to use because their hands are already on the keyboard rather than the mouse, and they can type what they want faster than they can scroll through a list. Plus, drop-down menus more than 10 items long can be very difficult to use on mobile devices.
10. You use the `<option>` tag with `<datalist>` to define list items.

Exercises

1. Open the site you are working on for this book and find the contact page. Adjust the form to use HTML5 input fields. If you don't have a contact page for the site, create one using HTML5 input fields.
2. Check the contact form in a small-screen browser like a smartphone or cell phone. Then go to your CSS and adjust your form to be more effective on small-screen as well as large-screen devices.

HOUR 19
Testing Responsive Websites

WHAT YOU'LL LEARN IN THIS HOUR:

- Why testing RWD is so important
- How to test responsive sites in a web browser
- How to handle testing if you don't have a mobile device

Testing is a critical but often overlooked part of web design. In many workflows, it happens at the end of the whole process, and most team members are probably tired of the designing and want to go live.

But it's better if you do your testing as you move through the design, not just at the end, when you think the project is done. When you're testing, you might find problems that cause you to have to rethink your entire design, and if you're only a few hours into the project, you will have less to lose than if you're near what you thought was the end.

Most web designers find testing boring, but in RWD, it's especially important that you do a lot of testing so you can be sure that your designs are progressively enhanced and responsive. This hour goes through some of the things you should consider when testing a responsive website, as well as how to test and what to do about scenarios you can't test.

CAUTION

Some Code Can Be Hard to Test Locally

Keep in mind that some browsers don't display things like JavaScript or cookies in a local page. And server-side languages like PHP don't run in a `file://` file. To test these, you need a server. But that server doesn't have to be on the live web. You can run WAMP and MAMP (Windows/Macintosh, Apache, MySQL, and PHP) servers on your local machine to do initial testing of dynamic files.

NOTE

Many WYSIWYG Editors Are Good for Testing

A lot of people believe that WYSIWYG editors are good for nothing but the scrap heap. You will be told that they write bad HTML and CSS, they mess up sites, and they really aren't WYSIWYG (what you see is what you get). While all this was true 10 or 15 years ago, it's really not true now. Professional web design tools like Dreamweaver, Macaw, and CoffeeCup Responsive Layout Maker offer a visual environment alongside a code editor. You can often see right away how the HTML or CSS is going to look, and the code is written cleaner than some designers write it. Plus, visual editors make testing as you go a breeze. While you should still open your pages in web browsers and mobile devices periodically, using a visual WYSIWYG editor is good for a quick first pass. Web pages can be written in basic text editors or fancy web editors, but don't be afraid of visual editors because of past misconceptions.

Testing in Your Browser

The first place you should be testing is in your web browser on your computer. This may seem like obvious advice, but many designers overlook it in their zeal to test on devices. The benefit of testing on your computer is that you don't really have to do anything special. Most web browsers open local web pages without a problem, and you can even resize the browser to do an initial breakpoint test.

Keeping Your Browsers Up-to-Date

A web browser is a key tool in doing responsive design, and for best results, you should use a standards-compliant browser, like Chrome, Firefox, Opera, or Safari. If you use a standards-compliant browser to test your site and it does well, you know that your HTML, CSS, and JavaScript will be standards compliant as well. This helps to future-proof your pages.

Once you have your web pages working in a modern, standards-compliant browser, you can get the pages working in less compliant browsers. This may seem like advice that is contrary to the progressive enhancement mantra, but in reality it's not.

Web browsers like Internet Explorer will work fine in your standard HTML. Yes, older versions like version 8 have some issues with a few HTML5 elements, but the pages will generally work. And then you can decide what features are critical to the pages and add workarounds to get them working on Internet Explorer 8.

It's important to have a number of different browsers on your computer to test on. While Chrome and Safari both use Webkit as their base, they still can have differences. And the more browsers you test in, the better your site will look.

TRY IT YOURSELF ▼

Set Up a Testing Regimen

One of the best things you can do for your web designs is test them continuously as you build. By setting up a regimen for testing, you can get in the habit of testing iteratively rather than in one giant batch at the end of the design phase.

1. Start by testing a design in your HTML editor. While you can design web pages using almost any text editor, I recommend using one that has some form of visual display or editor built in. There are a lot of good WYSIWYG HTML editors available, and many of the professional editors have code editors as well as WYSIWYG editors. My favorites include Dreamweaver (version CS5 and above), Macaw, and CoffeeCup Responsive Layout Maker Pro. I discuss these editors in more detail in Hour 21, "Tools for Creating Responsive Web Designs."

   You should get in the habit of looking at your pages in the visual editor every time you make a change. If you're editing in a code editor, get in the habit of checking your pages visually at least once for every hour of coding.

2. Check your pages in Chrome or Safari every four to six hours that you spend writing HTML, CSS, or JavaScript. The visual tools in most editors are good, but nothing beats seeing your pages in a real web browser. I recommend using Chrome or Safari because these browsers tend to be more up-to-date with modern web technologies.

3. At the end of the workday, check your pages in other browsers, like Firefox, Opera, and Internet Explorer. Note any issues you find to fix the next day.

4. Once you start writing your breakpoint CSS (see Hour 10, "CSS Media Queries," and Hour 11, "Breakpoints"), start testing at the different breakpoints every hour in your editor. The editors I list above offer the ability to set the visual editor to different breakpoints for testing.

5. Every four to six hours of coding, check your pages in a browser at the different breakpoints. You can either use either a web browser like Chrome or open the pages in a device that matches your breakpoints.

6. Get in the habit of checking your pages in as many devices as possible on a regular basis, preferably every day.

The key to testing responsive designs is to test your pages in several devices on a regular basis. It is easy to get complacent and assume that if something works in one browser and device width, it will work in them all. But that is exactly the attitude that results in problems right before you want to launch. By catching issues early, while you're still designing, you can fix them immediately and be confident at launch that everything is going to look good.

Resizing Your Browser to Test Different Breakpoints

One of the quickest ways to test a breakpoint change is right in the web browser. Figure 19.1 shows two Safari windows open to different widths to test breakpoints in a design. To do this testing, you simply resize the browser window.

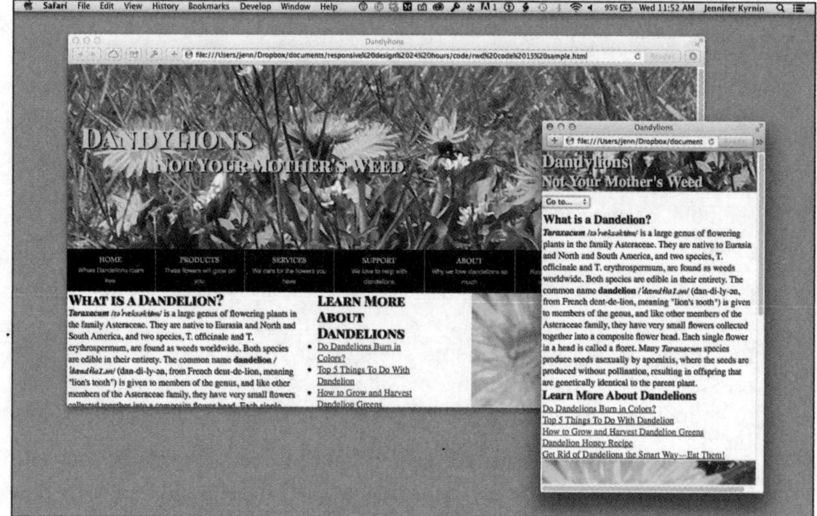

FIGURE 19.1
Two Safari windows testing the same page at different breakpoints.

This may seem obvious, but it is often overlooked, especially when you are focusing on mobile devices: Changing the width of the browser allows you to quickly test your pages in different breakpoints. And it can be pretty fun to drag your page through the different widths and watch it change.

Testing in a Device for All Your Breakpoints

It's a good idea to test your pages (using the regimen listed in the Try It Yourself) in a device that matches all your breakpoints. You need to test in a device as well as in a desktop browser because devices handle things differently in many cases. Figure 19.2 shows the same web page displayed in Opera at 320px wide and on an iPhone. And the two views look very different. The iPhone version has a lot more white space showing.

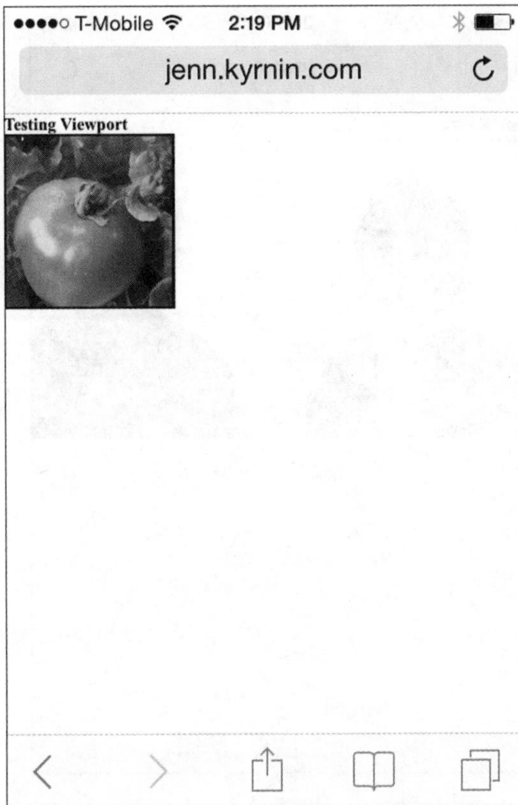

FIGURE 19.2
The same web page in a desktop browser (Opera) at 320px wide and on an iPhone 4S.

The iPhone (as well as other mobile devices) shows the page by default at a width determined by that manufacturer to be ideal for displaying web pages. In the case of the iPhone 4S, that is 980px. But as you can see from Figure 19.2, testing on a desktop browser would give you the wrong impression of the page.

It is very common on non-RWD sites to see web pages that are shrunken down and hard to read on a mobile device because the designer forgot to change the viewport and didn't test on a mobile device. Figure 19.3 shows a website I built a few years ago that has shrunk down until it's nearly illegible on my iPhone.

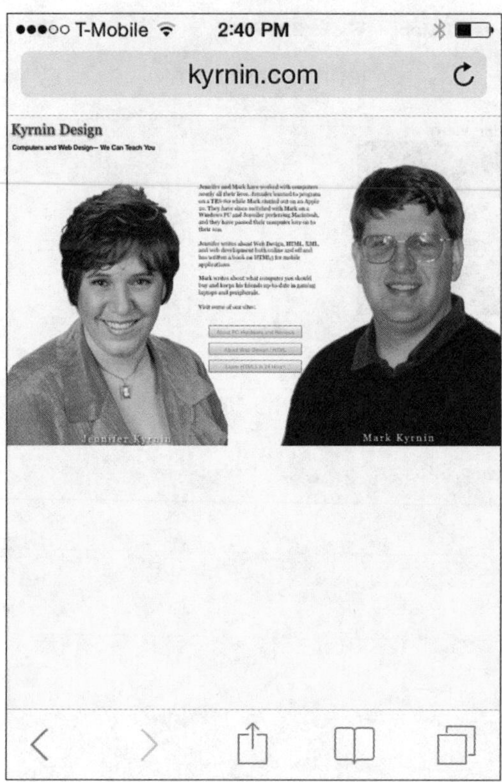

FIGURE 19.3
A non-RWD website on an iPhone.

Besides not being RWD, this website makes a big mistake for viewing on mobile devices. It doesn't use the `viewport` meta tag, like this:

```
<meta name="viewport" content="width=device-width">
```

This meta tag tells the browser that the viewable area of the web page should be the same as the device width, which on the iPhone 4S is 320px. Listing 19.1 shows the HTML to create the web page shown in Figure 19.2. This is the page without the `viewport` meta tag set.

LISTING 19.1 HTML Without the `viewport` Meta Tag

```
<!doctype html>
<html>
<head>
<meta charset="UTF-8">
<meta name="viewport" content="">
<title>Testing Viewport</title>
<style>
html, body, * { margin: 0; }
```

```
body { width: 600px; }
</style>
</head>
<body>
<h1>Testing Viewport</h1>
<img src="images/testing-viewport.png">
</body>
</html>
```

Just adding the `viewport` meta tag makes the page look much better on the iPhone, as you can see in Figure 19.4. Listing 19.2 shows the HTML.

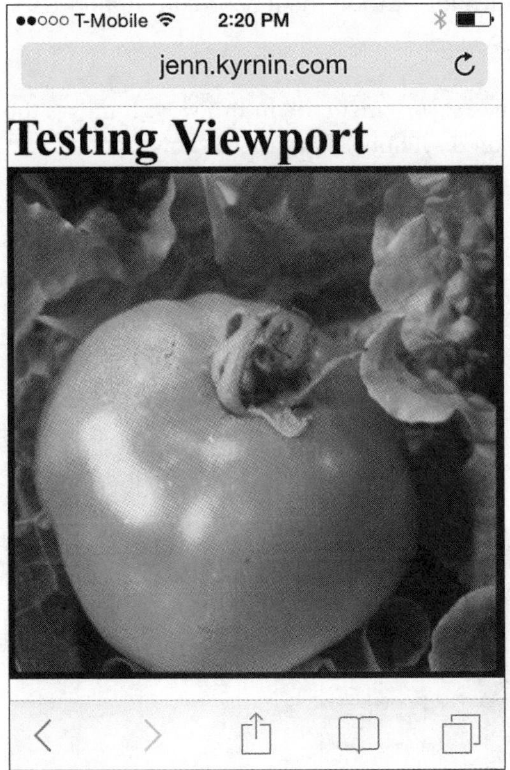

FIGURE 19.4
The same tomato web page as in Figure 19.2, now with the `viewport` meta tag.

LISTING 19.2 HTML with the `viewport` Meta Tag

```
<!doctype html>
<html>
<head>
<meta charset="UTF-8">
<meta name="viewport" content="width=device-width">
```

```
<title>Testing Viewport</title>
<style>
html, body, * { margin: 0; }
body { width: 600px; }
</style>
</head>
<body>
<h1>Testing Viewport</h1>
<img src="images/testing-viewport.png">
</body>
</html>
```

You can use the `viewport` meta tag to set the viewport to an explicit width. The web page in Figure 19.3 does use the `viewport` meta tag, but it sets it to a width that is much larger than the iPhone can support:

```
<meta name="viewport" content="width=1240">
```

I don't recommend using the `viewport` meta tag in this way. It makes the design much harder to read on an iPhone. Figure 19.5 shows that same page as Figure 19.3 with the viewport changed to `width=device-width`.

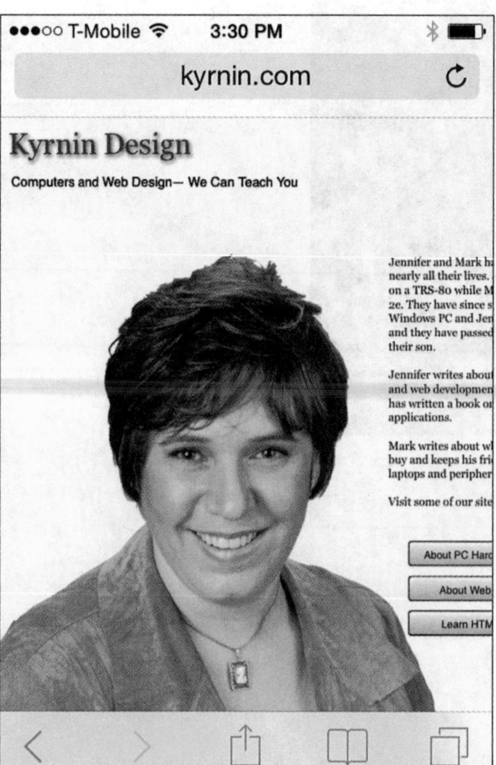

FIGURE 19.5
A non-RWD site with the viewport set to the device width.

As you can see, the page is still hard to read on an iPhone, but it's much more legible. It would be better if I made the site responsive, but for a quick fix, the `viewport` meta tag is a useful tool.

How to Test When You Don't Have the Devices

The challenge of testing responsive web design is the same as the challenge of testing any mobile website solution: There are dozens of different devices, device sizes, and device features, so how do you test them all?

When you are testing responsive web designs, there are three ways to test on mobile devices:

- Buy or rent a device.
- Borrow a device from a friend.
- Use a mobile emulator.

Most web designers can't afford to go out and purchase all the devices or even one in each category. To do a comprehensive test, though, you need to test on many different devices, including these:

- Small flip phones
- iOS phones
- Android phones
- Larger smartphones
- Phones on other operating systems, like Windows and Blackberry
- Small and large tablets in both Android and iOS operating systems

If you and your friends or co-workers don't own all these, you can rent them. There is a site called Rent Mobile Devices (`http://rentmobiledevices.com`) that allows device owners to lend out their phones or tablets and get paid for the lease. It doesn't have a lot of options right now but might get better as time goes on. Another site, Mobile Device Rentals (`http://www.mobiledevicerental.mobi`), offers tablets and laptops for rent. There are also other sites where you can find mobile phones and tablets for rent.

Your last resort, if you can't find a specific mobile device to test on, is an emulator. These are the desktop emulators that you can use to test your web pages before they go live:

- **Android SDK**—`http://developer.android.com/sdk/index.html` (This is part of the Eclipse environment, and not primarily an emulator.)
- **Blackberry**—`http://us.blackberry.com/sites/developers/resources/simulators.html`
- **iOS SDK**—`https://developer.apple.com/devcenter/ios/index.action` (You must log in as an Apple developer to download it.)
- **Opera**—`http://www.opera.com/developer` (You can download both Opera mobile and mini simulators.)
- **WebOS**—`https://developer.palm.com/content/api/dev-guide/tools/emulator.html`
- **Windows Phone Developer Tools**—`http://www.microsoft.com/en-us/download/details.aspx?id=13890`

There are also online emulators you can use to test pages that are on a live server:

- **Pixmobi Mobile Phone Emulator**—`www.mobilephoneemulator.com`. This emulator shows you several different devices (iOS, Android, Windows, and Blackberry). What's nice is that it shows you the device at approximately real size, based on your monitor size. But this site doesn't offer any tablet emulators.
- **iPad Peek**—`http://ipadpeek.com`. iPad Peek shows you an iPad, iPhone 5, or iPhone 4 emulation. I found the emulation to be a little off when I compared the same site on my iPad and this emulator.
- **Prism**—`http://prism.mobiforge.com`. There are a lot of devices to choose from on this site, but the emulation seems to be primarily just the size. And as with iPad Peek, the emulation here seemed a bit off to me.
- **Device Anywhere**—`http://www.keynotedeviceanywhere.com/mobile-testing.html`. This testing solution isn't free, but it offers a lot of options and devices for testing.

Emulators should always be a last resort because they aren't as accurate as they might seem. Plus, most mobile devices have touch screens, and there is a different way of interacting with web pages with a mouse than with a finger. But if you have one mobile device and need to test on other breakpoints, a mobile emulator along with your desktop browsers is a good substitute.

Don't forget about asking your customers for help with testing. You can put your site up at a testing server and ask for beta users to test how it works on their devices. If they find problems, they can send you a screen capture along with what device they are using. This is a great way to interact with your customers after the site is live as well.

Just remember: You can never do too much testing.

Summary

In this hour you've learned techniques for testing responsive websites. You've learned that you can use your desktop web browsers as well as WYSIWYG web editors to do initial testing. You've also learned some techniques for testing on mobile devices even if you don't have any to use.

Workshop

The workshop contains quiz questions to help you process what you've learned in this lesson. Try to answer all the questions before you read the answers.

Q&A

Q. Do *you* really do as much testing as you say is needed?

A. The amount of testing I do depends a lot on the project itself and how much the site owner wants. If there are a lot of mobile features like mapping or offline caching, I'll spend more time testing in as many devices as I can. For basic RWD sites where it's mostly layout changes for the different devices, I rely on the mobile devices I own (several different phones and tablets) for most of my testing. I have been doing web design since 1995, and I have a pretty good feel for what is going to work and what isn't.

Q. I use emulators all the time, and they work fine for testing my pages. Why are you so down on them?

A. Emulators work well as long as you understand their limitations. The most important thing to remember when using an emulator is that a phone or tablet is different from your computer. A link that is easy to click with a mouse might be too close to another to easily tap with a fat finger. Geolocation works much better on a device that moves around in space than on a desktop on a desk. A few years ago it was very common to find mobile web designs that had never been tested on a mobile device—only on emulators. And they often had usability issues that the computer-centric designers had failed to consider. As long as you are aware of the potential problems, emulators are a fine testing tool.

Q. What versions of Internet Explorer should I test with?

A. The correct answer to this is that it depends on your website. If you are writing a site that caters to people still using Windows XP, then you might have to test in Internet Explorer 6 or 7. A website that caters to cutting-edge designs might not have to go back any further than Internet Explorer 9. You should have a good understanding of your website audience before you start building so you know what versions of Internet Explorer you will need to support and test.

Q. How do I test with multiple versions of Internet Explorer?

A. One of the easiest ways to test older versions of Internet Explorer is to use a modern version of Internet Explorer and the developer tools that are built in. In Internet Explorer 8, 9, 10, and 11, you press F12 to access the developer tools, and from there you can choose to view the page in a different rendering engine, going back to Internet Explorer 6.

Quiz

1. Why is testing so important for RWD websites?
2. True or False: You should start testing RWD sites in a web browser.
3. True or False: Using visual or WYSIWYG editors is a bad choice for building and testing RWD sites.
4. True or False: You can test everything for a RWD site on your local machine.
5. Why should you use standards-compliant browsers for your preliminary testing?
6. What browsers are standards compliant?
7. How often should you check your pages in browsers other than your preferred standards-compliant browser?
8. Name two ways to test different breakpoints.
9. How often should you test your pages on mobile devices?
10. Name two ways to test in devices even if you don't own them.

Answers

1. Testing is important with RWD websites because these sites need to work on many different devices. It can be easy to fix a problem on one device or breakpoint only to have the fix cause another problem in another device or breakpoint.
2. True. Your web browser should be open the entire time you are working on a responsive site so that you can test regularly.
3. False. Using a visual editor that has code view built in can be a very good choice for editing RWD sites because these editors let you see how the page will look without requiring you to switch to a browser.
4. True. While you can't test things like PHP on your local machine without a web server, it is easy to set up a server using WAMP or MAMP for initial testing.

5. When you use standards-compliant browsers, you ensure that your pages will be standards compliant as well. And this makes them more future-proof.
6. Chrome, Firefox, Safari, and Opera are considered standards compliant. Internet Explorer 10 and 11 are getting closer, but many non-web developers still use older versions of Internet Explorer, so many web designers use the older versions, too.
7. You should check your web pages in several web browsers at least once every day that you work on a site.
8. You can test your breakpoints in an editor that lets you change the viewport size, in a web browser by resizing the window, or in a device that meets the breakpoint criteria.
9. Once you start adding breakpoints in your designs, you should test them at least once a day in mobile devices.
10. You can test on devices even if you don't own them by borrowing devices from friends, family members, and co-workers; by renting devices; and by using emulators.

Exercises

1. Open the site you've been working on for this book and test it in your web browser, in a resized web browser window, in at least two other web browsers on your desktop, and then on any mobile devices you have. If you've never done this for your entire site, make an effort to go to every page, or at least every type of page (home page, link lists, articles, contact forms, etc.). The more pages you look at, the more problems you will find and fix before your customers find them and leave.
2. If you don't have enough mobile devices to test in all the breakpoints you've created, borrow or rent one if you can and test the pages in them. If you can't borrow or rent a device, test out the pages in an emulator.

HOUR 20

Problems with Responsive Web Design

WHAT YOU'LL LEARN IN THIS HOUR:

- The most common problems with RWD
- How to solve those problems
- How to prevent new problems

Like everything in life, RWD is not a panacea. There are problems that you'll discover as you build responsive sites. It's possible to fix some of them and work around others, but some you just have to learn to live with.

This hour you will learn about some of the most common problems web designers and website owners have with responsive design, and it offers solutions for dealing with them.

Remember that just because a technology has problems doesn't mean you shouldn't use it. And if you're aware of the issues, they won't be a surprise if or when they appear.

Responsive Designs Can Be Slow

When you build a responsive website, you create more content, CSS, and decorative images than most of your users will see. This means that every time customers come to your site, they are downloading more than just the content they are using. And any extra download will cause your pages to be slower.

Impatient Mobile Customers

Needing to download extra content doesn't tend to affect a lot of computer users because they are viewing the page on a Wi-Fi or other high-speed Internet connection. But for a customer accessing your page on a cell phone network, the speed of a page can be a huge issue.

In several surveys, mobile customers have indicated that they expect the web pages they visit to be as fast as or nearly as fast as they are when viewing them on a computer. They claim that they will wait six to ten seconds for a page to load on their phone, but in practice the abandonment time is usually after around five seconds.

If your page has extra images or extra-large images that mobile customers must download—even if they aren't displayed in their version of the page—that will slow down the pages.

Speeding Up Your Pages

The best way to speed up your pages is to use the same best practices you use to create a fast site. Yahoo! has developed a list of 23 best practices for web performance. These are the ones I find easiest to implement:

- Minimize HTTP requests.
- Use a content delivery network (CDN).
- Put style sheets at the top.
- Put scripts at the bottom.
- Make JavaScript and CSS external.
- Reduce DNS lookups.
- Do not scale images in HTML.

There are many more recommendations for speeding up your site, and you can read about all of them at `https://developer.yahoo.com/yslow/`.

Minimizing HTTP Requests

Every time you put an image, a script, or a media file in your HTML, CSS, or JavaScript, the browser has to ask the server for that file, and then the sever sends it to the browser. And every request to the server takes some time. It may not seem like a lot, but it can add up.

The best way to minimize HTTP requests is to combine your files as much as possible. Use sprites for images. A sprite is a single image file that you crop to show individual icons and images using CSS. You should also collect all your scripts into one JavaScript file and all your styles into one CSS style sheet. You can use image maps to combine multiple images into one.

You can also use inline images and the `data:` URL scheme to embed an image into the HTML and CSS directly. This may increase the size of your documents, but it can help reduce HTTP requests.

Using a Content Delivery Network

Using a content delivery network (CDN) is a great way to speed up your pages because they rely on servers that are already cached on most customers' machines. It's best to use a CDN for content that a lot of people around the world will be using, like jQuery and other JavaScript libraries. Google hosts a lot of JavaScript libraries on its CDN, `https://developers.google.com/speed/libraries/devguide`.

Putting Style Sheets at the Top

You should place your style sheets at the top of your HTML, inside the `<head>` of the document. This makes the pages appear to load more quickly because the styles are loaded before the content of the page. This prevents content from appearing unstyled or a blank white screen from flashing as the browser decides how to render the content.

Putting Scripts at the Bottom

You might think that scripts should also go in the `<head>` of an HTML document, but placing scripts there can drastically slow down both the perceived and actual download times. This is because scripts are not downloaded in parallel with other items, so when the browser comes upon a script to download, all other downloads stop until the script is complete. If the page has already rendered, this delay isn't noticeable and makes the page usable for the customer that much faster. By putting scripts at the bottom of the HTML, rather than in the head, this ensures that the entire page has loaded before the scripts.

Making JavaScript and CSS External

This may seem to be a contradiction of the first recommendation to reduce HTTP requests, but it's not a contradiction because browsers cache both CSS and JavaScript files. If you include the styles and scripts in your HTML, you are not taking advantage of the cache.

The question is, do your customers stay on your site for more than one page? If they do—and this is true for most sites—then using one external JavaScript file and one external CSS file will reduce the HTTP requests for the site overall because those files are in the cache after the first load. However, if you are building a single-page site, your page will load more quickly with the CSS and JavaScript inline.

Reducing DNS Lookups

Every time you link a page element from a different domain, you force the browser to look up that address and return an IP address. This typically takes 20 to 120 milliseconds. Once a domain has been looked up, the browser caches the location for between a minute and an hour. By consolidating all your files (images, style sheets, scripts, media, etc.) on the same domain, you let the browser use the cached location rather than add time on looking up another domain.

Avoiding Scaling Images in HTML

Scaling images is the number-one reason RWD websites are so slow to download. As you learned in Hour 15, "Creating and Using Images in RWD," most RWD sites use flexible-width images. In other words, they create one image that is sized for the largest monitor or device viewing the page, and then they use CSS to change the width and height responsively. But this means that smartphones and cell phones are forced to download images that are much larger than they can easily view and that take a long time to download over a cellular network.

The Yahoo! best practices site specifically calls out not using a bigger image than you need and then setting the `width` and `height` attributes in HTML to the size you need, but using CSS does the same thing. CSS (and HTML) does not change the actual size of the file; it just changes how the file is displayed.

The best solution here is to use server-side scripts to deliver different images, depending on the device that is viewing them. In some cases, it might just be a resized version of the same large image that desktop viewers get, but instead of 10MB, it's only 10KB. You will learn more about how to do this in Hour 22, "Device and Feature Detection," and Hour 23, "Using RESS with RWD."

RWD Can Make More Work for Designers

A problem with responsive web design is how much work it can be for the web designers building the site. I've heard many designers complain that instead of having to build one site, they now have to build three (or more) for the same price. To some extent, this is true. For a website with two breakpoints, you need to create three separate designs: one for the smallest screens, the middle-sized screens (first breakpoint), and the largest screens (second breakpoint). You may have to create new images for the different designs, and you must work with the customer to determine what, if any, content is optional and can be removed from the smallest screens.

But if you've read the first 19 hours in this book, you already have a good understanding of how to do that efficiently. Back in Hour 4, "Progressive Enhancement," you learned how to start with the smallest screens and build on content, designs, and interactivity from there.

The other thing you should realize is that by doing RWD, you are delivering a better package for your customers, so you should be able to charge more for the work. If you find you can't charge more, then you should work smart. Here are some examples of how to work smart:

- **Limit the number of breakpoints your design will support.** The more breakpoints a design has, the more responsive it is, but this also means more work for designers.
- **Limit the design changes.** As with breakpoints, if the changes are minimal, the amount of work required is also minimal.
- **Limit testing.** In Hour 19, "Testing Responsive Websites," I suggested that you should test every hour or so to make sure your designs are working, but this can slow things down. I still recommend doing testing while you're designing, but if you do it less frequently, you might speed up the project.
- **Become an expert at RWD.** The better you know how to build an RWD site, the faster you will be able to do it. Plus, you'll be able to implement more solutions without needing as much testing, as you'll know what works and what doesn't.

Another solution would be to not do RWD and seek out only customers who don't want it. But that would ultimately hurt your ability as a designer. RWD is a popular solution, and as more and more people move to mobile devices, it is going to be more popular.

Not All Customers Like Responsive Sites

This is one of those facts that many designers don't like to face, but it's true. There are customers who don't like or want RWD sites. I've found that there are generally two groups of people who don't want RWD: web design clients and mobile web customers.

NOTE

Be Sure to Build and Test for the Client's Devices

It's embarrassing to admit how many times I've been nearly done with a project only to have the client say to me, "I was checking out the new site on my Blackberry yesterday, and there's a problem." I have been doing web design since 1995, and you would think that I would know by now to build and test for my clients' mobile devices. At the very least, by knowing what devices your client has, you know you can test with them.

The Expense of RWD

While there are many clients out there who come to a web designer saying they want their site to "be responsive," there are others who see responsiveness as a drawback. In fact, they might see it as just another way for you to charge more for the same services.

While it's true that you may be doing more work to build a responsive website, if customers don't see the need, they will object to the charges. And often if you try to explain why RWD is important, unless you keep it very high level, most clients will get bored and disagree with the need. Most clients want their websites to work on the devices they use, and they forget that other customers might use other devices.

I don't recommend including specific charges for responsive design in your contracts unless clients are asking for something beyond the usual layout and design changes. Instead, you should focus on how your design techniques will deliver a site that looks great on smartphones and large monitors and devices in between. And then set your prices accordingly.

Expecting More from Mobile Sites

A problem with RWD that designers would like to pretend isn't true is that mobile customers want more than just a scaled-down version of the site on their phones. There are apps out there that do some really amazing things, so they know their smartphones are just that—smart! But when you visit some dumbed-down mobile and responsive sites, it's clear that the designers don't like building mobile designs.

As mentioned earlier in this book, mobile customers want to get the same experience on their small devices as they get on full-sized computers. But even more importantly, they want *more* than they get from their computers. Mobile devices offer features that you can't always get on desktops, like these:

- **Geolocation**—A device with this feature knows where the user is and can show maps and directions that respond to the person's movement. Websites that include geolocation where appropriate can improve the experience on a mobile device.
- **Built-in cameras**—A device with a camera can take photos and videos, and users want apps and websites that let them interact in that way. There are even apps you can use to play augmented reality games on the phone. This is harder for websites to do, as the camera is often blocked from the browser, but there are ways to work around this.
- **Other built-in hardware**—Many devices now have pedometers, altimeters, levels, and other hardware features that can be used in apps but are often hard to access from a website.
- **Offline access**—This is less a feature than a fact: Not all mobile devices are connected to the web at all times. And sometimes the customers don't want to connect because of the costs. Websites that don't have offline capability won't get used.

The best responsive sites use technology like I teach in my book *Sams Teach Yourself HTML5 Mobile Application Development in 24 Hours*. And by using server scripts, as you'll learn in Hour 22 and Hour 23, you can deliver even more powerful mobile versions of your responsive website.

RWD May Break Advertising

This is the elephant in the room when it comes to doing responsive web design: Advertising is the biggest problem holding back RWD.

The main problem with advertising is that advertisements on the web are delivered at fixed sizes. These sizes are chosen to look good at one size only, and they are designed to fit into websites of a certain size. They are usually sold based on their size and position on the page. Figure 20.1 shows a web page with two advertisements mocked up on it.

Dandylions
Advertisement
DANDYLIONS
NOT YOUR MOTHER'S WEED
HOME
Where Dandelions roam free
PRODUCTS
These flowers will grow on you
SERVICES
We care for the flowers you have
SUPPORT
We love to help with dandelions
ABOUT
Why we love dandelions so much
READING
Read more about this wondrous plant
CONTACT
Ask us about your dandelion needs
WHAT IS A DANDELION?
Taraxacum /təˈræksəkʉm/ is a large genus of flowering plants in the family Asteraceae. They are native to Eurasia and North and South America, and two species, T. officinale and T. erythrospermum, are found as weeds worldwide. Both species are edible in their entirety. The common name dandelion /ˈdændɨlaɪ.ən/ (dan-di-ly-ən, from French dent-de-lion, meaning "lion's tooth") is given to members of the genus, and like other members of the Asteraceae family, they have very small flowers collected together into a composite flower head. Each single flower in a head is called a floret. Many Taraxacum species produce seeds asexually by apomixis, where the seeds are produced without pollination, resulting in offspring that are genetically identical to the parent plant.
LEARN MORE ABOUT DANDELIONS
Do Dandelions Burn in Colors?
Top 5 Things To Do With Dandelion
How to Grow and Harvest Dandelion Greens
Dandelion Honey Recipe
Get Rid of Dandelions the Smart Way—Eat Them!
Ad

FIGURE 20.1
A responsive page with some ads in a mockup.

But, as you see in Figure 20.2, the banner won't fit on the page at the smallest breakpoint. The logical solution would seem to be to make the advertising image responsive as well.

The problem is that advertisers are paying for the placement of the ad as well as its size. If you change the size responsively, they aren't getting what they paid for. And if you change the placement in the layout, they also aren't getting what they paid for.

But more than position and size, advertisers are also paying for prominence. If you make your advertisement flex with the size of the screen, it might take up more space than the advertiser paid for, but more likely it will take up less. And this is when advertisers start to object. And advertisers object by taking their money elsewhere.

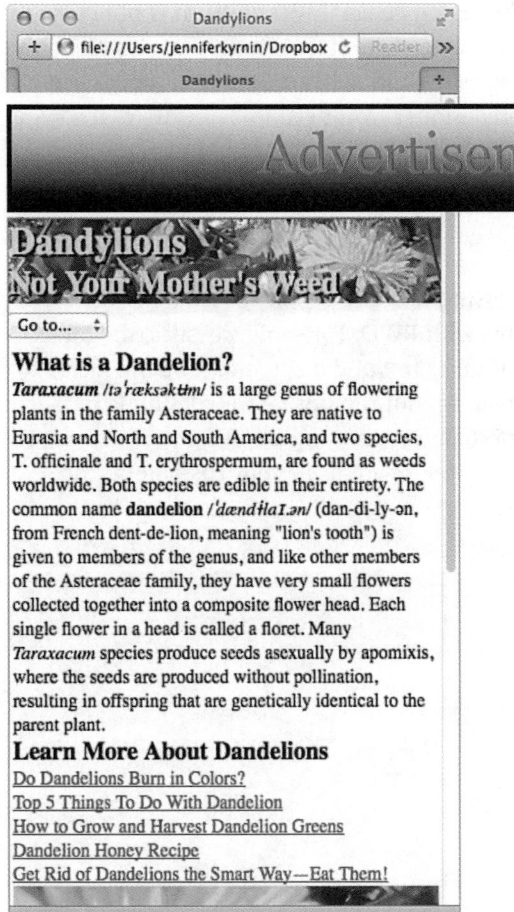
Dandylions
file:///Users/jenniferkyrnin/Dropbox
Reader
Dandylions
Advertisem
Dandylions
Not Your Mother's Weed
Go to...
What is a Dandelion?
Taraxacum /tə'ræksəkʉm/ is a large genus of flowering plants in the family Asteraceae. They are native to Eurasia and North and South America, and two species, T. officinale and T. erythrospermum, are found as weeds worldwide. Both species are edible in their entirety. The common name dandelion /'dændɨlaɪ.ən/ (dan-di-ly-ən, from French dent-de-lion, meaning "lion's tooth") is given to members of the genus, and like other members of the Asteraceae family, they have very small flowers collected together into a composite flower head. Each single flower in a head is called a floret. Many Taraxacum species produce seeds asexually by apomixis, where the seeds are produced without pollination, resulting in offspring that are genetically identical to the parent plant.
Learn More About Dandelions
Do Dandelions Burn in Colors?
Top 5 Things To Do With Dandelion
How to Grow and Harvest Dandelion Greens
Dandelion Honey Recipe
Get Rid of Dandelions the Smart Way—Eat Them!

FIGURE 20.2
The banner doesn't fit at the smaller screen size.

Luckily, advertisers are starting to address this issue themselves. Some ad companies are offering new forms of responsive advertising:

- Some companies sell advertising packages rather than slots, so the designer can provide three ads in a two-breakpoint site without changing what the advertiser purchased.
- Some companies sell slots just in specific breakpoints. This allows advertisers to target specific devices, and they might end up spending more for those ads.
- Some companies sell sponsorship and other site-wide promotions. Then advertisers can create ads for every version of the site.

I am confident that the advertising-versus-RWD problem is not going to be around much longer as advertisers start getting comfortable with the new way of designing websites and delivering content to customers. But as a responsive web designer, you need to be aware of it so you can plan for it in your designs.

Summary

This hour might seem depressing to some people, as it's a discussion of some of the biggest problems with RWD. For some websites, the advertising problem or the time it takes to build a site might be the factor that keeps RWD from happening. But responsive web design is considered a best *practice*, not *perfection*. By being aware of some of the ways RWD can go wrong, you can prepare yourself, your customers, and your websites ahead of time.

Workshop

The workshop contains quiz questions to help you process what you've learned in this lesson. Try to answer all the questions before you read the answers.

Q&A

Q. What about search engine optimization (SEO)? Does RWD cause problems with search engines viewing and indexing the content?

A. No. One of the best features of RWD is that, when done right, the content for the site is included in the HTML, and that is what the search engines are cataloging. A search engine will not see a responsive site any differently than it sees a nonresponsive site. Where you get problems with SEO is when a site is not well designed. If your pages don't use mobile-specific keywords and you don't have a well-defined information architecture for the site, your pages will not show up well in search. But this is true whether your site is RWD or not.

Q. My scripts use `document.write()` or other functions that require them to be placed somewhere else in the document than at the bottom. Will that slow down my page?

A. The best scripts use unobtrusive JavaScript, as I mentioned in Hour 7, "Unobtrusive JavaScript." If you are using a `document.write()` to insert content, you should review how to convert that to unobtrusive JavaScript so that the page can load before the JavaScript loads. If you don't, yes, that will slow down your page's load time.

Quiz

1. True or False: The problems surrounding RWD make it impossible to implement for most websites.
2. True or False: Mobile customers don't mind waiting for web pages to load.
3. How long will most mobile customers wait for a page to load?
4. True or False: Mobile customers do not want a different experience from desktop customers.
5. Name two ways you can speed up an RWD website.
6. Where is the best place to put your JavaScript files to keep your pages loading quickly?

7. Name three ways you can make designing RWD sites faster and easier.
8. Name two things mobile customers want on web pages that desktop browsers can't always do.
9. What makes most advertising not responsive?
10. Name one way advertisers can address RWD sites with their ads.

Answers

1. False. Some of the problems are difficult and can create a lot of extra work for designers, but there are ways to get around most of them.
2. False. While mobile customers will state that they are willing to wait, in reality they wait only between 5 and 10 seconds.
3. They claim they will wait 6 to 10 seconds, but users typically abandon a page after 5 to 8 seconds.
4. True. Mobile customers expect their smartphones to be able to deliver websites as robust and interactive as those on their desktops.
5. You speed up an RWD site the same ways you speed up a non-RWD site. Some examples listed this hour are minimize HTTP requests, use a content delivery network (CDN), put style sheets at the top, put scripts at the bottom, make JavaScript and CSS external, reduce DNS lookups, and avoid scaling images in HTML or CSS.
6. You should always place a link to your external JavaScript file at the end of your HTML, right before the closing `</body>` tag.
7. To reduce the time spent developing, you should limit the breakpoints, layout changes, and testing of your RWD pages. Plus, by becoming an RWD expert, you will speed up the design time.
8. RWD cannot deliver features like geolocation, offline caching, access to built-in cameras, and other technology.
9. At this point, most advertising is not responsive because it is written with explicit pixel widths and heights.
10. Advertisers can buy and sell packages of ads rather than specific sizes, they can buy and sell ads for specific breakpoint sizes and slots, or they can buy and sell sponsorship deals where they advertise on the entire site.

Exercises

1. If your site has (or you want it to have) advertising, begin looking for ways to deliver responsive ads or sell packages of ads that change depending on the breakpoint. Consider checking out a service like ResponsiveAds (`http://www.responsiveads.com`) to generate the ads for your site.

2. Go through your site HTML, CSS, and JavaScript to speed it up. Install YSlow (`https://developer.yahoo.com/yslow/`) in your browser and check your site's speed grade. Follow the instructions in the YSlow evaluation to improve your speed.

HOUR 21
Tools for Creating Responsive Web Designs

WHAT YOU'LL LEARN IN THIS HOUR:

- Some of the many tools available for RWD
- How to use RWD tools effectively
- Issues to watch out for with some RWD tools
- Several web editors that have RWD built in

There are many tools you can use to help plan, design, build, test, and maintain your responsive websites that there is no way I could cover them all in an hour. But in this hour I will show you some of the tools I use and find valuable for doing RWD.

If you read only one section of this hour, make it "Web Editors for Building Responsive Web Pages." It describes the three web editors I've found that do responsive design right. But in this hour I also cover some other excellent tools. I share tools for every step of the process, including these:

- Tools for planning your RWD site
- Tools for helping you get started designing
- Specific tools for HTML elements like tables and forms
- Tools for helping with CSS media queries and breakpoints
- Testing tools that really work for testing RWD

With the tools mentioned in this hour, you will have all you need to build a robust responsive website.

Planning and Designing Your RWD Site

As mentioned in earlier hours, the first step in building a responsive site is planning. And there are a lot of tools you can use to help make your planning more effective.

When I'm first thinking about a design, I like to draw on paper. I have sketched designs on napkins, and I've used the backs of my son's old school papers as well. But when you want to show clients your sketches, a more polished look can be better. Jeremy Palford's Responsive Web Design Sketch Sheets (`http://jeremypalford.com/arch-journal/responsive-web-design-sketch-sheets/`) provides a simple template to sketch out a layout for four device sizes. As you can see in Figure 21.1, you can even open the PDFs in Photoshop and sketch on your computer if you prefer.

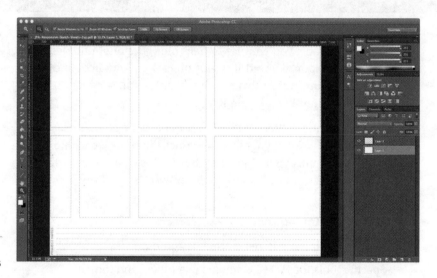

FIGURE 21.1
Edit the sketch sheet in Photoshop for online sketching.

But if you're like me, once you start editing a file like this on the computer, you start wanting the elements of the page designs to look nicer. Your sketch of a button on a bar napkin might look like a blob. Even an early mockup needs to look good when you're showing it to clients.

This is where I move to wireframe tools. There are a number of apps for both tablets and computers that you can use to create great-looking mockups of websites. It's important to remember to create mockups for all the devices you want to support. And it's a good idea to record where you think the breakpoints should be. These numbers may change once you start building the site, but wireframes can give you a good start.

NOTE

Remember That Wireframes Are Mockups

I often see beginning web designers get caught up in creating picture-perfect mockups. I knew a web designer who would use Photoshop to create amazing pictures of the websites he planned. The drawings were great, but this guy was often disappointed by the end results of the web pages because he couldn't get them pixel perfect like his pictures. Wireframes are useful tools, but remember that they are just that—tools. While it can be fun to create mockups in wireframe tools, it's more fun to create a working responsive website.

These are some of the more popular wireframe tools:

- **Axure** (`http://www.axure.com`)—This desktop app gives you a lot of prototyping tools and features. You can create really nice-looking mockups and then convert them to HTML to publish online. The pro version allows you to create Word templates and work in teams. This is a fairly expensive software product, but it does a lot and is very popular with web design firms.
- **Balsamiq** (`http://balsamiq.com/products/mockups/`)—Balsamiq Mockups offers both a web application you can use on a subscription basis and a desktop application you can purchase outright. Using this product is much more like drawing than other apps.
- **MockFlow** (`http://www.mockflow.com`)—The free version of this product allows one project with one user and four pages. You can also have up to two co-editors and unlimited reviewers. This is a desktop application, but it also includes features to let you create a website and build a mockup for a web app, among others. I am not a huge fan of this product because to get more team features, you have to pay a subscription. But lots of web design teams use this tool very effectively.
- **Moqups** (`https://moqups.com`)—You can play with this online HTML5 mockups tool without an account. But it's also a subscription model with no desktop application. There are a lot of stencils to choose from, and if you just want to do a quick mockup online, you can use the playground and then take a screen shot.
- **Pencil Project** (`http://pencil.evolus.vn`)—This is an open source GUI prototyping tool. It's not as fancy as some of the other paid products, but it does offer templates and stencils for lots of different shapes and operating systems.

Once you've got an idea of how you're going to design your pages, you can start working on the pages themselves, and there are tools for that, too. The most commonly used tools are frameworks.

A *framework* is a package of HTML, CSS, and often JavaScript files that make building a website easier. They provide a common structure so that you, the web designer or developer, don't have to reinvent the wheel while designing your site.

Responsive frameworks provide you things like the following:

- CSS to create a grid system for laying out your web pages
- Typography styles so you don't have to figure out the best sizes and line heights
- Styles and scripts to support older browsers and browser versions

These are some of the best responsive frameworks:

- **Responsive Grid System (`http://www.responsivegridsystem.com`)**—This company claims its tool isn't a framework or a boilerplate, but it provides all the features you need to create a great responsive website quickly and easily. It includes basic mobile breakpoints but uses percentages so that it will scale to any browser width. I like to use this system.
- **Foundation (`http://foundation.zurb.com`)**—This is one of the first frameworks I've found that cares about speed—but not speed for developers. No, no…Foundation is a framework that is faster for the end users. But it does care about speed for developers, too; for example, it includes a command-line tool to help create projects faster. It's a lot to learn, but Foundation provides a semantic, mobile-first environment for your responsive websites.
- **HTML5 Boilerplate (`http://html5boilerplate.com`)**—This is one of the first frameworks I ever used. I liked it because it was small and easy to use. It's mobile friendly and includes Google Analytics built in.
- **Bootstrap (`http://getbootstrap.com`)**—Twitter created this framework, which uses both LESS and SASS to help speed up your CSS. It offers lots of components, like drop-downs, buttons, thumbnails, typography, and more.

Some people don't like using frameworks because they often include more overhead than many smaller sites really need. The solution to this is to get familiar with web design patterns and include only the patterns you need for your site.

Design patterns are snippets of HTML, CSS, and JavaScript code that solve specific problems on websites. The best-known list of web design patterns is the Yahoo User Interface (YUI) Library (`http://yuilibrary.com`).

While it's possible to generate your own patterns, many patterns have already been developed, so you don't have to reinvent anything. Here are some of my favorite website patterns sites:

- **Responsive Patterns** (`http://bradfrost.github.io/this-is-responsive/patterns.html`)—I like this site because it offers more than just layout and navigation patterns. A few of the patterns aren't linked correctly, which is disappointing, but there are a lot of choices to find the pattern you need for your site.
- **RWD Table Patterns** (`http://gergeo.se/RWD-Table-Patterns/`)—These patterns can be imported into the Bootstrap framework. They are built mobile first with progressive enhancement, and they include JavaScript fallbacks for tables.
- **Responsive Email Patterns** (`http://responsiveemailpatterns.com`)—These patterns are for email specifically but can be used on websites, too.

HTML Element and CSS Tools

Once you get started building the HTML and CSS for your website, you'll find a lot of tools that can help you with the specifics.

CSS Media Query Tools

Once you've built 100 media queries, you might not need any tools to help you build them. But until then, take a look at these tools, which can make building media queries much easier:

- **Media Query Snippets** (`http://nmsdvid.com/snippets/`)—This page offers a couple dozen snippets for different devices and screen sizes.
- **@media.info** (`http://atmedia.info`)—This tool gives you information for the device currently viewing the page, which allows you to create a media query for a specific device.
- **CSS Media Queries Test** (`http://mediaqueriestest.com`)—This is another tool that gives you the various attributes of the device viewing the page. What's nice about this tool is that it's responsive and adjusts to the screen width. But it also includes optional extensions you can test for, or you can run your own custom media queries to see if the current screen supports them. Finally, this page has a QR code you can scan with a mobile device to get that device's results quickly.

Type Tools

As you learned in Hour 14, "Responsive Fonts and Typography," dealing with typography in responsive design can be frustrating. Luckily there are all kinds of helpful tools, from scripts to add to your pages to type testers and more. These are some of my favorite type tools for responsive design:

- **Type Tester** (`http://www.typetester.org`)—This tool is useful for more than just responsive web design. It gives you a great visual of how a font will look. You can change the size, leading, tracking, alignment, word spacing, decoration, color, and background color.
- **IcoMoon** (`http://icomoon.io`)—Using icons is a great way to add images to your pages because they load much more quickly than actual images. IcoMoon offers a free app to build a font with exactly the images you need for your site. Then you just use web fonts to display the images at whatever size you need.
- **Lettering.js** (`http://letteringjs.com`)—Yes, it's another jQuery plug-in, but it gives you a lot more control over your type. You can easily kern type, control the type design, and manage the code that does it.
- **FitText** (`http://fittextjs.com`)—This jQuery plug-in is by the same folks who made Lettering.js. This one helps you make your giant headlines fit on multiple devices.
- **PXtoEM** (`http://pxtoem.com`)—This tool helps you use ems for measuring more than fonts. You set your base font size and can then define exact pixel widths, using ems.

Image Tools

Images are an important part of web pages. And as you learned in Hour 20, "Problems with Responsive Web Design," images are a major problem in responsive web designs. The following tools can help you adjust image sizes on-the-fly and deal with the problems images cause in RWD:

- **Adaptive Images** (`http://adaptive-images.com`)—You can use this PHP and JavaScript tool to detect screen size and then deliver rescaled versions of the images. You don't need to change any markup beyond adding the script. The only drawback I've found is that if you don't have PHP and htaccess available on your website, you can't use it.

- **Picturefill** (`http://scottjehl.github.io/picturefill/`)—The `<picture>` element allows for HTML to provide different source files for images, much the way that the `<video>` and `<audio>` elements do. But it's not supported in browsers. This tool provides a polyfill to make it work.

The other place that images can cause problems is on Retina and other high-resolution devices. You can choose to force every device to see the Retina-ready images, but this causes the pages to load more slowly, and it provides no benefit for any non-Retina devices. These tools help solve this problem:

- **Foresight.js** (`http://codevisually.com/foresight-js-request-hi-res-images-according-to-device-pixel-ratio/`)—You use Foresight.js to determine whether the device viewing the page can view high-resolution images (as Retina devices can) and then request the appropriate image.
- **Retina Images** (`http://retina-images.complexcompulsions.com`)—This tool uses PHP, htaccess, and JavaScript to detect the device ratio and then serve high-resolution images to the devices that can do it. This tool can adjust both HTML and CSS images.
- **Is This Retina?** (`http://isthisretina.com`)—Steve Jobs has been quoted as saying that when you hold a device 10 to 12 inches from your eyes, images that are 300px per inch are indistinguishable from text. So if you have a device that has a smaller PPI, if you hold it farther from your eyes, you won't be able to distinguish it from print. In other words, at a certain viewing distance, every screen is "Retina." I'm not sure how useful this is, but it is fun. This tool tells you how far away a customer needs to view a page on various devices and have them appear to be "Retina."

Table Tools

Tables are challenging for mobile devices, but there are a bunch of tools you can use to automatically adjust tables, depending on the device viewing them. Here are a few:

- **Zurb Responsive Tables** (`http://zurb.com/playground/responsive-tables`)—This combination of CSS and JavaScript helps your tables adapt to small screens.

- **Stacktable.js** (`http://johnpolacek.github.io/stacktable.js/`)—This script can use two ways to display a table on smaller screen. You can also use this tool in your media queries to adjust tables.
- **FooTable** (`http://css-tricks.com/footable-a-jquery-plugin-for-responsive-data-tables/`)—This jQuery plug-in takes the features of other table tools and combines the best into the ultimate responsive table tool.
- **TablePress** (`http://tablepress.org/extensions/responsive-tables/`)—If you use WordPress with a responsive template, this plug-in will help your tables be responsive.

Form Tools

Forms are another difficult thing to make responsive. These tools help make it easier:

- **CoffeeCup Web Form Builder** (`http://www.coffeecup.com/web-form-builder-lite/`)—CoffeeCup offers dozens of responsive form themes to work with this program. Or you can build your own designs and make them responsive. This link is to the free version, and there is also a paid version available.
- **Formstack Responsive Web Form Builder** (`http://blog.formstack.com/2013/responsive-web-form-builder/`)—This online form builder allows you to design responsive forms. It also does the form submissions and hosts forms for you.
- **Multi-Language Responsive Contact Form** (`http://wordpress.org/plugins/responsive-contact-form/`)—This WordPress plug-in helps make WordPress forms responsive.

Speed Tools

The speed tools I use most often are those that help minify, or make my CSS and JavaScript smaller. I recommend that you do minification on your files only when you're sure you have them the way you want them. I also recommend that you keep an un-minified version of the files as a backup.

NOTE

How Minification Works

Minification is a process where the extra spaces and carriage returns are removed from the scripts and CSS. This makes the files hard to read, but the removal of all the extra white space characters can make a big difference in the size of the script and CSS files.

Here are two minifiers:

- **CSS Minifier (`http://cssminifier.com`)**—This minifier works as both a form where you can paste your CSS and an API you can use to automate the process.
- **JavaScript Compressor (`http://minifyjavascript.com`)**—This minifier compresses JavaScript files. You can also use it to uncompress minified JavaScript files.

The other tool I use all the time is the YSlow analyzer (`https://developer.yahoo.com/yslow/`). This tool is great for finding out where your pages are slow and for getting suggestions on how to speed them up.

Testing Tools

Testing can be one of the trickiest parts of doing RWD because you have to have devices of different sizes and specifications to test with. But there are a few tools that can help make this easier:

- **Can I Use (`http://caniuse.com`)**—I reference this site all the time to find out what features of CSS3, HTML5, and JavaScript are supported by browsers. This changes all the time, as browsers release new versions and mobile browsers come out with more features.
- **MobiReady (`http://ready.mobi`)**—This site lets you test for mobile readiness. I don't consider this site as useful for RWD sites as it used to be because the focus is more on cell phones than smartphones that have better mobile support. But for smaller devices, the advice on this site is good.
- **Adobe Edge Inspect (`http://html.adobe.com/edge/inspect/`)**—This tool works for testing designs on devices you already own. It integrates into browsers and into several Adobe products. It is available with a Creative Cloud subscription.
- **Responsive Design View in Firefox (`https://www.mozilla.org/en-US/firefox/new/`)**—This is one of the only browser-based tools I've found that actually works for testing responsive designs.

▼ TRY IT YOURSELF

Test a Page in the Responsive Design View Tool

Firefox has a lot of tools that are useful for web designers to build and test web pages—both regular pages and responsive pages. The Responsive Design Tool is especially great for testing because it really does work to test RWD and not just window sizes.

1. Open Firefox and navigate to the page you want to test.
2. In the Tools menu, go to the Web Developer section and choose Responsive Design View. You can also find this in the "hamburger" icon under Developer.
3. Choose a browser size and reload the page.

This tool allows you to test your pages at different breakpoints and see the changes in the browser window. But what's even nicer is that you can test touch events along with clicks and take screen shots to show others what the page might look like at different sizes.

Beware of Online Testing Tools That Don't Work

Many websites offer free responsive website testing tools that simply don't work. These sites and tools claim to help you test responsive designs. You can find dozens of them if you do a search for "responsive design testing tools." Figure 21.2 shows one of these tools in action.

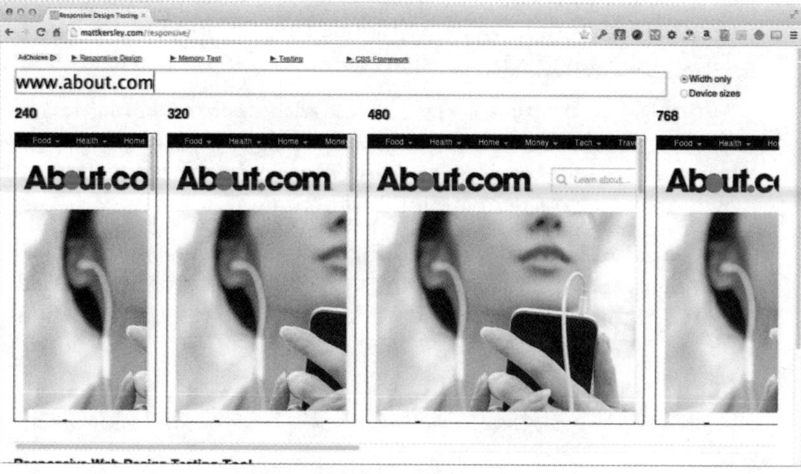

FIGURE 21.2
An RWD testing tool in action but not showing responsive designs.

The page I tested in Figure 21.2 is www.about.com, and it has at least one breakpoint, but when you load the page in the testing tool, there appear to be no breakpoints whatsoever. Figure 21.3 shows the same page, viewed on an iPhone 4.

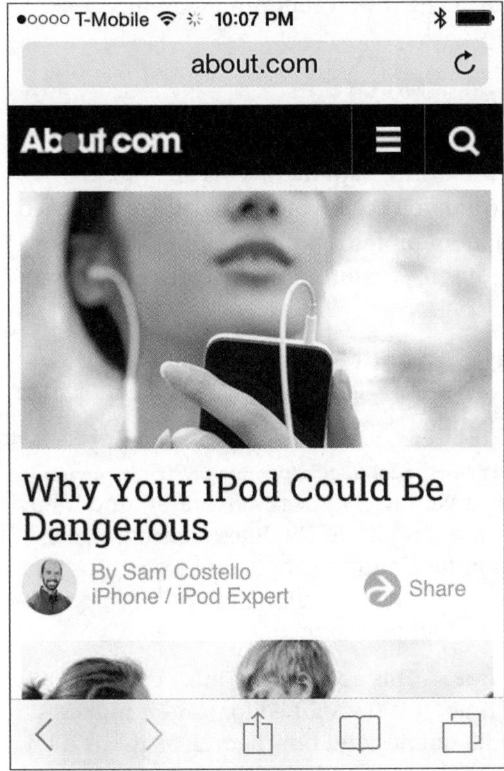

FIGURE 21.3
The same site as in Figure 21.2, but on a real iPhone.

When you compare that result to the result shown in Figure 21.2, it's clear that the testing tool is not showing a responsive version of the page but rather how the page would look if it were not responsive.

I recommend not using online testing tools except for minor testing to get an idea of page sizes. It's better to simply open your pages in a web browser and then resize the browser.

Web Editors for Building Responsive Web Pages

The last tools you should consider are the editors you use to build your pages. While it's reasonable to use a basic text editor to build RWD pages, you might find a more focused web editor more useful.

Professional Design Editors

There are a lot of professional web design editors. And regardless of what you may have heard, they write high-quality HTML and CSS code—even the WYSIWYG (what you see is what you get) editors listed below. But while there are a lot of professional web editors, there are not a lot (yet) that have features to support responsive design. These are the three I like the best:

- **CoffeeCup Responsive Layout Maker (`www.coffeecup.com/responsive-layout-maker-pro/`)**—This is a new visual editor from CoffeeCup. It makes creating responsive layouts very easy.
- **Dreamweaver (`http://www.adobe.com/products/dreamweaver.html`)**—Dreamweaver is a very well-known web editor, and it has had support for RWD for a long time. The latest version, which is part of the subscription for Creative Cloud, offers good support for RWD, but even the previous version, CS6, provides support for visualizing media queries and testing them.
- **Macaw (`http://macaw.co`)**—This editor is the most exciting editor I've tried in a long time. It is a visual editor, and it makes it very easy to create media queries and test them. Plus it has a lot of support for CSS3 properties that go beyond just media queries.

Online Editors

If you are looking for tools for your clients to use, online editors can be a good solution. They are often very easy to use and include hosting along with the web editing. These editors include a lot of responsive templates to help get a site started:

- **Squarespace (`http://www.squarespace.com`)**—Squarespace is a newer online editor that is gaining a lot of traction. It offers lots of modern templates and features as well as lots of customization.

- **Weebly (`http://www.weebly.com`)**—Weebly offers a lot of templates, but what I like best is the access to HTML and CSS to customize your sites. It also has good ecommerce tools built in.
- **Wix (`http://www.wix.com`)**—Wix offers hundreds of templates you can use to create your site. It has a drag and drop tools and great support.

These tools are more for beginners than for professional web designers, but they can be fun to use and can help you create some nice-looking sites really quickly.

Summary

In this hour you've learned about a lot of tools you can use to create responsive websites. There are a lot of tools available to help you plan and build sites as well as test them once they are built. You've also learned about the dangers these tools can pose, both in getting too engrossed in them and in getting bad information. It's important to use tools to be more effective in your web design work and not get used by them.

Workshop

The workshop contains quiz questions to help you process what you've learned in this lesson. Try to answer all the questions before you read the answers.

Q&A

Q. You mention the Firefox developer tools, but you don't mention the tools in Chrome—specifically the emulators. Why not?

A. Even though the Chrome tools for testing mobile devices are called emulators, they don't work like emulators. I don't recommend using the Chrome emulators for anything except seeing how your page would look in those devices if there are no media queries to make the pages responsive.

Quiz

1. If you like to sketch your designs before you start working on them, what is a good tool to do that with?
2. What do you use a wireframe tool for?
3. Name an open source wireframe or prototyping tool.
4. What is a framework?
5. Why might you want to use an online editor like Wix or Squarespace?
6. Why should you use font icons as images on a responsive site?
7. Why is it bad to force all devices to load Retina-ready images?
8. What does a minifier do?
9. What testing tool is included in Firefox?
10. Name two professional web editors that provide good support for RWD.

Answers

1. Jeremy Palford's Responsive Web Design Sketch Sheets provides a good starting point for sketching designs on paper. Plus you can load your drawings in Photoshop and sketch on your computer as well.
2. A wireframe tool is used to create a prototype or mockup of a website.

3. The Pencil Project is an open source wireframe tool. All the others listed in this hour are not open source.
4. A framework is a package of HTML, CSS, and often JavaScript files that are used to make building a website easier.
5. Online editors like Wix and Squarespace are easy to use and a good choice to allow clients to edit their own pages. They include responsive templates, and usually include hosting as well as editing in the cost.
6. When you place font icons as images, you can then scale them up or down as large or small as you need them to be. This makes them more responsive than normal images.
7. Retina-ready images are larger than the images needed for non-Retina devices. This means that the non-Retina devices have to download more than they can use, which slows down the page.
8. A minifier removes the extraneous white space characters (like space and carriage return) in order to make CSS and JavaScript as small as possible.
9. Firefox includes a web developer tool called the Responsive Design View. This tool lets you see how pages look at various dimensions with your different breakpoints.
10. This hour lists three professional web editors that can support RWD: CoffeeCup Responsive Layout Maker, Dreamweaver, and Macaw.

Exercises

1. Check out some of the tools listed in this hour to see if they would be useful for you or your website. I recommend trying a new tool for at least a couple days to really get a feel for whether it will do what you need it to do.
2. Test your page by using the Mobi.Ready site to see how your site would fare on a mobile phone. Don't be discouraged if you score low; just take a look at the recommendations and see if you can implement any of them.
3. Test your page in YSlow. Examine the most important problems it finds to see if you can adjust your page to be faster. The faster your pages load, the more users will like them.

HOUR 22
Device and Feature Detection

Device and feature detection are often seen as an old-school approach to the problem of mobile web design. They are often what web designers used before they started using RWD. But in this hour, you'll learn that there is still a place for detection scripts, and they can solve many of the problems mentioned in Hour 20, "Problems with Responsive Web Design." In this hour I will teach you two ways to do detection: feature detection and device detection. You will also learn the benefits of both and when to consider using them.

WHAT YOU'LL LEARN IN THIS HOUR:

- What detection scripts are used for
- The difference between feature detection and device detection
- When and why to use each type
- How to use Modernizr for feature detection
- How to use WURFL for device detection

Why Use Detection Scripts

A *detection script* is a script that detects information about the device viewing a page. There are two types of detection scripts:

- Feature detection scripts
- Device detection scripts

Feature detection scripts look at a device's features and determine whether particular features works on the device. A feature detection script is most often used with JavaScript.

Back in the early days of the web, when JavaScript was still new, web developers realized that they could determine what browser their customers were using through the user agent string. This led logically to the creation of pages specific to certain browsers or user agents. Because they were writing scripts that optimized the site for specific browsers, developers started putting up buttons announcing what browser their customers should use to view the page, as in Figure 22.1.

FIGURE 22.1
Best viewed with Internet Explorer and Netscape buttons.

The developers used these browser detection scripts to try to prevent problems in browsers that didn't support all the same features. And usually the easiest way to prevent the problems was to give a dumbed-down version of the page to any browser with a user agent string they didn't support.

But as you can see from the number of user agent strings listed at User Agent String.com (`http://useragentstring.com/pages/useragentstring.php`), this very quickly became a losing battle. In order to keep your browser detection script up-to-date, you'd have to have hundreds of checks. You would also need to know exactly what each browser supports at all times.

And you can't assume that the user agent is even correct. Nearly every user agent claims to be a Mozilla-based user agent. But that is only true for Gecko browsers like Firefox and Netscape. Any other browser using that term in the user agent will also claim "compatible" because it really is only compatible with the Mozilla user agent, not actually based on it.

Plus, there are many security tools and even features in the browsers themselves to allow customers to change the user agent string the browser sends.

▼ TRY IT YOURSELF

Change the User Agent in Safari

In the Safari Developer tools, you can change the user agent to whatever you want it to be. Follow these steps to learn how:

1. Open Safari Preferences and go to the Advanced pane.
2. Make sure the Show Develop Menu in Menu Bar box is checked.
3. Close Preferences and go to the Develop menu.
4. In the User Agent menu, as shown in Figure 22.2, choose a user agent you want to switch to.
5. If you want to write your own user agent, click on Other and then fill in your own user agent string.

TRY IT YOURSELF ▼

Change the User Agent in Safari

continued

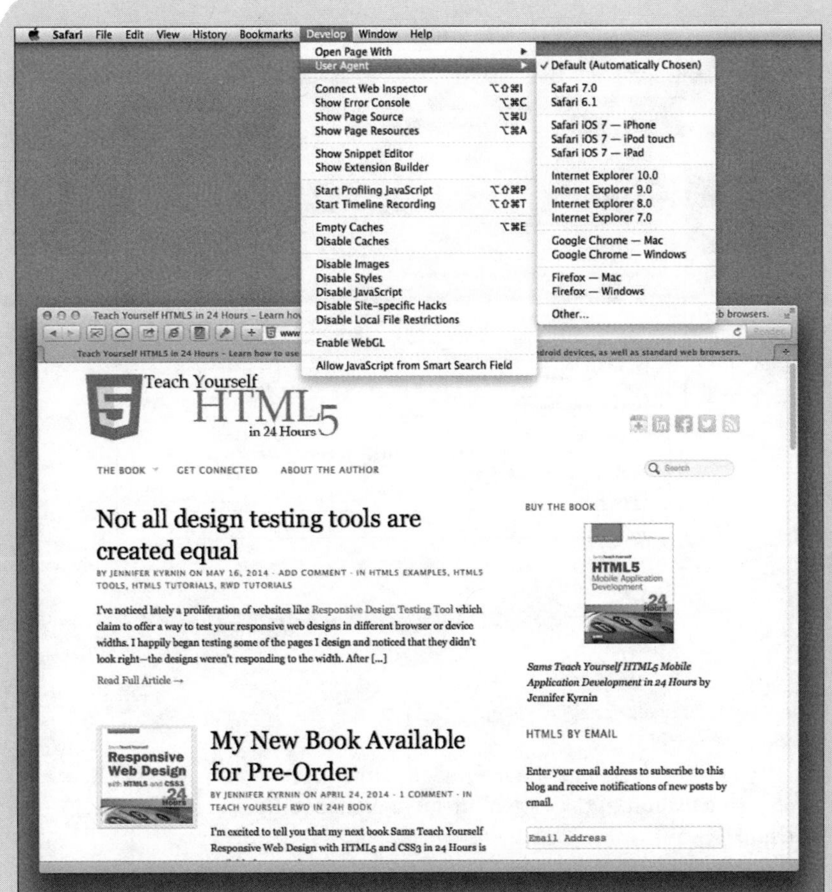

FIGURE 22.2
User agent choices in Safari.

You can test this by going to `http://useragentstring.com` and changing the user agent string to whatever you want, as you can see in Figure 22.3.

▼ TRY IT YOURSELF

Change the User Agent in Safari

continued

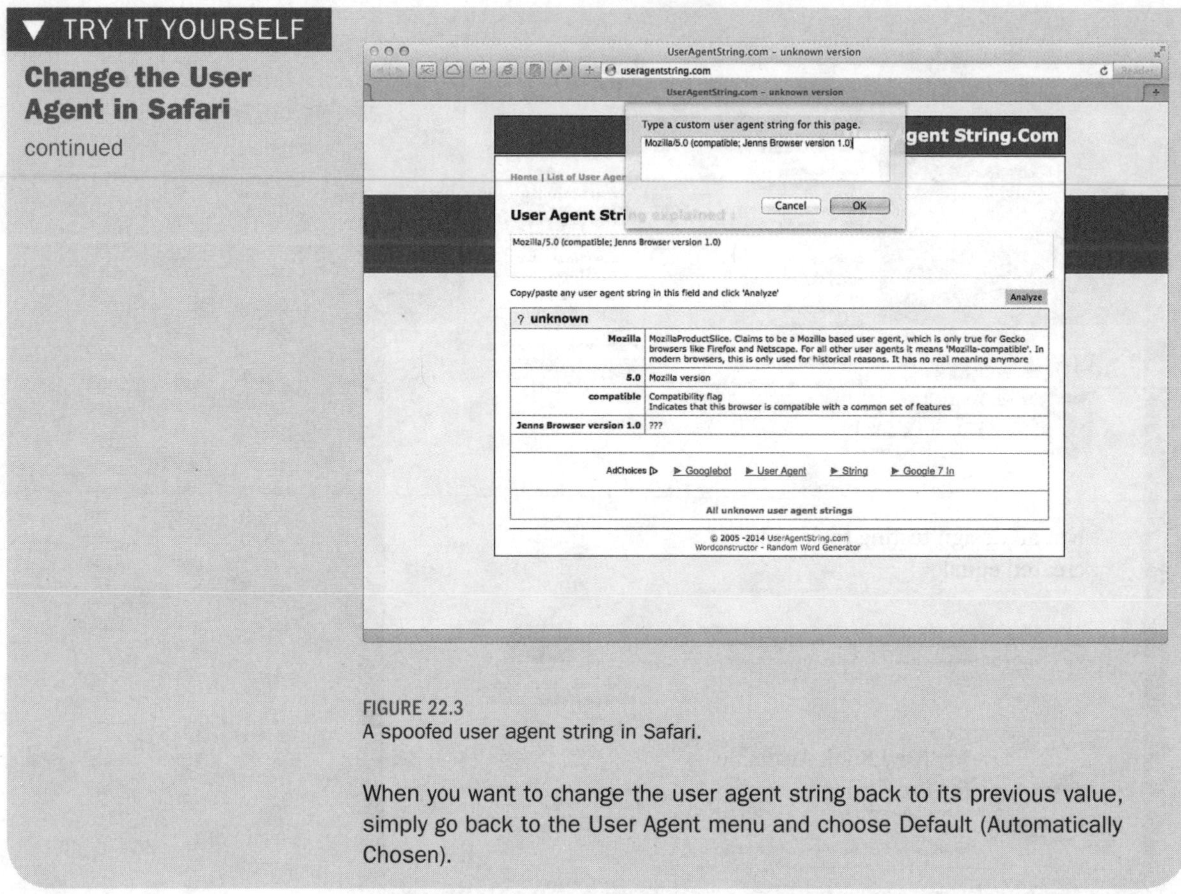

FIGURE 22.3
A spoofed user agent string in Safari.

When you want to change the user agent string back to its previous value, simply go back to the User Agent menu and choose Default (Automatically Chosen).

NOTE

What Is a Polyfill?

Remy Sharp coined the term `polyfill` in 2009. He wanted a word that meant a script that could replicate an API using JavaScript (or whatever) if the browser doesn't have it built in. A polyfill isn't progressive enhancement because it requires JavaScript to work. But you can use a polyfill to provide alternatives when a feature detection script determines that the customer doesn't have the feature you need.

Feature detection came about as an answer to these problems with browser detection. With feature detection, instead of trying to keep up with what browsers support what features, you set your script up to detect the features you need to support. If a feature isn't there, you can create a fallback for customers who won't have access to that feature.

The most popular feature detection script is Modernizr (`http://modernizr.com`).

Device detection scripts try to determine exactly what device is accessing the page so that it can be compared to a database of features that that device has. These databases are maintained by humans and can give more information than a feature detection script because they can indicate gradations of support as well as point out areas where feature detection fails.

If you carefully read the earlier section describing browser detection, you may now be wondering how device detection is any better. After all, if there are hundreds of different browsers and user agents out there, there are thousands of different combinations of devices and browsers. So the problems of getting good device detection are magnified because of the sheer number of possibilities.

But the difference between device detection and browser detection is how it's implemented. Browser detection was typically done by one web developer writing a script to try to guess at the user agents that needed to be supported. This was slow and inefficient. Plus, with the ability to fake user agents mentioned earlier, it could be very difficult to get an accurate result.

Good device detection solutions use a detection engine and an API that connects to a centralized database. You can go as simple as just determining whether the device is mobile, but more complex systems provide details like what the devices support, their sizes, and the manufacturer and model number of the device.

Some of the best mobile device detection systems include Apache Mobile Filter (`http://apachemobilefilter.org`), DeviceAtlas (`https://deviceatlas.com`), and 51Degrees (`http://51degrees.com`). The most popular device detection script is WURFL (`http://wurfl.sourceforge.net`).

Modernizr

Modernizr is a small JavaScript library that you can include in your websites to do feature detection quickly and easily. As of this writing, Modernizr detects more than 40 modern HTML5, CSS3, and JavaScript features. And it lets you develop more cutting-edge features in your websites while being confident that your designs are still progressively enhanced.

How to Install Modernizr

Modernizr is easy to install. You can choose to just point to the entire script on a CDN and use it just like that. CDNJS (`http://www.cdnjs.com`) offers the minified Modernizr development build for you to point to. You add this script to the <head> of your document after your style sheets:

```
<script src="http://cdnjs.cloudflare.com/ajax/libs/modernizr/2.8.2/
➥modernizr.min.js"></script>
```

Then you can start using Modernizr however you need to within your scripts. Note that this goes against the general best practice of placing scripts at the bottom of your documents, but Modernizr recommends placing it in the <head>. This ensures that the HTML5 shim that lets HTML5 elements work in older versions of Internet Explorer loads before the <body> tag loads. Plus, if you're using any Modernizr CSS classes, this will prevent a flash of unstyled content (often called FOUC). If you don't need to support Internet Explorer 8 or lower and you don't need to worry about the FOUC, then you can include Modernizr wherever you want to.

CAUTION

The Development Version of Modernizr Is Large

The drawback to using the development version of Modernizr is that it is almost certainly more than you really need. That is, you end up forcing your customers to download more than they have to, which slows their page load times. It is better to customize your version of Modernizr to include only the features you need to detect for your site. You can do that on the Modernizr download page (`http://modernizr.com/download/`).

Using Modernizr

There isn't a lot to learn about using Modernizr. For the most part, after you've installed Modernizr, you either need to do nothing to get support for a feature or you need to run a simple script to determine whether the feature is supported.

In the "do nothing" category is how Modernizr shims Internet Explorer 8. A common place where web designers get hung up is with HTML5 elements in Internet Explorer 8 (and lower). Since Internet Explorer 8 doesn't support HTML5 elements, Modernizr runs a loop to make Internet Explorer 8 recognize HTML5 elements that you can style in CSS. Modernizr does this automatically when you install it in your pages.

What most people want with Modernizr is feature detection. Modernizr uses JavaScript objects that are typically given a Boolean (true/false) value. Then you just create a script that tests for one of those objects. If the object is present, you can use it; otherwise, you use a fallback option. Listing 22.1 shows a simple Modernizr script to detect for geolocation support.

CAUTION

Modernizr Won't Make Internet Explorer 8 Support the `<video>` Element

One of the common misconceptions is that by using Modernizr, you can get Internet Explorer 8 and other older browsers that don't support HTML5 elements to automatically support them. Unfortunately, this is not true. Instead, Modernizr tells those browsers about the new HTML5 elements so that if your site uses an <article> element instead of <div>, Internet Explorer 8 won't ignore the tag or any styles on it.

LISTING 22.1 Script to Detect for Geolocation Support

```
if (Modernizr.geolocation) {
  // add your geolocation functions here
  alert("This browser supports Geolocation.");
} else {
  // add your fallback functions here
  alert("This browser does not support Geolocation.");
}
```

Modernizr offers a lot of feature detection for websites—much more than I can discuss in a single hour. If you feel that feature detection is right for your site, then I recommend that you get familiar with the Modernizr documentation at `http://modernizr.com/docs/` so that you can better understand how to use this powerful tool.

WURFL

WURFL stands for Wireless Universal Resource FiLe. It is a community-based effort to do mobile device detection. It contains thousands of devices and hundreds of properties to create a database matrix of capabilities that web developers can use to manage their websites.

There are many WURFL APIs you can use, including Java, PHP, Database, and ASP.Net. This hour focuses on the PHP API with file-based data.

CAUTION

Is WURFL Free?

Licensing issues related to WURFL can be confusing. Using the WURFL APIs is licensed under the Affero General Public License, version 3 (AGPL), an open source license. The XML database has a restricted license that allows it to be used only with a WURFL API. If you can comply with the AGPL restrictions, you can use WURFL for free.

But here's where it gets tricky: AGPL considers running the software on a server as distribution. And if you distribute the APIs, you need to open source the derivative works—and most people don't want to open source their web applications. If this is the case for you, you need to buy a commercial license from ScientiaMobile (`http://scientiamobile.com/`).

Getting Started with WURFL

Before you can use WURFL, you need to download and install the PHP API, which you can get at `http://sourceforge.net/projects/wurfl/files/WURFL%20PHP/1.4/`. You install it in a directory that your web server can access. Then go and get the latest XML file at `http://wurfl.sourceforge.net/wurfl_download.php`. You need to agree to the licensing agreement to download it. Once you have that file, rename it `wurfl.xml` and put it in the `examples/resources` directory of your WURFL PHP installation. Finally, you need to edit the `examples/resources/wurfl-config.xml` file so that the `<main-file>` element looks like this:

```
<main-file>wurfl.xml</main-file>
```

If you have trouble getting it going, chances are it's because of permissions on the files. Make sure that Apache can write to the data files.

Once you get WURFL installed, you can try it out by using the demo script to provide some device capabilities. I installed WURFL on my local MAMP (Macintosh Apache, MySQL, and PHP) server and tested by going to `http://localhost/wurfl/examples/demo/` in my web browser. That page looks as shown in Figure 22.4.

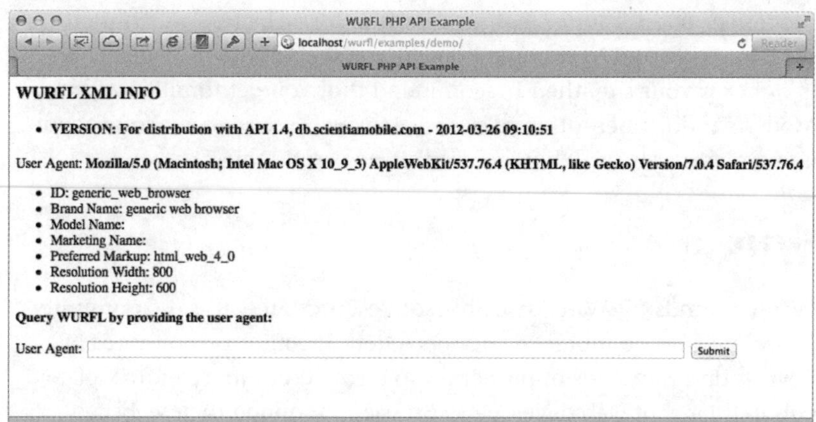

FIGURE 22.4
WURFL showing information on my browser.

Then you can see what information WURFL will provide for other user agents. I found a random mobile user agent for an Opera Mini browser and typed it in:

```
Opera/9.80 (J2ME/MIDP; Opera Mini/9.80 (S60; SymbOS;
➥Opera Mobi/23.348; U; en) Presto/2.5.25 Version/10.54
```

Figure 22.5 shows that WURFL delivers different information for this device.

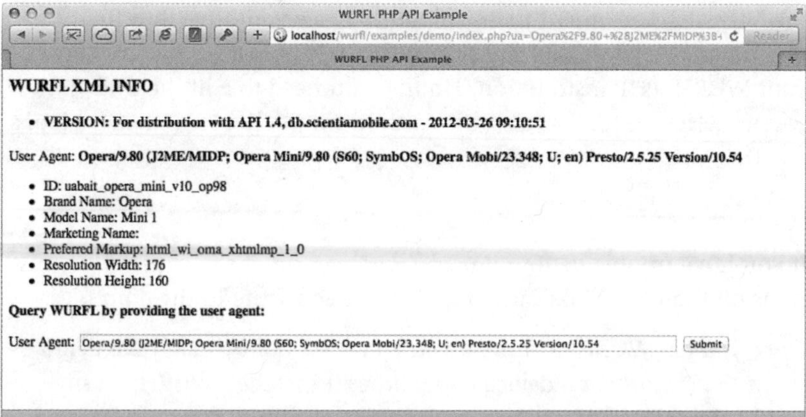

FIGURE 22.5
WURFL showing information on an Opera Mini device.

How WURFL Works

WURFL looks at more than just the user agent to determine what the device is and return its capabilities. And it combines all those things into a matrix that it can quickly reference to provide you with information on specific features.

WURFL assumes that while different browsers are different, they have things in common with one another. Plus devices from the same manufacturer often use the same hardware and software, so the differences between them are minimal. Finally, devices from different manufacturers may run the same software. For example, Android runs on lots of different phones and tablets. This allows WURFL to compact the device data and keep the update process as simple as possible. And this makes getting the information quick and reliable.

Summary

In this hour, you've learned about feature and device detection. You've learned what these detection scripts are for and how to use them. You've learned the history behind feature detection and how much better it is than browser detection.

You've also learned about how to install and get started using Modernizr, a great feature detection script. And you've learned how to install and get started with WURFL, a complicated but powerful device detection script.

Workshop

The workshop contains quiz questions to help you process what you've learned in this lesson. Try to answer all the questions before you read the answers.

Q&A

Q. I don't like the licensing options for WURFL. Are there other open source alternatives?

A. WURFL is the only device database that offers an open source license. DeviceAtlas (`https://deviceatlas.com`) is the closest alternative, and DetectRight (`http://www.detectright.com`) and 51Degrees (`http://51degrees.com/Products/Device-Detection`) also offer solutions that might work.

Another option that you might find more useful is the WURFL.js (`http://wurfljs.com`) solution provided by ScientiaMobile. As long as your website is publicly available and does not require fees or a paid subscription, you can use this for free and have a JavaScript API as well.

Q. Where can I get more information on how to use WURFL?

A. A great place to start is the ScientiaMobile WURFL forums (`http://www.scientiamobile.com/forum/index.php`). The API forums can help answer your questions and get you started using WURFL quickly and painlessly. I also found a good tutorial on mobiForge (`http://mobiforge.com/design-development/introduction-wurfl`).

Q. If I don't have PHP, can I still use WURFL?

A. As mentioned above, there are lots of different API languages for WURFL, including ASP.Net and Java. But one that I didn't mention is the Cloud offering (`http://scientiamobile.com/cloud`). Using it is a very easy way to set up and run a WURFL web application, with fewer of the open source licensing issues. Plus, there is a free license available if you just want to test or need only a few capabilities.

Quiz

1. Name two types of detection scripts.
2. What replaced browser detection scripts?
3. Name three ways browser detection scripts don't work very well.

4. True or False: A polyfill is an example of progressive enhancement?
5. What is a polyfill?
6. What makes device detection better than browser detection?
7. What does it mean that Modernizr shims HTML5 for older browsers?
8. If you saw a script that started with `if (Modernizr.webfont) { ... }` what do you think it would do?
9. What does WURFL stand for?
10. What assumptions does WURFL make about mobile devices?

Answers

1. This hour discusses browser detection, feature detection, and device detection.
2. Feature detection replaced browser detection as a more effective way of checking whether a feature works in the browser.
3. Browser detection scripts don't work very well because there are too many browsers to keep track of, the user agent strings change constantly and they can be spoofed by the customer, and web designers have to know exactly what features each browser and corresponding user agent string support.
4. False. Polyfills require the use of JavaScript to work, and so they won't work on devices that don't support JavaScript. This makes them not progressive enhancement.
5. A polyfill is a script that replicates a web API that the browser does not currently support.
6. Device detection is done on the server and combines the attributes of the devices into a matrix that can be queried quickly to get basic features of a device.
7. Modernizr shims HTML5 elements so that they can be used in web pages, and even older browsers (specifically Internet Explorer 8 and lower) can display styles on those elements.
8. A script that starts with `if (Modernizr.webfont) { ... }` would check whether the current browser supports web fonts. If it does, then the script would implement web fonts on the system.
9. WURFL stands for Wireless Universal Resource FiLe.

10. WURFL assumes that while different browsers are different, they have things in common with one another. Plus, devices from the same manufacturer often use the same hardware and software, so the differences between them are minimal. Finally, devices from different manufacturers may run the same software; for example, Android runs on lots of different phones and tablets.

Exercises

1. Examine your site and see what features you are using for which you could add a Modernizr check. Once you know what features you're using, download a custom build of Modernizr and set up fallback options for the features.

2. Set up a WAMP or MAMP server on your local machine. Then install WURFL and try out the demo script.

HOUR 23
Using RESS with RWD

WHAT YOU'LL LEARN IN THIS HOUR:

- ▶ What RESS is
- ▶ How to use RESS on responsive web pages
- ▶ How RESS will improve your site
- ▶ How to create a simple RESS page

RESS is not just another acronym in an industry that is full of them. It is a system for doing web design that you may already be considering, even if you don't know it. That is because RESS really is just a combination of server-side and client-side scripts to help create the best possible responsive website.

In this hour, you'll learn what RESS is and how to get started using it. You'll apply some of the things you learned in Hour 22, "Device and Feature Detection," as well as the rest of the book.

What Is RESS?

RESS stands for Responsive Web Design + Server Side Components. It was first described by Luke Wroblewski in 2011 as a way to help make RWD more effective. RESS is considered a hybrid design because it relies on more than just client-side technology to work.

Client-side technology—including HTML, CSS, and JavaScript—is what most web designers focus on when building web pages. These technologies work in the browser without needing a server for activation.

But if everything is maintained on the client, that means everything has to be stored there. This results in the biggest problem of RWD: file sizes. Because you have to create style sheets and scripts to support all the devices, the files are going to be much larger than non-RWD files.

And while it might not matter how large the files are on your desktop computer at work, when you start delivering huge data files to your mobile customers, your site can slow to a crawl, which could cost your customers lots of money in data charges.

RESS uses server-side technology such as PHP to customize the RWD as much as possible, based on feature and device detection.

Benefits of Using RESS

The biggest benefit of using RESS on a responsive website is that you can address some of the common problems discussed in Hour 20, "Problems with Responsive Web Design." RESS can speed up your site delivery by delivering only the page components that the user's device can handle. In other words, with RESS using both client-side feature detection and server-side device detection, you can deliver Retina-ready images to an iPhone 5 while delivering non-Retina to a basic flip phone.

RESS allows you to create device-specific elements for your site. You can target specific devices for special designs and make mobile web pages that use all the capabilities that the phones and tablets have to offer.

But the benefit that most web designers will appreciate the most is the size optimization. When you do RESS right, you can reduce the size of images, JavaScript, and CSS significantly for most customers. And this will speed up your site for everyone.

Getting Started with RESS

In Hour 15, "Creating and Using Images in RWD," I showed you a site built with responsive design. Figure 23.1 shows you how it would look at three device sizes. And Listing 23.1 and Listing 23.2 show the HTML and CSS.

FIGURE 23.1
The same page at three sizes.

LISTING 23.1 HTML for a Basic RWD Website

```
<!doctype html>
<html>
  <head>
    <meta charset="UTF-8">
    <title>Dandylions</title>
    <link href="rwd code 23.2.css" rel="stylesheet">
    <script src="http://ajax.googleapis.com/
➥ajax/libs/jquery/1.6.2/jquery.min.js">
    </script>
  </head>
  <body>
    <div id="main">
      <header>
        <h1>Dandylions</h1>
        <h2>Not Your Mother's Weed</h2>
      </header>
      <nav>
        <ul id="navigation">
          <li><a href="#">Home<br>
          <small>Where Dandelions roam free</small></a></li>
          <li><a href="#">Products<br>
          <small>These flowers will grow on you</small></a></li>
          <li><a href="#">Services<br>
          <small>We care for the flowers you have</small></a></li>
```

```
      <li><a href="#">Support<br>
      <small>We love to help with dandelions</small></a></li>
      <li><a href="#">About<br>
      <small>Why we love dandelions so much</small></a></li>
      <li><a href="#">Reading<br>
      <small>Read more about this wondrous
      plant</small></a></li>
      <li><a href="#">Contact<br>
      <small>Ask us about your dandelion needs</small></a></li>
    </ul>
    <select id="mobileNav">
      <option value="">Go to...</option>
      <option value="/home">Home</option>
      <option value="/products">Products</option>
      <option value="/services">Services</option>
      <option value="/support">Support</option>
      <option value="/about">About</option>
      <option value="/articles">Reading</option>
      <option value="/contact">Contact</option>
    </select>
  </nav>
  <div id="bodyContent" class="clearfix">
    <article id="mainarticle">
      <h3>What is a Dandelion?</h3>
      <p><span class="pronounce"><strong><em>
      Taraxacum</em></strong> <em>/tə'ræksəkʉm/</em></span> is
      a large genus of flowering plants in the family
      Asteraceae. They are native to Eurasia and North and
      South America, and two species, T. officinale and T.
      erythrospermum, are found as weeds worldwide. Both
      species are edible in their entirety. The common name
      <span class="pronounce"><strong>dandelion</strong>
      <em>/'dændɨlaɪ.ən/</em></span> (dan-di-ly-ən, from French
      dent-de-lion, meaning "lion's tooth") is given to members
      of the genus, and like other members of the Asteraceae
      family, they have very small flowers collected together
      into a composite flower head. Each single flower in a
      head is called a floret. Many <em>Taraxacum</em> species
      produce seeds asexually by apomixis, where the seeds are
      produced without pollination, resulting in offspring that
      are genetically identical to the parent plant.</p>
    </article>
  <div class="sidebars">
  <aside id="links">
    <h3>Learn More About Dandelions</h3>
    <ul>
      <li><a href="do-dandelions-burn-in-colors.htm">
      Do Dandelions Burn in Colors?</a></li>
      <li><a href="10-uses-for-dandelions.htm">
      Top 5 Things To Do With Dandelion</a></li>
      <li><a href="How-To-Grow-Dandelion-Greens.htm">
      How to Grow and Harvest Dandelion Greens</a></li>
      <li><a href="bljelly9.htm">
```

```
          Dandelion Honey Recipe</a></li>
          <li><a href="kill_dandelions_2.htm">
          Get Rid of Dandelions the Smart Way&#8212;Eat
          Them!</a></li>
        </ul>
      </aside>
      <aside id="sidebar">
        <p><img src="images/dandy.jpg" width="400" height="300"
          alt=""/></p>
        <p><img src="images/seeded.jpg" width="400" height="300"
          alt=""/></p>
      </aside>
        </div><!-- end sidebars -->
      </div> <!-- end bodyContent -->
      <footer>
        <p>Text from
        <a href="http://en.wikipedia.org/wiki/Dandelion">
        Wikipedia</a></p>
      </footer>
    </div><!-- end main -->
    <script>
    $(function() {
    $("nav select").change(function() {
    window.location = $(this).find("option:selected").val();
    });
    });
    </script>
  </body>
</html>
```

LISTING 23.2 CSS for a Basic RWD Website

```
/* CSS Document */
@import url(
http://fonts.googleapis.com/css?family=Playfair+Display+SC:900
)
screen and (min-width: 400px);
/* styles for all browser widths */
/* very basic reset */
* { font-size: 100%; }
*, *:before, *:after {
  padding: 0;
  margin: 0;
  -webkit-box-sizing: border-box;
  -moz-box-sizing: border-box;
  box-sizing: border-box;
}
.clearfix:after {
  content: ".";
  visibility: hidden;
  display: block;
  height: 0;
```

```
  clear: both;
}

h1, h2, h3 { font-family: 'Playfair Display SC', serif;
  line-height: 1.2; }

h1 { font-size: 2em; }
h2 { font-size: 1.7em; }
h3 { font-size: 1.3em; }
p, ul, ol, dl { font-size: 1em; line-height: 1.275; }
#bodyContent, footer { margin: 0 0.2em; }

/* images */
img { width: 100%; max-width: 100%; height: auto; }

/* nav bar */
nav {
  width: 100%;
  margin: auto;
}
nav ul {
  list-style: none;
  overflow: hidden;
  background: #000;
}
nav li a {
  display: block;
  float: left;
  width: 14.28%;
  padding: 10px;
  background: #000;
  border-right: 1px solid #fff;
  color: #fbd91f;
  font: 400 13px/1.4 bitstream_vera_serifbold, Baskerville,
    "Palatino Linotype",
  Palatino, "Times New Roman", serif;
  text-align: center;
  text-decoration: none;
  text-transform: uppercase;
}
/* small text */
nav small {
  color: #aaa;
  font: 100 11px/1 Helvetica, Verdana, Arial, sans-serif;
  text-transform: none;
}
/* default to smallest browser size */
nav ul { display: none; }
nav select { display: inline-block; margin: 0.5em 0; }

/*header */
header {
  background: url(images/dandy-header-bg-small.png) bottom
```

```
    left no-repeat;
  color: #EDEE6A;
  text-shadow: 3px 2px #000000;
}

/* styles for smartphones and tablets */
@media screen and (min-width: 400px)  {
        h1 { font-size: 3em; }
        h2 { font-size: 2em; }
        h3 { font-size: 1.5em; }
  #bodyContent { margin-right: 0; }
  header {
    background: url(images/dandy-header-bg.png) bottom
      left no-repeat;
  }
}
/* styles just for smartphones */
@media screen and (min-width: 400px) and (max-width: 970px) {

  /* two columns */
  #mainarticle {
    width: 50%;
    float: left;
    padding-right: 2em;
  }
  .sidebars {
    width: 48%;
    float: right;
  }

  /* header */
  header {
    height: 10em;
  }

}
/* change to full nav for larger screens */
@media screen and (min-width: 481px) {
  nav ul { display: block; }
  nav select { display: none; }
}
/* styles for the largest screens */
@media screen and (min-width: 971px) {
  /* three columns */
  #mainarticle {
    width: 40%;
    float: left;
    padding-right: 2em;
  }
  .sidebars {
    width: 60%;
    float: right;
  }
```

```
  .sidebars #links {
    width: 30%;
    float: left;
  }
  .sidebars #sidebar {
    width: 65%;
    float: right;
  }
  /* header */
  header {
    height: 20em;
  }
  header h1 {
    padding-top: 1.5em;
    padding-left: 0.5em;
  }
  header h2 {
    padding-left: 6em;
    padding-top: 1em;
  }
}
```

You need to save the HTML as a PHP file. Because PHP uses HTML inside, you don't have to make any changes to the HTML; you just need to rename the file from `index.html` to `index.php`.

If you're following along on your own server, you should make sure that you have WURFL up and running correctly (see Hour 22) because this hour you're going to use it.

Adding WURFL for Server-Side Device Detection

The first file you need to create on your server is the `wurfl.php` file. You will include this file by using the PHP `include()` method in every file on which you want to do device detection. The best way to create the `wurfl.php` file is to modify the `wurfl_config_standard.php` file found in the `examples/demo/inc` folder of the WURFL PHP API. You need to change the `$wurflDir` and `$resourcesDir` variables to point to your WURFL installation. Then you include that file at the top of your PHP document, as in Listing 23.3.

LISTING 23.3 WURFL PHP

```
<?php
// Include the configuration file
include_once '/wurfl/inc/wurfl.php';

$wurflInfo = $wurflManager->getWURFLInfo();

if (isset($_GET['ua']) && trim($_GET['ua'])) {
  $ua = $_GET['ua'];
  $requestingDevice =
    $wurflManager->getDeviceForUserAgent($_GET['ua']);
} else {
  $ua = $_SERVER['HTTP_USER_AGENT'];
  // This line detects the visiting device by looking at its
  // HTTP Request ($_SERVER)
  $requestingDevice =
    $wurflManager->getDeviceForHttpRequest($_SERVER);
}

$isMobile =
  $requestingDevice->getCapability('is_wireless_device');
?>
```

Listing 23.3 gets information about the viewing device and gives you a Boolean variable `$isMobile` that you can use to start defining features for mobile devices. If it is mobile, the `$isMobile` variable is set to `true`; otherwise it is set to `false`.

If you want to grab the brand name of the device, you can add another variable line, like this:

```
$brand = $requestingDevice->getCapability('brand_name');
```

Or if you want to find out if a Google Glass user is visiting your site, you can assign a variable, like this:

```
$glasshead = $requestingDevice->getCapability('is_google_glass');
```

But be aware: When I tried to see if my iPad is a Google Glass masquerading as an iPad, I got a fatal error message, as in Figure 23.2. Some of the capabilities might not be fully supported.

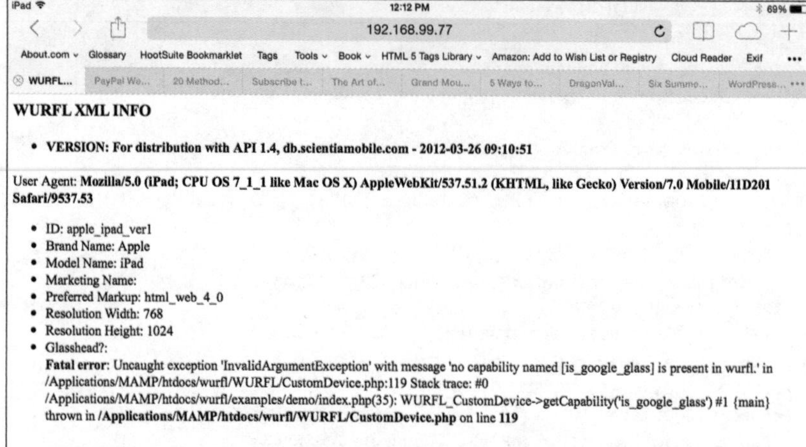

FIGURE 23.2
My WURFL can't test for Google Glass yet.

Using Cookies to Store Data

Once you have data from WURFL or Modernizr or some other source, you should store that data in a cookie for that device. That way, your pages don't have to recheck every time they load; they can bypass the check if the cookie is set.

You should store any details your scripts need to create effective and efficient pages for your mobile and desktop clients. I recommend storing them only for the current session because things change.

When to Use RESS

You can use RESS for almost anything you can imagine. Here are some of the ways I find it valuable:

- **Resizing images on-the-fly**—By collecting information about the devices viewing your site, you can use the GD library of PHP to resize images to fit exactly the dimensions of a device viewing the page.
- **Changing the images you display**—If you don't want to do dynamic resizing, you can still get speed gains with RESS by creating several versions of an image in different sizes. Then with the detection features of RESS, you can display the `image_retina.png` version to Retina devices, the `image_tiny.png` version to the smallest cell phones, and the `image.png` version to desktop computers.

- **Swapping out advertising blocks**—You can create a media query to hide ads at the smallest sizes and then use RESS to deliver an appropriately sized ad block to larger screens.
- **Adding phone- or tablet-specific features**—Phones and tablets have features like vibrate, the ability to dial phone numbers, touch screens, and so on. By using RESS device detection, you can take advantage of such features on your web pages.
- **Providing specific messages for specific devices**—Assuming that the previously mentioned `is_google_glass` capability is supported, it might be nice to have a greeting that gets seen only by people viewing the page on their Glass. Or if you want to target Nokia customers with a special offer, or need to block apps from viewing something on your page, you can provide specific messages to specific devices. All of these things can be evaluated in WURFL and then acted on with RESS.

In Figure 23.3 I added a simple script with JavaScript (see Listing 23.4) to access the WURFL data to find out whether the viewer is on a wireless device.

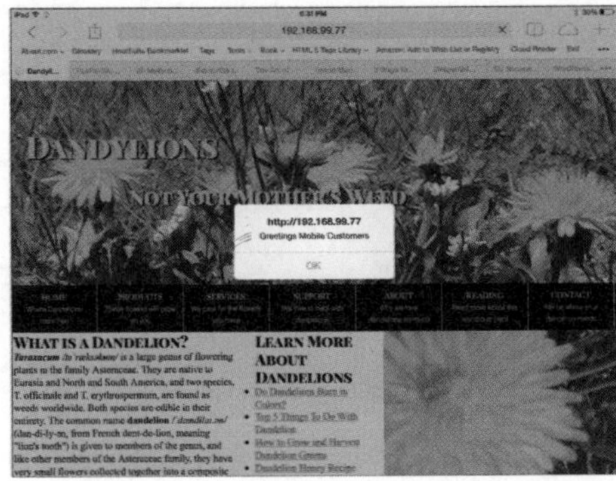

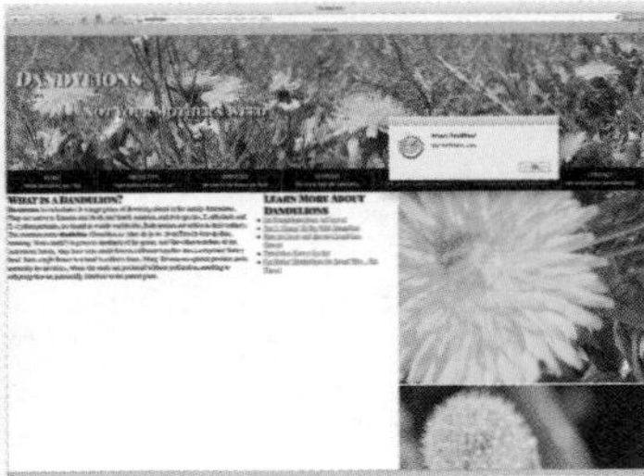

FIGURE 23.3
The web page on an iPad (left) and desktop (right), showing a JavaScript message for the viewers.

LISTING 23.4 Simple JavaScript Message

```
var isMobile = "<?php echo $isMobile; ?>";
if (isMobile === 'true') {
  alert ("Greetings Mobile Customers");
} else {
  alert ("Not on Mobile, I see");
}
```

Notice that the PHP in the first line of Listing 23.4 references the variable I set in the PHP in Listing 23.3.

Summary

RESS is a powerful tool for web designers, and there are so many ways to use it that it almost requires its own book, not just a single hour. In this hour you've learned a little more about how to use WURFL and client-side programming to create a website that is responsive both with CSS and server-side components.

Workshop

The workshop contains quiz questions to help you process what you've learned in this lesson. Try to answer all the questions before you read the answers.

Q&A

Q. You showed how to get some information about the capabilities of mobile devices using WURFL, but what other capabilities is it possible to find out?

A. There are hundreds of capabilities you can look for with WURFL. ScientiaMobile maintains a list of them at `http://www.scientia.mobile.com/wurflCapability/`.

Q. Where can I go to learn more about RESS and how to use it?

A. I've found two articles especially valuable. One is "Getting Started with RESS" (`http://www.creativebloq.com/responsive-web-design/getting-started-ress-5122956`). This article takes you through building a fully responsive and RESS-enabled site that changes the images displayed, depending on the screen size, creates a carousel with Modernizr, and adjusts the ad sizes. The other is "Lightening Your Responsive Website Design with RESS" (`http://www.smashingmagazine.com/2013/10/08/responsive-website-design-with-ress/`). This uses PageSpeed and DeviceAtlas to resize the images on-the-fly to fit the screens. It also shows how you can optimize your JavaScript and CSS for speed and how to use connectivity detection to further decrease the size of your pages for low-end mobile devices.

Quiz

1. What does RESS stand for?
2. Why is RESS considered a hybrid design?
3. What are two benefits to using RESS?
4. Can you use RESS to modify CSS?
5. Can you use RESS with plain HTML?
6. Is WURFL client side?
7. What is a WURFL capability?
8. What do you think the code snippet `$requestingDevice->getCapability('brand_name')` does?

9. Why should you store WURFL or Modernizr data in a cookie?
10. Name three ways to use RESS on your site.

Answers

1. RESS stands for Responsive Web Design + Server Side Components.
2. RESS is considered a hybrid solution because it uses both client-side and server-side scripts to make pages more responsive.
3. With RESS you can deliver optimized images, CSS, and JavaScript to the devices that need it, you can provide the different-sized ads needed by different devices, and you can create device-specific web pages.
4. You can use the information you get from RESS scripts to modify any part of your web page you want, including the CSS.
5. Plain HTML doesn't have server-side connectivity. RESS is usually done with PHP files, but it can be done with any server-side scripting languages.
6. WURFL is not typically client side; it is accessed through server-side languages.
7. A WURFL capability is a test that WURFL checks on the browsers and devices that access it.
8. The code snippet `$requestingDevice->getCapability('brand_name')` provides the brand name of the device viewing the page.
9. When you store WURFL or Modernizr results in a cookie, every page can load even more quickly with the results of the RESS data collected.
10. You can use RESS for resizing images on-the-fly, changing what images you display, swapping out advertising blocks, adding phone- or tablet-specific features, providing specific messages for specific devices, and anything else you can think of.

Exercises

1. Look into converting your site to PHP or another server-side scripting language so that you can use RESS with it.
2. If you don't have PHP or don't want to go that route, investigate using WURFL Cloud (`http://www.scientiamobile.com/cloud`).

HOUR 24
RWD Best Practices

If you've read the first 23 hours of this book, you have already learned about a lot of the best practices for doing responsive web design. But it's helpful to see them all in one place.

In this hour you will get tips and tricks for creating the best possible RWD site for your clients, your customers, and yourself. By following the best practices listed in this hour, you can be sure that you'll be building a responsive site that works well and delivers what your customers want and expect.

WHAT YOU'LL LEARN IN THIS HOUR:

- How to get the most out of RWD
- Creating breakpoints that work for your customers and your design
- Tips for making flexible pages, images, and fonts
- How to keep the costs of RWD as low as possible—but not too low

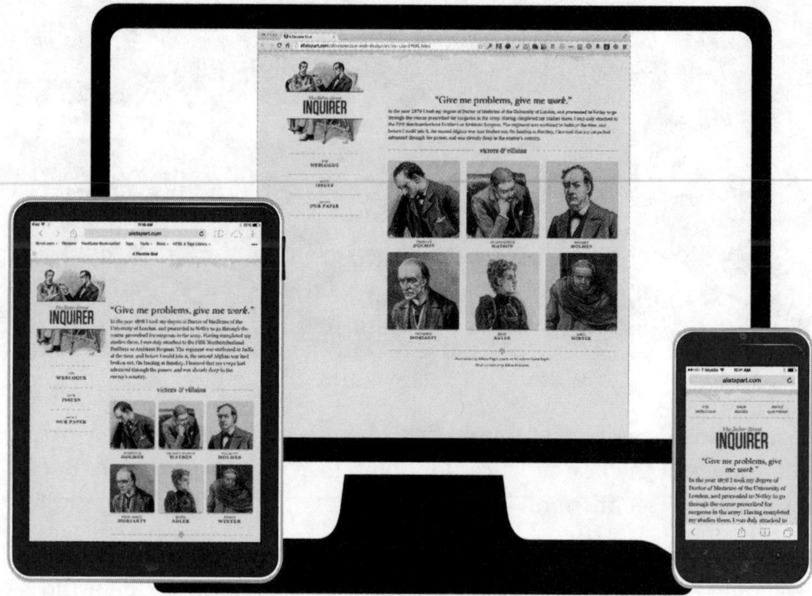

FIGURE 24.1
Possibly the first responsive web page from A List Apart, http://alistapart.com/d/responsive-web-design/ex/ex-site-flexible.html.

Interspersed through this hour are screen shots of some RWD sites that have inspired me. I include the URL along with each screen shot, and I highly recommend that you visit them on some combination of your phone, tablet, and computer to really get a sense of what makes them responsive.

Give Everyone the Best Experience

When you're working on a responsive website, it's easy to get hung up on one experience, but whether your customers are on tiny phones or 30-inch monitors, they all expect to get the best experience possible.

This means you need to build websites so that the experience your customers get is universally good. It doesn't have to be identical across devices, but it does need to be awesome.

Remember Mobile First

As discussed in Hour 9, "Mobile First," focusing first on the smallest and often most limited customers is a critical step in creating a responsive site. By building a site for the devices that have the most limitations, you ensure that they get everything they need. And then because you're building on that foundation, every other device gets everything, too.

FIGURE 24.2
Andersson-Wise Architects,
`http://www.anderssonwise.com.`

This also means that you need to be thinking responsively from the get-go. If you're creating a wireframe of a site, you should create a wireframe for each iteration of the site you're going to build. Don't just assume that you'll know "what to remove" from a desktop wireframe. Spend the time building wireframes for phones and tablets, too.

Keep Your HTML Simple

As you learned in Hour 5, "HTML for Responsive Web Design," you need to keep your HTML as simple as you can. But it means more than that. You need to focus on specifics like these:

- **Write semantic HTML.** The best pages use semantic markup that tells the browser what the contents are. You don't need to go all out and use RDF (Resource Description Framework) or micro-formats, but if you are posting an article, use the `<article>` tag rather than the `<div>` tag.

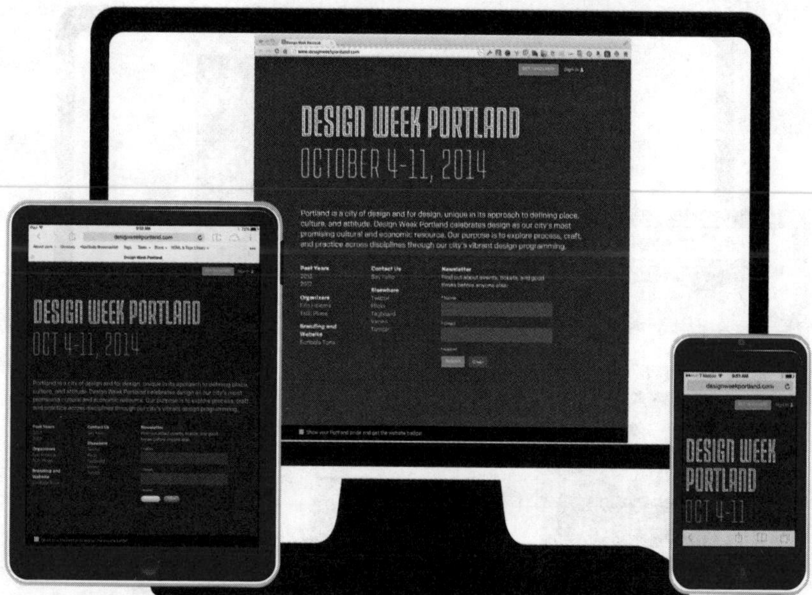

FIGURE 24.3
Design Week Portland, `http://www.designweekportland.com`.

- **Use modern HTML.** HTML5 offers a lot of new elements that can be useful on new web pages. And all modern browsers support the vast majority of them.
- **Use modern CSS.** CSS3 is also well supported in modern browsers, and CSS3 offers a lot of things that you used to be able to do only with images like gradients, rounded corners, and so on.

Use the Best Breakpoints You Can

As you learned in Hour 11, "Breakpoints," there are an infinite number of breakpoints you can use for responsive sites. But there are several sizes you should be aware of:

- **Less than 320px wide**—While there are some smaller phones, this is the smallest you really need to worry about. What will your design look like on these older, lower-resolution devices? Even if you don't add a breakpoint for these, you should consider how your pages look here.

FIGURE 24.4
Snohomish Aquatic Center, `http://www.snohomishaquatic.com`.

- **Less than 480px wide**—Many older smartphones fall into this range. And while you may have the newest HTC One M8 or iPhone 6+, your customers may still be limping along on something less cutting edge.
- **Less than 768px wide**—Larger smartphones and smaller tablets often land here.
- **Less than 1024px wide**—Here you'll find smaller laptops and some desktop computers, as well as larger tablets. There may even be some smartphones at this breakpoint.
- **Greater than 1024px wide**—Here you'll find the larger laptops and desktops, including the really wide-screen monitors. There are also some newer tablets in this range.

FIGURE 24.5
Mr. Simon Collison, http://colly.com.

Most of my sites use two breakpoints with three versions: small, medium, and large. I don't usually put breakpoints right at the dimensions listed above, but rather I put them in when the design starts to break.

Be Flexible and Think Small

Web design has always required designers to have a more flexible outlook than more traditional print designers need to have. Web pages can be viewed on so many devices with so many different features that it can be hard to ensure that the content even displays, let alone looks identical in all situations. But a responsive designer needs to be especially flexible.

You need to consider the following:

- **Your layouts need to flex with the screen.** One of the main ways you can recognize a responsive website from a non-responsive one is in how the layout changes depending on what device is viewing it. The easiest way to create flexible layouts is to use percentages for the layout elements.

FIGURE 24.6
About Family Crafts, `http://aboutfamilycrafts.com`.

- **Images need to adjust to screen sizes, too.** The very best responsive designs use RESS to resize images for the different device sizes. But if you don't do that, it's a good idea to use adaptive sizing (typically percentages, ems, or rems) to define the image sizes.
- **Video and other media needs to be small and adaptive.** Like images, your videos should be only as large as you need them, and no larger. If you don't plan to provide an HD-sized area for viewing your movies, then don't upload an HD-sized video to display there.
- **You should compress everything you can.** Compress your images, minify your CSS and JavaScript (and HTML, if there's a lot there), and make everything as small as you can. And once you've compressed everything, consider adding Gzip compression to your website so that it loads even faster.
- **You should use only one or two web fonts.** I love web fonts, and it can be tempting to install tons on a site because you can. But web fonts can cause your page to take longer to load. Plus, not all mobile devices support web fonts; older phones won't see web fonts, but they still have to download them.

Keeping your pages as small as you possibly can will help keep your responsive site working well.

FIGURE 24.7
Food Sense, `http://foodsense.is`.

Don't Forget the Content

Content is important. It's what makes a web page. But I don't agree with those people who advocate deleting content for mobile customers. Mobile customers are just customers who happen to be on a phone. You should make it easy for them to see the content you have, not limit them to content you want them to see. But that doesn't mean that every page must have all your content on it or linked to it. No one likes cluttered web pages, whether on a desktop or a cell phone.

There are many reasons to not create cluttered pages—and those reasons go well beyond just RWD. Search engines appreciate pages that stick to one topic. Customers find pages with too much clutter hard to read and follow.

FIGURE 24.8
Internet Images, `http://interim.it`.

There are some specific things you can do to improve your content:

- **Be clear and concise.** Shorter content is often appreciated on small devices, as it's easier to read without having to scroll. But if you must write a lot (and there's definitely value in long pages), make sure it's easy for those on both small and large screens to read and digest.
- **Use bullet points.** Bulleted and numbered lists are easier to read than flat blocks of text. And both your mobile and non-mobile customers will appreciate them.
- **Don't pile up your links.** Remember that multiple links in close proximity can make it hard for a user of a phone (especially a small one) to tap on the right link. Use CSS to space out links or separate them with non-clickable text.
- **Use images for decoration and declaration, but don't go overboard.** Images are the number-one place that most responsive sites get too slow to download.

FIGURE 24.9
BBC News, `http://www.bbc.com/news/`.

If you have content that was never intended for a mobile audience, you might consider removing it. But I always return to the thought that mobile customers are just customers using small screens. What you think isn't appropriate for mobile might be just fine with them. Plus, more and more of the world's populations are getting smartphones, and in some parts of the world, these are the *only* way of viewing the web. If you had to choose between someone seeing your page on a phone or not seeing it at all, which would you choose?

Manage Costs

The last best practice is to remember that RWD costs money, just like anything else. And most clients don't have an unlimited budget when it comes to building websites. So you need to make sure you keep costs down where you can. To keep design costs down, you can do things like the following:

- Limit the number of breakpoints you design for.
- Change only one aspect of the site, such as the layout for each breakpoint.

- Minimize the use of things like tables and forms that require a lot of work to make responsive.
- Automate making images Retina-ready or resized for different devices. (This is a good use of RESS.)

FIGURE 24.10
City of Snohomish, Washington, `http://ci.snohomish.wa.us`.

Before you start slashing your budget, remember that while RWD costs more than doing nothing or doing your design the way you did last year or 10 years ago, the costs of designing in an old-fashioned way may be higher than you or your clients think. By creating a site that ignores the growing mobile market, you condemn your pages to be ignored by that market.

Plus, responsive design, as outlined in this book, is intended to be responsive to the unexpected and unplanned as well as what we already know about. And while I can't guarantee that your responsive website will look amazing on the new 3D web widget coming out next month, chances are it will at least be viewable.

Summary

In this hour you've seen 10 inspirational RWD websites. These images have shown you what good RWD can look like and have provided ideas for how to improve your own RWD designs.

You've also learned best practices surrounding giving everyone the best design and content possible, saving money on the design process, improving your content so that it's mobile and computer ready, and creating images that are flexible and quick to download.

Workshop

The workshop contains quiz questions to help you process what you've learned in this lesson. Try to answer all the questions before you read the answers.

Q&A

Q. You mention using Gzip compression on your website, but how do you do that?

A. It's fairly easy if you have an Apache website with htaccess. I have instructions on About.com: `http://www.html5in24hours.com/2014/09/gzip-compression/`.

Q. Do you know of other places I can find inspirational RWD designs?

A. I post sites that inspire me to my HTML5 in 24 Hours website. I created a special post just for the inspirational sites listed in this book: `http://www.html5in24hours.com/2014/05/inspiring-responsive-web-designs/`. All the sites listed in this hour are posted there.

Quiz

1. True or False: RWD designs should strive to make the pages look identical on all devices.
2. What is more important: giving a customer a good experience or getting the design to match your mockup?
3. If you have a site with three planned breakpoints, how many mockups should you create (at a minimum)?
4. If you build a web form, should you use the `<input type=email>` tag to collect email addresses? If not, what should you use instead?
5. What is the smallest-width device you should consider?
6. How many breakpoints do I use on most of my sites?
7. Should your breakpoints match the width of the devices you want to support?
8. Name three ways you can keep your pages small.
9. Name three ways you can reduce costs on RWD design.
10. How is RWD cheaper, in the long run, than non-RWD design?

Answers

1. False. RWD designs should strive to make the content accessible on all devices, but the actual design does not need to be identical.

2. While mockups are important, giving the customer the best experience possible should always be your major goal.

3. You should create at least four mockups of a site with three planned breakpoints. Make a mockup for every version of the site.

4. You should use the `<input type=email>` tag on your modern web forms. Using new HTML5 elements makes your pages more future-proof.

5. You should consider the size of the smallest device that will visit your site, but in general that means around 320px wide or less.

6. I usually use two breakpoints on most of my designs, and I create a version of the site for each of three devices sized: small, medium, and large.

7. While you can attempt to match the breakpoints to your commonly used device widths, it's better to add a breakpoint where the design breaks down. Thus you might have two breakpoints, but since the design looks fine up to 480px wide, that would be where your first breakpoint should be.

8. Keep your image and video sizes small, compress everything that you can by minifying the code, and use only one or two web fonts.

9. You can reduce RWD costs by limiting the number of breakpoints you design for, changing only one aspect of the site for each breakpoint, minimizing the use of things like tables and forms that require a lot of work to make responsive, and automating making images Retina-ready or resized for different devices.

10. Ignoring RWD might end up costing a site more in lost customers and revenue. Plus, a responsive site is better set up to handle unexpected changes in the devices that view web pages.

Exercise

Go out and find two or more responsive websites that inspire you. Look on search engines like Bing, check out the sites I mention this hour, and ask your friends for their recommendations. Share what you found in the comments on my site (`http://www.html5in24hours.com/2014/05/inspiring-responsive-web-designs/`).

INDEX

SYMBOLS

NUMBERS

A

B

D

E

G - H

I

J

K - L

M

P

Q - R

S

U

V

W

X - Y - Z

Learning Labs!

Learn online with videos, live code editing, and quizzes

SPECIAL 50% OFF – Introductory Offer
Discount Code: STYLL50

FOR A LIMITED TIME, we are offering readers of **Sams Teach Yourself** books a **50% OFF** discount to **ANY online Learning Lab** through Dec 15, 2015.

Visit **informit.com/learninglabs** to see available labs, try out full samples, and order today.

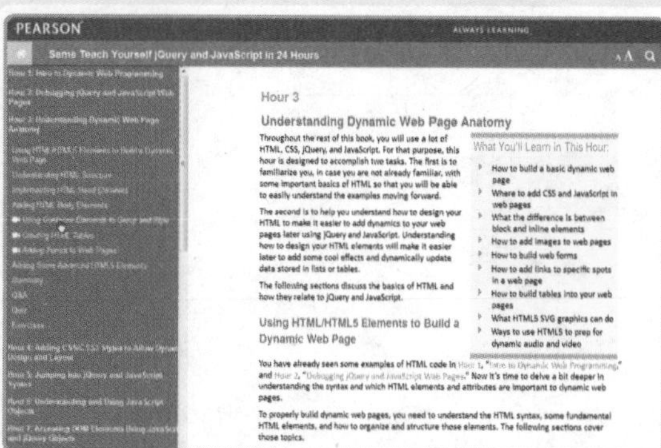

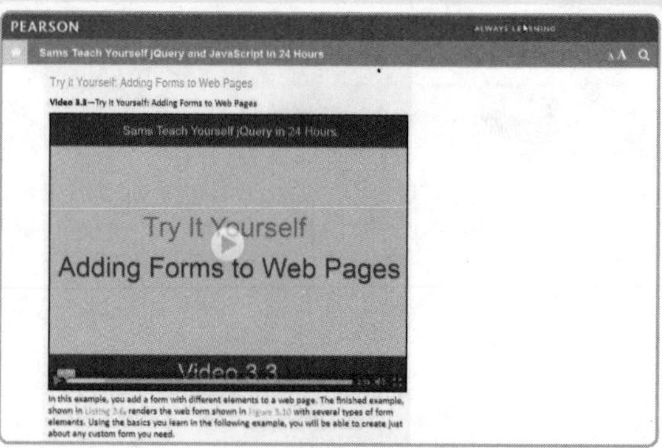

- **Read** the complete text of the book online in your web browser
- **Watch** an expert instructor show you how to perform tasks in easy-to-follow videos

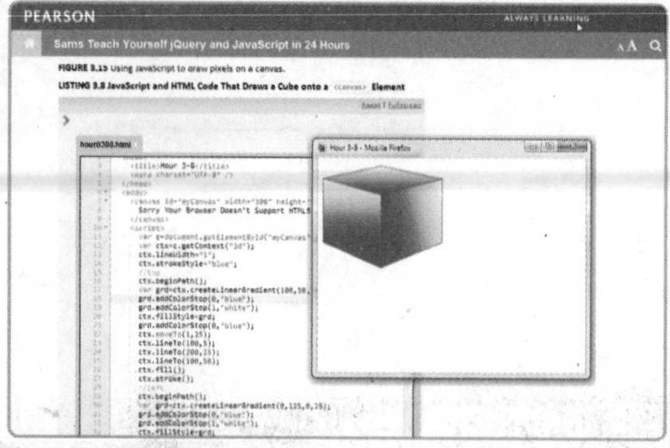

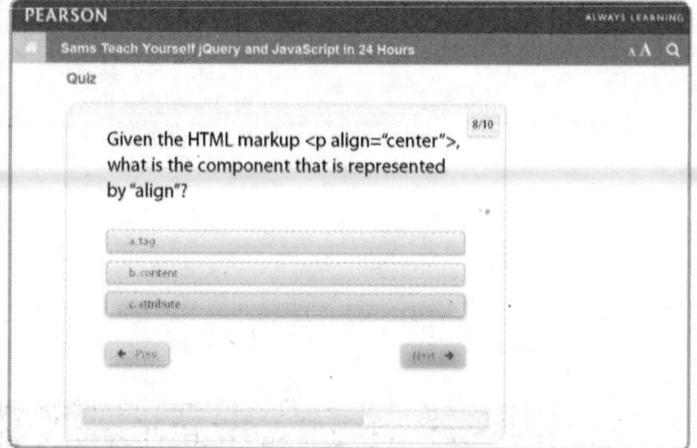

- **Try** your hand at coding in an interactive code-editing sandbox in select products
- **Test** yourself with interactive quizzes

ALWAYS LEARNING PEARSON